75

Another Chance

Another Chance

Hope & Health for the Alcoholic Family

Sharon Wegscheider

Science and Behavior Books, Inc.

For my children
Patrick, Sandra, and Deborah,
who gave me support, encouragement,
and understanding during my years
of writing

Illustrations by Mary Burkhardt
Book design by Al Burkhardt
Jacket design by Anita Scott

SCIENCE AND BEHAVIOR BOOKS, INC.
701 Welch Road, Palo Alto, CA 94306
Copyright © 1981 by Science and Behavior Books, Inc.
Printed in the United States of America. All rights reserved.
This book or parts thereof may not be reproduced in any form without
written permission of the publisher.
ISBN: 0–8314–0059–5
Library of Congress Catalog Card Number: 81–50908

Contents

THE TREATMENT PLAN

APPENDICES

ACKNOWLEDGMENTS

Of the many people to whom I am indebted for help in writing this book, I would like to give special recognition to:

Patricia Kollings, who contributed long hours of editing and rewriting; she used her expertise and skill, creativity and imagination to weave a script that will be understood and appreciated by many.

Don Wegscheider, who spent many hours writing, talking, and sharing with mc as I developed the contents of the book; he made an invaluable contribution.

Virginia Satir, who gave me support and believed in me before I believed in myself; her training and nurturance guided me in developing the concepts presented here.

Wheelock Whitney, who encouraged me to use my knowledge about family systems for a better understanding of larger systems such as industry, education, and communities; in doing so, we have learned to create healthier climates in which families can work and grow.

Irene Whitney, who understood my family concepts and philosophy long before they were accepted extensively by the treatment field; her encouragement gave me hope even in times of adversity.

Anne Roelandt, my mother, who along with my brother, my sister, and me struggled through our family battle with alcoholism; through her perseverance and love I learned a great deal about family togetherness, a lesson that underlies the philosophy of this book.

Emil Roelandt, my father, who lost his life to the disease of alcoholism; I am blessed with memories of his warmth and love from which I can take courage and strength.

DeLois, Bob, Elaine, Ed, Sue, Ron, Evie, Lee, Joan, Dick, and Mona, loyal friends who, during the past few years of hard work, unpredictable schedules, and a testing of friendship, have been consistently available to me; with them I have laughed, cried, dreamed, and prayed.

To them all my warmest thanks!

Foreword

BY VIRGINIA SATIR, M.S.W.

Family Therapist and Human Systems Consultant;
Author of *Peoplemaking* and *Conjoint Family Therapy*

WE HEAR A LOT about stress these days—how widespread it is, what serious health problems it causes, what can be done about it. But actually we Americans of the twentieth century didn't invent stress. It's been around a long time. I suspect that every human being in every time and place has experienced stress of one sort or another.

The particular circumstances that cause stress vary according to one's age, culture, socio-economic status, and other factors, but they usually come down to a few basics, such as:

Imbalance. Too much work and too little play, for instance, can lead to feelings of being overburdened. Some parts of the self steal all the time and energy while other parts, also valued, have no chance for expression at all.

Conflict. When two strong yet apparently irreconcilable needs come into conflict, a person feels trapped and helpless. ("I must always make the right decision, yet here there *is* no right decision." Or, "I must never suffer a loss, yet here I am bound to lose one thing or the other.")

Survival needs. One person may be threatened by economic worries ("If I don't have money, I'll die"); another by ill health ("If my body isn't functioning well, I'll die"); still another by feeling alone, abandoned, unloved ("If no one loves me, I'll die"). All of these survival fears bring with them a sense of hopelessness.

Competition. Fighting the competitive battle of modern urban society may be one of the greatest sources of stress today. It leads to

9

feelings of resentment and blame, both toward others and toward one-self. ("If I'm not on top, I'm not worth much.") And the battle is never over. Typically, a business executive or an elected official will endure terrible stress for years to get to the top, only to find that the stress of staying there may be even worse. Often he has to prostitute his very deepest values to do so—a severe blow to his self-worth.

To relieve the discomfort of their stress-filled lives, millions of people turn to alcohol and drugs. Like stress itself, these pain-killers are far from new. People have been turning to chemicals as a panacea for thousands of years; nearly every culture has had some kind of mood-altering substance. In our Western world today alcohol is the most widely used drug, though certainly not the only one. It offers a cheap, easily available, and socially sanctioned way to cope. In fact, in many segments of our society it has become an expected part of every social occasion.

For the majority of users alcohol seems to be a relatively safe relaxant. But not for all. For that unhappy minority who cannot control their drinking, the price of alcohol is enormous. The pain it relieves is nothing compared to the pain it brings as they slowly become dependent on it. Eventually, they weaken or destroy all the parts of the self that give life meaning—the very parts they were trying to protect when they started to drink.

The breakdown in an alcoholic's inner system of parts, of "personal potentials," is reflected by a parallel breakdown in the family or other intimate human system of which he is a part. In time, as a result of their close relationship to him and his symptoms, the other members of his family experience a breakdown of their potentials as well.

In the first ten chapters of this book, Sharon Wegscheider gives us a detailed and sensitive description of these losses, their magnitude, and how they come about. Step by step, she traces the development of the "family disease," as she calls it, and of the role-playing by which individual dysfunction masquerades as love and help. The picture she draws of the alcoholic family, as surprising or even shocking as it may be to many readers, is totally consistent with all that I know about the way families operate.

A family, like any other system, is always trying to maintain its stability. When one member introduces an unhealthy element, such as alcohol abuse, the whole system becomes unhealthy in order to maintain its balance. The support system that once supported the person now supports his disease.

Though drugs and addiction have been around since long before people were able to record the problem, the ways we are learning to deal with those problems *are* new. In the last fifty years we have finally stopped treating the alcoholic as bad and realized that he is sick. Instead of punishing him, we started trying to help him get well. At first most of the effort was spent persuading him to stop drinking. That was right, of course—the alcoholic *must* get dry and stay dry. But if nothing else is done, if we don't help him improve his life at the same time, just trying to stay sober will become a grim, white-knuckle thing. The odds are great that sooner or later the person will relapse. If he doesn't start drinking again, he'll find a new addiction, develop a physical disease, adopt some unrewarding role, or otherwise become dysfunctional again.

The treatment plan presented in the later chapters of this book recognizes that for lasting recovery the alcoholic must become more than sober; he must become whole. In fact, this is the first truly holistic treatment program for alcoholism that I know of. It treats the whole family and the whole person of each family member. It offers them not only recovery but continuing growth to realize more and more of their personal wholeness. It envisions a counselor who is pursuing his own wholeness, and it draws on the whole pool of available insights and experience, from alcoholism treatment, group therapy, and family therapy to Alcoholics Anonymous.

I believe that in *Another Chance* Sharon Wegscheider has written one of the best books available on alcoholism and substance abuse. It is, at the same time, one of the best books on family therapy. It will not only give "hope and health" to alcoholic families, but also serve as a practical guide for therapists at all levels of experience.

Foreword

BY KENNETH H. WILLIAMS, M.D.

Medical Director, Maple Grove Treatment Center, Detroit, Michigan;
Class A Trustee, General Service Board, Alcoholics Anonymous

MILLIONS OF American families are trapped by the stigma and warped by the effects of alcoholism. Afraid to speak out about the "family secret," other family members become compulsively involved with the drinking member and his behavior. His repeated intoxication, decreased work efficiency, blackouts and other memory problems, failing health, and withdrawal symptoms lead to an inconsistent family life and widespread effects on the personal lives of all the members.

The family with alcoholism is an unstable one. Studies have demonstrated high rates of divorce, separation, marital strife, wife abuse, and child neglect and abuse. Because of his disease the alcoholic faces a much higher risk of sudden, violent death from suicide, homicide, or accident; a life expectancy shortened by more than ten years; and an increased risk of disease caused by the medical complications of addiction. Because of the damaging effect of alcoholism on trust and sharing, clinicians experienced in working with alcoholic families, such as psychiatrist Ruth Fox, have questioned whether love can exist at all between spouses when one is an active alcoholic.

The spouse of the alcoholic is at higher risk of both emotional and physical problems, while the children are at increased risk of depression, hyperactivity, school and behavior problems, and child abuse. They also have an increased likelihood of themselves developing alcoholism or drug abuse, or of marrying into another family with alcoholism, thereby perpetuating their high-risk situation. Certainly anyone who has been raised in a family with alcoholism knows the tremendous impact of the disease on family life.

Why then, one might wonder, is alcoholism as a family illness given so little emphasis in professional schools that train the health care professionals who will be working with alcoholic families? Repeatedly one finds that community and other health care agencies dealing with children and families ignore the presence or possibility of alcoholism. In many cases health care professionals do not even ask the correct questions to enable them to diagnose alcoholism in the family. Even where they are aware of the problem, it rarely receives the appropriate attention and treatment. As a result the disease progresses needlessly. We now know of excellent family intervention techniques and many treatment modalities that are associated with an increased likelihood of recovery, Alcoholics Anonymous and Al-anon among them.

The family is probably the first to feel the impact of a growing alcoholism problem in one of its members. With early intervention the likelihood of recovery is greater; the longer the disease goes untreated, the poorer the prognosis. Why is there not more education directed to families to enable them to recognize and deal with the problem if it arises?

Family members are probably the therapist's strongest allies in work with an active alcoholic, for their therapeutic leverage offers the best opportunity for successful intervention and treatment. Why is the family not included more often in alcoholism treatment programs?

The biologic offspring of the alcoholic are the highest at-risk group for later development of addiction. Why are there no prevention programs directed here?

My hope is that this book may serve as a wedge to correct many of these deficiencies. With an extensive clinical experience in working with alcoholic families, Sharon Wegscheider has opened the door on the "family secret" and described in fascinating detail the typical patterns of malfunction as they appear in these families. Certainly this book makes a great contribution to our knowledge of addicted families.

Prologue

The undertaker's small parlor is filled with family, familiar faces yet they somehow make the room all the more unfamiliar. There's a murmur of conversation, the voices hushed as voices are on such occasions. But there's more than sorrow in the bits of conversation I pick up, something uncomfortable, a guarded edge. Friends seem a little embarrassed, not sure what to say. Family members simply seem bewildered and ask one another, What happened? What made him do it? Why didn't he ask for help?

The voices fade in and out, and a wave of pain and confusion wash over me.

I stifle a voice inside that wants to scream out its own questions— Why can't we be honest? Why can't we just cry together, then hold and comfort each other? Why couldn't we do it all these years?

I see Mother across the room, huddled by the oil burner. She looks so cold and alone! I wonder what she is thinking, and feel a pang of worry for her. Then I remember my own children, so young and so many miles away. I had to leave them suddenly when I got the news, with little chance to explain. Yes, I must get back to them now.

As I go to find my coat, a mirror catches my eye, and in it an unfamiliar figure. Black wool skirt, black sweater, black hair—the picture of a mourner. Her face is pale, her eyes dry and glazed, as though the tears were frozen and unable to flow. How many times his eyes looked like that. Were they misty with pain, too? Now I understand! His eyes were always a little puffy, even in the happier days, and my eyes have the same look. For years I've tried to hide it with make-up, but I resolve not to try anymore. These eyes are part of me and part of my connection with my father.

Over one black shoulder the mirror reflects a window, and beyond it the twinkling colored lights on a neighbor's tree. I remember that other families are celebrating the last days of Christmas. Somewhere out there, there is still joy.

I ask Mother if she is ready to go home. No, she thinks she'll stay on for a while. Couldn't sleep anyway. But will I stop by the house and lock up on my way back to the city? I promise that I will and give her a parting hug.

So I start the drive home, more than two hundred miles through the long, cold Minnesota night. At a familiar alley the car turns, almost automatically, and I pull up to the back door of my parents' house.

On the kitchen table empty coffee cups and brimming ash trays wait where they were left. On the counter are a stack of cake pans and casserole dishes that had been our neighbors' quiet way of saying they cared and were sorry. Some of the pans bore name tapes to identify their owners. In time they'd be returned, and the giver would take that opportunity to offer Mother a cup of coffee and an expression of concern about how things were going.

Silently, I thank them all and busy myself clearing away the coffee cups. The old kitchen brings back memories. My sister and I setting the table, and Mother's voice warning, "Sharon, keep your hands out of the olives!"—the wonderful smells of pot roast and chocolate cake—the smell of Dad's cologne that meant it was Sunday—the table opened large for relatives and friends, who always loved to come to our house—everyone talking and laughing and sharing . . .

I dry the last cup and find myself climbing the stairs to my old room. It is dark, and I remember the years of nights when I would lie there in the dark listening to voices I knew so well saying things that sounded so strange. One night is still especially clear. Dad sounded very, very angry. So did Mother. She said he shouldn't have come home like that. A little while later, after I heard her come up to bed, I slipped out of my room and crept down the dark stairs.

Now the memory of it guides my feet unconsciously back to the steps, a small, confused child once more. As I reach the bottom, I turn again toward the kitchen, where we always used to keep a low light burning all night. That fateful night I headed toward it. Nearing the doorway, I suddenly caught sight of a body stretched out on the floor. Just as I was about to scream, I realized that it was Dad!

After the first shock, I saw that he was not dead or even hurt. He was drunk! To me, he looked like a lonely little boy, his hands tucked under his head for a pillow, his legs pulled up to keep warm. All he needed was a teddy bear. I took a blanket from the closet to cover him, kissed his forehead, and asked God to be with him.

As I stand in the empty kitchen now, I remember feeling those same feelings and offering that same prayer as I kissed him goodbye tonight, before they closed the coffin.

It's late, and home is still many miles away. I put on my coat and take a last, wistful look around the house. In that moment I know that I'll never return to my childhood home again. Even though business may bring me back here, it won't be the same. It will be an empty house, for tonight I've gathered up all the memories and I'm taking them with me. All the memories and all the questions—those disturbing questions! What was it that happened in my family? What, oh what, happened?

Preface

It is hard to say just when this book began. An easy answer would be 1974, when I started a journal to document my experiences with families who were living with, or recovering from, the pain of chemical dependency in someone they loved. Or perhaps 1971, when I first began to work with these families and learn from them.

But I think it may really have been many years before, when I was trying to deal with the personal anguish that resulted from my father's death; or earlier yet, as I was growing up in a family that was painfully trapped in his advancing alcoholism.

Actually, each of these experiences led naturally to the next, all of them reinforcing what has become the central quest of my professional life: to understand what happens in the families of chemical dependents and to help them understand, too, so they may find their way back to health and joyful living.

At the time of my father's death I was still in my early twenties, busy with the responsibilities of being a wife and the mother of two small children. Suddenly, there was a funeral to be arranged, a younger brother and sister to be cared for, my mother to be supported and comforted, the family business to be closed. For a while it was easy to hide from my feelings by repressing them and submerging myself in practical demands. But the truth was that my hurt and confusion were so great that I could endure them only by refusing to look them in the face.

It was many years before I regained enough strength and courage to go back and sort out what had happened. I was able to do it then only because of the caring and support of a growth group in which I was participating. Encouraged by them, I enrolled in a special program on the problems of chemical dependency that was just being developed at Metropolitan Community College in Minneapolis. Up to that time, alcoholism and drug addiction had been seen as distinct and separate problems. The new, experimental program in which I was about to take part would prepare people to work in all aspects of chemical abuse. It was here that the term *chemical dependency* emerged to identify the more basic addiction process that includes dependency on both alcohol and other drugs.

During this training I found answers to many of my questions about what happens to a person who becomes chemically dependent, questions that had been haunting me ever since my father's death.

On completing the program and receiving my certification in 1973, I began an internship at the Johnson Institute, a well-known center in Minneapolis which at that time offered intervention and after-care services to the families of alcoholics. There I continued to learn.

New ways were being found to identify alcoholism early and to intervene with the alcoholic in order to arrest the disease. It became increasingly clear to me, however, that while we were doing a great deal to help alcoholics, we were not yet doing much for their families.

For many months Mary McMahon, a counselor at the institute, shared her office and her clients with me. My days were spent listening to the wives, husbands, and children of chemical dependents as they poured out their anger, fears, frustration, and hopelessness. To my surprise, I discovered that my childhood family had not been alone. While the details of our experience were unique to us, something similar had happened and was still happening to millions of other families. With each family I interviewed, the same pattern emerged. They all felt the same shame, the same personal desperation, the same solitary suffering.

At about this time I joined Al-anon—an organization that could have offered the kind of support I had so desperately needed a few years earlier, if only I had found it then. Late as it was, I saw in Al-anon a wise and powerful philosophy for living, with or without the problems of alcoholism. It also provided an opportunity to view this central question in my life from yet another perspective.

Members talked a lot about family stress, about kids who were showing all kinds of symptoms, about marital relationships that had not really improved much after sobriety. Families had improved, of course —if by improvement we mean they had learned to cope with alcoholism. But coping did not seem to end the stress and bring happiness.

What is more, the teenagers in many of these families were beginning to show signs of incipient alcoholism themselves. This observation was consistent with what I was seeing in my work with youngsters who were becoming dependent on drugs, including alcohol: the majority of them had an alcoholic in the family. What was happening here?

The more I learned, the more convinced I became that it was not enough to work with the alcoholic. We had to work with the family, too.

When my internship at the Johnson Institute was completed, I began to visit other treatment centers, hoping to talk with other counselors and compare what we were finding. I was also looking for a setting where I might get on with the work I wanted to do. To my disappointment, I found no one was very interested. I knocked on the doors of at least fifteen treatment centers. I even volunteered to work free if only they would let me work with families. But the resistance was unanimous. Everyone agreed that families had problems, but they saw those problems as secondary to the problems of the alcoholic. Besides, they said, offering programmed help to families was "impractical." Discouraged, I realized that if I was to learn more about how these families operated, I was not going to learn it in the field of alcoholism counseling.

My husband, Don, is also a counselor, and he shared my concern. Together we began to look for someone else who could teach us about family dynamics. We found that person in Virginia Satir. Impressed by the practical wisdom of her ideas in *Conjoint Family Therapy*[1] and *Peoplemaking*,[2] we decided to seek her out.

Since that time we have participated in a number of Virginia's training workshops on family systems, holistic health, personal self-worth, and other themes. She has become without question the most influential single person in our lives, her work one of our prime sources of understanding and inspiration. She has also taught me a great deal about myself and what happened to me growing up in an alcoholic family.

The more I learned about families in general, the more I wanted to learn about the families of alcoholics in particular. But just as alcoholism counselors were not interested in families, it seemed that family therapists did not see alcoholism as a problem different from any other family problem. I felt totally alone.

So, in addition to starting my training with Virginia Satir, I decided to open my own agency, the Family Factory. With the support of my husband and a few others who shared my convictions, I managed to find

[1]Satir, *Conjoint Family Therapy*. Palo Alto, CA: Science and Behavior Books, 1964, 1967.
[2]Satir, *Peoplemaking*. Palo Alto, CA: Science and Behavior Books, 1973.

board members and arrange for incorporation. For $15 a month we rented a tax consultant's office that would be vacant for a few months. It was minimal but well located—next door to an alcoholism referral center. A lot of troubled families would be walking by. Optimistically, we hoped that maybe a few would wander in.

Four part-time volunteers and a college intern made up our staff. We had some skills in alcoholism counseling, group therapy, and working with children but could not really offer much formal programming—no one knew yet what programs families needed. There was little choice but to learn from our clients. As members of Al-anon we did have access to a lot of families needing help, so we began to invite family members to come and share their problems with one another and with us.

At first we did not charge for our services. I felt we had no right to, since we knew so little about what we were doing. Mostly we were just listening and learning. But there were months when I had to borrow to pay for the room, so we began to assess each family a dollar a month, netting barely enough to cover rent and postage. People continued to come.

Minnesota is a real mecca of help for alcoholics. In 1973 there were already more treatment beds for inpatients than in any other state. No one, however, was offering personal help to the members of these alcoholics' families, and there was a great hunger for it. Very few agencies were working with youngsters who had alcohol or drug dependencies either.

It did not take long for the word to get around that the Family Factory was a place one could go for these kinds of help. Within five months after we opened, we were working with three hundred people. We had found larger quarters, and two more interns had joined us.

The dynamics of alcoholic families were becoming clearer and clearer. By this time we had enough data to begin developing services that would be based on Virginia Satir's ideas about what happens to people in families, yet be tailored to the special needs that alcoholic families have. We offered a variety of programs—children's groups, teen groups, adult groups, family counseling, individual counseling, educational workshops.

It was rewarding, and awesome, to watch individuals and whole families who had come to us so hopeless now getting well. My private belief in a Higher Power was confirmed almost daily by the apparent miracles in people's lives. But facilitating those miracles had its price. We worked ten- and twelve-hour days, sharing the duties of counselor, administrator, snow shoveler, group leader, bookkeeper, and toilet cleaner. Still, it all seemed worth the effort. A shared hope and excitement permeated everything we did.

While we ourselves were jubilant about our success, the landlord was not. Other tenants might object to "that kind of people" going in and out, he said. He would rent to us only for evening and weekend use. Somehow, by working almost around the clock on weekends, we managed to squeeze our busy program into those few permissible hours.

The shortage of time and space had been plaguing us for several months when one day I received a phone call from Ward Nerothin, pastor of Elim Lutheran Church. We had never met, but he had heard about our work with alcoholic families and thought it could be equally valuable for other troubled families. Would I consider developing a church-sponsored program that would be open to all families in stress, whether or not their problem was related to chemical use?

Two hours later we were walking through an old house that the church owned in a Minneapolis suburb. It was to serve as the proposed agency's quarters. My first impulse was to cry. The ceilings sagged visibly, and wallpaper hung away from the walls where the water of many rains had poured through the leaky roof. Floors and windows were bare, and the basement smelled of mildew. But at least we were wanted here, and we had already learned about miracles.

So, for the second time in less than a year, I went through the ordeal of incorporating, choosing a board, and the other labors of birthing an agency. With the loving help of many, we were ready two months later to open the doors of "The House," a community counseling center offering help to any family where someone was showing symptoms of stress. We specialized in therapy for children.

When the clients started coming in, we noticed an interesting thing. Although we were not an alcoholism treatment center, more than 70 percent of the families had an alcoholic somewhere in a three-generation span! And it did not seem to make any difference whether the alcoholic was recovering or still using—the families were still in stress. We could only conclude that during the period of active alcoholism the other family members had developed dysfunctions of their own.

The House continued to welcome all families, but drawing on our experience at the Family Factory, we began to design special programs for alcoholic families. And as before, individuals and whole families began to get better.

Meanwhile, whenever possible, I took further training from Virginia Satir. A personal friendship was developing between us. Her published work and live workshops had already become one of my prime sources of learning and inspiration. Now I had direct and informal access to her wisdom. Even more important to me were her personal interest and encouragement in my growth, both as a human being and as a counselor.

In the spring of 1974, shortly after we had opened The House, Virginia asked if she might do my family reconstruction (a powerful technique she has developed for studying family dynamics through role-playing). The session was to be filmed for training purposes.[3]

That reconstruction proved to be a valuable source of learning and healing for me. It gave me new ways of looking at what had gone on in my family—why my parents did the things they did and why I felt as I did. Three especially poignant insights stand out in my mind:

1. Coming to know my parents as people, not just as Mother and Dad; this enabled me to accept myself as a person, too, not just as Daughter.
2. Discovering what was really happening between my mother and me; while I was perceiving her as critical, she was actually still struggling with her relationship to her own parents.
3. Being able to say good-bye to my father and let him go; I found I could hold onto the good times and the gifts he gave me, yet accept the reality of his death, integrating it as part of my own development.

In 1976 another significant woman came into my life—Irene Whitney. She and her husband, Wheelock, individually and together, had pioneered several innovative programs in the Twin Cities area, a number of them for alcoholics and their families. (They have since played important roles in my life and the work I am trying to accomplish.) At that time, Irene was on the board of the Johnson Institute and had been charged with finding someone with experience who could expand the institute's services for families. Though we had never met before, there was an instant sense of our shared mission and feeling for people in need of help.

The decision to leave The House was difficult. In three years I had invested much of myself in it. But alcoholic families were still my first concern, and a large, specialized center like the Johnson Institute would give me the opportunity to help many more.

Immediately upon my return to the institute, I was asked to set up two programs: one that would offer treatment for every family member

[3]*Reconstruction*, film produced by John Goodell. Inquiries should be directed to ONSITE Training & Consulting, Inc., 1645 Hennepin Avenue, Minneapolis, MN 55403.

when one member got help for alcoholism, the other a training program to teach counselors from other centers what we had learned about alcoholic families. In the four years that followed, thousands of families came to the institute in pain and left able to understand what was causing it and to develop new ways of coping and growing together. The gospel of the "family illness of chemical dependency" was spreading. Today treatment centers in at least sixteen states have added family care as an integral part of their programs.

For some time now people have been urging me to publish the wealth of clinical findings from the past nine years, along with the models of family illness and treatment that have grown out of them. This book is a response to those requests. I did write a preliminary pamphlet in 1976, focusing chiefly on family roles, but there is more to be said and much to be added since it was written.

Because of the nature of the illness, professional work with chemically dependent persons and their families requires highly specialized training. Much of my own time is now spent on workshops for counselors, presenting the philosophy and treatment strategies that I have been evolving. The number that I can speak to personally, however, is small compared to the need. By including much of the same material in this book, I hope to reach many others who are trying to bring relief to suffering families.

It is not my intent to provide here an exhaustive handbook on either chemical dependency or family therapy. Excellent works in both fields are already available. But there is little in print on either the specific dynamics of the chemically dependent family or the treatment strategies for modifying them—certainly nothing that grows out of direct experience with so many clinical cases (more than four thousand).

Nor should the reader expect to find in this book a thorough review of the research that has been done on families with addiction or the clinical techniques that have been tried with them. Rather, my purpose is to present a philosophy, one that ties together Virginia Satir's approach to family therapy and the approaches of Gary Forrest,[4] Vernon Johnson,[5] and Mary McAuliffe[6] to chemical dependency.

Specifically, my goals are to:

[4]Gary Forrest, *Diagnosis and Treatment of Alcoholism.* Springfield, IL: Charles C. Thomas, 1975.

[5]Vernon Johnson, *I'll Quit Tomorrow.* New York, NY: Harper & Row, 1973.

[6]Robert & Mary McAuliffe, *Essentials of Chemical Dependency.* The Chemical Dependency Society of America (5001 Olson Memorial Highway, Minneapolis, MN 55426), 1975.

1. Provide a simple, bias-free language for understanding and talking about the dynamic system that grows up around a chemically dependent person.
2. Describe the feelings, behavior, and interactions observed consistently in a large sample of chemically dependent families.
3. Offer a model of the illness in these families and a plan for their recovery that will speak to the needs of each family member.
4. Help counselors understand the confusing tangle of behavior that expresses the aching isolation, low self-worth, and "stuckness" of these families.
5. Help counselors guide family members to rediscover their individual strengths in order first to face the problems of addiction and then to heal relationships within the family system.

As a certified alcoholism specialist, a therapist, and a member of Al-anon (which, of course, shares the AA philosophy), I am in a rather uncommon position, and increasing cooperation between these groups is a matter of passionate concern to me. In this book I am speaking to all of them—and drawing on their combined wisdom and experience. Each has valuable insights and skills to share, but too often they don't hear one another. Though we all come from our individual conceptual bases, I hope that we can begin to learn and to share, and even to appreciate the richness arising from our differences. In my experience, there is no one right way to do anything. Effective treatment is usually the result of pooling resources.

While I am speaking primarily to professionals, I realize that this book will find its way into the hands of readers who are facing the problems it describes in their own families. To them I would like to say, take comfort—you are not alone. I hope that this book will bring you the insights you need to become aware of your own feelings and behavior, seek out an understanding counselor, and join the thousands of other people who are working their way out of the painful trap of chemical dependency.

A NOTE ON LANGUAGE

The terms I prefer are *chemical dependency,* for the disease of which we are speaking, and *chemically dependent person,* for its victim. I use them frequently throughout this book, often shortening the latter to *dependent* or *Dependent* (where I am speaking of the person in his family role). Since alcohol is the chemical used by the greatest number of dependents, and many readers may feel more at ease with the familiar terms *alcoholism* and *alcoholic,* I also use these. It is important to be aware, however, that whatever is said about these can be applied to dependency on another drug as well. The family illness we are studying is basically the same no matter what chemical is being abused—alcohol, prescription drugs, marijuana, cocaine, street drugs, whatever.

In discussing the family roles, I usually use *he* to refer to the Dependent and *she* to refer to the spouse. I will speak more of this later. For now I only wish to assure the reader that the choice of pronouns has nothing to do with either feminist prejudice or the odds of addiction.

I might add that my editorial collaborator, Patricia Kollings, has wrestled with the larger *he/she* question on virtually every page of this book. Our English language, reflecting the world's long history of sexual inequality, offers us no gender-free pronouns by which we can refer to the unidentified individual. The customary usage of *he, him,* and *his* where the antecedent may be either male or female is offensive to many thoughtful people today. The alternatives (*he and she, he/she,* or the unpronounceable *s/he*), however, are clumsy at best and often interfere with the smooth flow of communication. As women, we can only hope that someone will invent a more satisfactory substitute soon. In the meantime, we have reluctantly decided to stay with the time-honored— and discriminatory—masculine pronouns in the interest of readability.

Even more important than the language I use is the language I will try to avoid. Many expressions describing use and abuse of chemicals mean different things to different people. Many also carry a heavy load of emotion, bias, or both. A word that is common jargon for one group of people concerned about drinking or alcoholism may for that very reason bring a negative response from another group. A classic example is *temperance.* The virtue—defined in the dictionary as "moderation" —is one most Americans would probably endorse. Yet, mentioned in connection with drinking, the word is sure to arouse resistance because of its popular association with Prohibition.

So I have tried to stay with simple, human, everyday language wherever possible, language that cuts across the many disciplines and viewpoints concerned with chemical dependency. I believe that precise, accurate, and neutral terms for the concepts we are working with can do much to bring the various factions in this field together in a common effort to increase understanding and ease human pain.

CHAPTER 1

Old Myths,
New Insights

AS A CHILD I never heard my father's alcoholism mentioned. *Alcoholic* was not a familiar word in the small Minnesota town where I grew up. The very concepts of alcoholism and chemical dependency were simply not part of most people's frame of reference. If a man drank heavily, he was said to be "getting a buzz on," "feeling mellow," "getting high" or "plastered" or "pie-eyed." If the drinker was a woman, she might be called "tipsy" or "disgusting" or "loose"—words spoken in whispers with knowing looks. The language was vague and so were the perceptions it expressed.

My own image of the chemically dependent person was a mixture of my meager personal experience with drinking (outside the family) and the stereotypes I had picked up around me: a man with bloodshot eyes, a red nose, and a big belly, shouting and looking for a fight; a woman with flashy clothes and too much makeup, slurring her words and staggering; a teenager drinking at "keg parties," sneaking pills, or "smoking dope" in someone's car.

These images do, of course, describe some individuals. The problem is that there are so many cases that do not fit the pigeonholes. There is no place, for instance, for the apparently successful executive whose problem with alcohol is hidden by both his company and his family; or the housewife who plans her life around the daytime hours when no one is home and she can drink secretly; or the quiet teenager who takes liquor from his parents' supply when they are not at home; or the aging person who lives and drinks alone, unheeded by the busy world.

A lot has been learned about alcoholism since I was a child, and some effective efforts have been made to educate the public about it. But attitudes have not kept pace. The old stereotypes are still all too common. Joan Jackson's description of the situation twenty-five years ago remains true for many families.

> Alcoholism in a family poses a situation defined by the culture as shameful but for the handling of which there are no prescriptions which are effective or which permit direct action not in conflict with other cultural prescriptions. While in crises such as illness or death the family members can draw on cultural definitions of appropriate behavior for procedures which will terminate the crisis, this is not the case with alcoholism.[1]

No wonder most families feel they have no alternative but to hide the truth, often even from one another, and endure the same lonely pain that my family did many years ago.

Among most helping professionals, of course, those old notions have long since disappeared. They realize that the alcoholic is genuinely ill, suffering from a diagnosable, progressive, ultimately fatal disease. There is no permanent cure for it—a relapse is always as close as the next drink—but it can be arrested, and with proper help the alcoholic can regain health and sobriety. Treatment centers all over the country are now providing such help.

Forty years' research has failed to reveal any particular personality pattern that predisposes one to alcoholism. About the only reliable basis for predicting the odds of addiction is the presence of another alcoholic person in the family. (And those odds are high.)

Behavior, however, *is* predictable, once the disease process takes over. It follows a pattern that has become all too familiar to alcoholism workers, providing a visible manifestation of the gradual but accelerating disintegration of the whole person that is the mark of alcoholism. Eventually, every human potential is destroyed.

Bill Wilson, founder of AA, sensed this when he described his alcoholism as a three-pronged illness: *physical, mental,* and *spiritual.*[2] Vernon Johnson, author of *I'll Quit Tomorrow,* adds *emotional* to the list.[3] In my own work with alcoholics and their families, I have found that *volitional* (will) power and *social* interactions are also affected. So as we look at the whole person in this book, we will be considering all six personal potentials.

While we can isolate the individual to talk about him, we must

---

[1]Joan Jackson, "Family Adjustment to Alcoholism," *Quarterly Journal of Studies on Alcohol,* 15 (1954): 562–586.
[2]Robert Thomsen, *Bill W.* New York, NY: Harper & Row, 1975; Author's note.
[3]Johnson, *I'll Quit Tomorrow.* New York, NY: Harper & Row, 1973; p. 6.

remember that he actually lives in a context, most often within a family. There the various members interact dynamically, complicating the picture immeasurably and contributing to either the growth or the destruction of each individual. Not so many years ago, we would have found this process far too complex to understand. In the past twenty years, however, much has been learned about the systems, rules, and communication patterns that determine what goes on in a family.

Fundamentally, the family is a system, just as a machine or a human body is. In the interests of their own personal survival, the members of the family assume behavior patterns that will maintain a balance (homeostasis) in the system. A distorted balance, such as occurs when one member starts becoming dependent on a chemical, causes psychological and/or biological symptoms in the other members.

Alcoholics suffer from very low self-worth. As a result, they are incapable of either maintaining a healthy marriage relationship or encouraging children to develop high self-worth, both of which require an adult who feels secure about his own worth. Soon each family member's growing sense of worthlessness feeds every other member's. Without outside help the entire family will begin to show symptoms of one kind or another—some remarkably like those of the alcoholic. In time they will follow the same long, slow path to personal disintegration, both individually and as a family unit. Even if the alcoholic eventually gets professional help, it will probably come too late to prevent damage to the rest of the family.

As early as 1969 a study documented that pathological drinking becomes integrated into the family system and leads to predictable, compulsive behavior, both in individual family members and in the interactions among them.[4] Between 1972 and 1974, I worked with some 4,000 people in over 600 families, and I came to the same conclusion.

Statistics have since confirmed our clinical observations. For example, one study reported that 52 percent of the alcoholics in the sample were themselves children of alcoholics.[5] When we remember that an estimated 15 to 17 million children in this country have an alcoholic parent,[6] and countless more have a parent addicted to some other drug, the immensity of the risk is clear.

---

[4]Jody Kellerman, *Alcoholism, A Merry-Go-Round Named Denial.* New York, NY: Al-anon Family Group Headquarters, Inc., 1969.
[5]Jill Pierce, "Alcoholism: A Family Disease." In *Alcoholism & Recovery Within the Naval Service,* 1976.
[6]Willard Foster, from conference on "Our Nation's Drinking Problem," National Council on Women in the United States (NIAA *New York Times,* March 3, 1976), p. 39.

Becoming alcoholic themselves is only one of many hazards for these children. Another study found that among the nonalcoholic wives of alcoholics, 60 percent had had an alcoholic father.[7]

Still another study, published in 1976, examined a whole range of problems in alcoholics' children. Comparing them to a control group of children whose parents were considered disadvantaged but not alcoholic, the researchers stated that "in every way the children of alcoholics are worse off than their counterparts":

- Three times as many children of alcoholics had to be placed in foster homes (31 percent to 11 percent).
- Twice as many married under the age of sixteen (6 percent to 3 percent).
- Juvenile delinquency was much higher (50 percent to 31 percent).
- Twice as many were mentally ill (21 percent to 11 percent).
- Suicides were attempted by some children of alcoholics but not by those of the disadvantaged (7 percent to 0).[8]

The destructive interaction between the alcoholic and his family is not, of course, a one-way street. As other family members become caught up in the disease, they begin to have a reciprocal effect on the alcoholic. By the time he eventually finds his way to a treatment center, his counselor has a number of sound reasons for involving the family, if only for the patient's welfare:

- Family members are often helpful in confirming or correcting the history obtained from the patient.
- Family members are statistically more likely than most people to be alcoholic themselves and thus to affect the patient in exactly the same way he is affecting them.
- A family member frequently proves to be functionally or psychiatrically "sicker" than the patient, again exerting a strong influence on whether or not he recovers.
- Even if family members are sober and relatively healthy, some or all of them unconsciously *enable* the patient's dependency, perpetuating it and making successful treatment much more difficult.

In the face of all this evidence, both clinical and empirical, it seems surprising that workers in the field of alcoholism have been so slow to

[7]Stephen Wolin, *Alcohol Transmission via Family Ritual* (unpublished), 1973.
[8]Cynthia Parson, "Alcoholic Parents: Children Show Greater Damage," *Christian Science Monitor*, June 14, 1976.

accept it as a *family disease* and provide treatment accordingly. The magnitude of the problem in terms of physical and mental illness, delinquency, economic cost, and sheer human suffering is overwhelming.

In the last five years, however, an increasing number of alcoholism counselors and others have begun to appreciate the importance of treating the family along with the alcoholic, and an increasing number of treatment centers have begun to offer programs for doing so. The Second Special Report to the U.S. Congress on Alcohol and Health called family therapy "the most notable current advance in the area of psychotherapy for alcoholism."[9]

Although the effects of family treatment on individual families can be seen almost at once, it may be many years before we can fully appreciate its broader benefits. Since we are discovering that families who have received treatment do not develop new chemical dependencies, *family treatment may be our best hope for preventing alcoholism and drug dependency in the next generation.*

In the chapters that follow, we will look first at the healthy person and the healthy family, then consider what happens to them as one member becomes dependent on a chemical. We will examine what are coming to be recognized as classic roles in the drama of chemical dependency and watch as the various family members play them out to their inevitable conclusion in either treatment or tragedy.

Then, turning to brighter things, we will talk about the new approaches to family treatment that are now bringing health and happiness back to chemically dependent families after they had thought all hope was gone. Treatment strategies, from initial work with family members, through intervention to help bring the dependent person to treatment, to the final phases of after-care and recovery—all will come in for attention. Finally we will look at the role of the counselor, the challenges that working with chemically dependent families presents, and the techniques and personal qualities that will help him meet those challenges effectively.

[9]Peter Steinglass, *Experimenting with Family Treatment Approaches to Alcoholism,* (unpublished) 1950–1975. (The preparation of this paper was supported by Grant No. R01 AA, 01441 from the National Institute of Alcohol Abuse and Alcoholism.)

CHAPTER 2

The
Whole-Person
Model

WHETHER we choose to work with one client or a whole family, our basic concern as counselors and therapists is the individual person. After all, the family's sole reason for being is the welfare of its individual members.

Early in our counseling careers, my husband, Don, and I sensed our need to have a clear picture of the healthy, fully functioning person if we were to help a client move toward becoming one. We discussed this question often, discovered that our mental pictures were very much alike, and began to develop what we call the "whole-person concept," a model that I find as effective with chemically dependent families as Don does with families in other kinds of stress. We use it both in assessing clients' problems and strengths, and in planning appropriate treatment. It has also proved to be a valuable tool for helping clients to understand themselves.

Very simply, this model shows that, just as crystals of a given compound have a certain number of facets, or flowers of a given species have a certain number of petals, so the human person has certain fundamental dimensions of being—I call them *personal potentials*. Within this framework, however, there is a great deal of room for individual variation, including the possibility that one or more dimensions may have failed to develop properly or may have been damaged after development.

In the beginning of our evolution as a separate species, mankind was no doubt dependent chiefly on his physical capacities, as most other mammals are. But through tens of thousands of years we have gradually

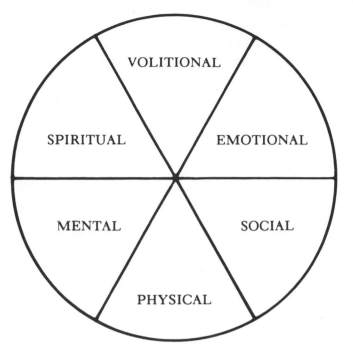

The Whole Person Wheel

developed other sides to ourselves, until today, in our present stage of evolution, we evidence six distinct personal potentials: physical, emotional, social, mental, spiritual, and volitional. To say that a creature possesses those six capacities is, in effect, to define it as human.

We like to picture the whole person geometrically as a circle—long recognized by students of myths and dreams as a symbol of wholeness. In our model the circle is made up of six separate and equally important segments. When any one is incomplete or damaged, the entire circle loses its integrity.

In order to keep the model simple, and therefore useful, we have limited it to the *structure* of the person. It does not show that structure in operation. Actually, each personal potential, though distinct, is in dynamic contact with every other, affecting and being affected constantly. If we imagine for a moment that the circle is a wheel, it becomes clear what a strong effect deformity in one segment can have on the functioning of the whole.

In any given real-life situation our feelings and behavior are the result of several, or even all six, of the potentials interacting in various proportions. Altogether, they offer their possessor a rich variety of possibilities for relating to himself, other persons, his environment, and the universe. Let us take a closer look at each of them.

THE PHYSICAL POTENTIAL

Each of us is born with a body. The one we have is uniquely our own, a set of possibilities that no other human being shares. It provides us with the horizons of what we can experience and what we can accomplish physically if we choose.

Some minimal amount of physical potential is necessary for us simply to survive as living creatures, but its value goes far beyond that. It is our first line of contact with the world around us. It holds all of our receptors for perceiving what is out there, and all of our equipment for responding to what we find. It is the foundation of health, strength, endurance, swiftness, agility, dexterity, grace, beauty, energy, sexuality, sensory awareness, communication, and much more.

All of our other potentials must rely on the physical to bring them the information they need and to translate their functioning into practical expression. But the physical potential is not totally independent either. One can see immediately how volitional power might affect health, or emotional power sensory awareness, or indeed all of the other potentials might affect, say, beauty.

A well-developed physical potential can be our key to many of the satisfactions of life. Seeing a loved one's face, hearing beautiful music, making love, creating a work of art, enjoying nature—nearly every pleasurable experience has at least some measure of physical functioning involved. The body can perceive itself as well as the world around it, so it can monitor its own well-being and enjoy its own functioning, as in dancing or sports. It can even find satisfaction in the absence of functioning—in rest.

It is obvious, however, that pleasure is not the body's only potential. It can also be a source of pain. Which we experience depends in part, of course, on chance and our natural endowment. But no one is born without at least some positive potential, and most of us have far more than we ever tap. Usually, the pleasure or pain our bodies give us is a result of how we use what physical potential we have. When we experience pain, either physical or emotional, from our physical functioning, the chances are either that we have never developed our potential fully or that, once developed, it has been allowed to deteriorate.

Deterioration of all aspects of the physical potential is rarely seen so dramatically as in the victims of alcoholism. As their disease progresses, the accompanying stress brings about a slow erosion of the physical potential, not only of the victim but of the entire family. (This is in addition to the devastating pharmacological effects of the chemical on the victim.) To the observant professional, illness, overweight, and other physical symptoms in any of the members are warning signals that dependency may exist somewhere in the family. Conversely, when treatment is underway, the physical potential can be used as a base for restoring some of the personal satisfactions that have been lacking in these people's lives for so long.

THE EMOTIONAL POTENTIAL

Developing the emotional potential, unlike the physical, calls for no nurturing, no practice. The whole range of emotions springs naturally in each of us, giving life zest and flavor. We have only to allow them, whatever they may be, to rise into the full light of consciousness and then use them in positive, healthy ways. Simple as that may sound, it turns out to be no easy matter.

Emotion is just another word for *feelings*—our inner response to both inner and outer events. We all have feelings; any person who acts as if he did not, seems to us little more than a robot. The popular student, the successful salesman, the beloved friend are all likely to be people who are at ease with their emotions, neither hiding them nor being controlled by them.

However they may admire another who responds to them with feeling, many people nevertheless find their own emotions a source of fear. Not knowing how else to handle them, they resort to pretending their feelings do not exist. This ostrichlike solution would not work for long if the game had to be played continuously at a conscious level. But, as every therapist knows so well, the human unconscious learns quickly how to block uncomfortable emotions before they ever appear on the screen of conscious awareness. Thus the game goes on and sometimes even appears to succeed—but the cost of playing is high.

Feelings, honestly felt, give life its pulse and color. They allow that part of ourselves that we experience as human to reach out and relate dynamically to the material world and the humanity of those around us. Being in touch with them is the most reliable barometer of our personal reality at any given moment, opening us to valuable intuitive insights.

Directly expressed, feelings give us credibility, let others know where they stand with us, and generally inspire trust. Responsibly expressed, they make others feel safe, knowing that our emotions will neither be allowed to run wild nor be bottled up until they explode. The emotional potential, thus channeled and harnessed, can provide an ever-flowing wellspring of energy to power the action that will convert our life choices into realities.

All these gifts are lost to the person who refuses to risk facing his feelings. Furthermore, he must invest great amounts of energy in restraining the natural pressure of emotions to make themselves manifest.

Part of his fear lies in the pain that experiencing certain feelings can bring; he does not realize that the pain caused by *not* experiencing them is far worse. Part of it lies in a belief that certain feelings are bad and that he is bad to feel them; he does not realize that all feelings are healthy and that only the way one expresses them can be "bad," or unhealthy. Yet another source of fear lies in his realization of the power of feelings and his doubts about his ability to control them. While this last fear may have some basis in reality, most people can, with help, find healthy ways to express any emotion, no matter how powerful. It is the counselor's job to provide that help.

Faced with a strong emotion, each of us has a number of choices in deciding how to respond. Some are healthy; some are not. Let us suppose for a moment that someone has publicly insulted me. Instantly I feel embarrassed, hurt, angry. My face flushes, my skin feels prickly, my teeth clench, there is a surge of energy in my arms and shoulders. I face the problem of how to respond. Some of my choices are to:

- punch the insulter in the nose, releasing my anger but doing little about my hurt and possibly adding to my embarrassment.
- insult him in return, which is merely punching him with words instead of fists.
- say and do nothing now, but carry the anger around, nursing it and throwing small bits of it at the insulter whenever I have a chance.
- deny all my unpleasant feelings and pretend that nothing has happened.

These are all unhealthy choices. They either make the situation worse by arousing the same unpleasant feelings in the other person, or they fail to give me an outlet for my own feelings and hence allow them to accumulate dangerously, ever ready to explode when a new situation brings the pressure of additional emotion.

But these are not my only alternatives. I also may choose to:

- tell the insulter then and there how I feel, but without accusing him of anything or insulting him in return.
- wait until a more appropriate time and then tell him how I feel.
- refrain from either verbalizing or acting on my feelings, but find some other way to give vent to the energy they have aroused in me.

These are all healthy choices. They acknowledge that both he and I have feelings, and they attempt to make us both as comfortable as possible. Which I choose in any given situation will depend upon the circumstances.

As people discover that they need not be helpless victims of their emotions, as they learn to make fewer of the unhealthy choices and more of the healthy ones, they begin to enjoy the rewards their emotional potential can bring.

THE SOCIAL POTENTIAL

None of us really lives alone. We may not share our home or apartment, but we all share a neighborhood and a nation, an office or factory or classroom, a club or a church congregation. Some of our greatest problems lie in our contacts with other people, and so do some of our greatest joys. To be cut off from all contact with others, as in solitary confinement, is viewed by many people as torture.

We draw on the social potential in even our most superficial relationships—with our work associates, our butcher and our banker, all the various individuals in various roles whom we encounter casually in day-to-day living. If it is functioning well, it can make all those contacts more pleasant and effective. In our society considerable importance is given to developing this level of the social potential, to learning skills that make us attractive to others and enable us to manipulate life situations to our advantage. The emphasis is not so much on the quality of the interchange as on what we can get from it.

Unfortunately, that focus does not teach—in fact, it discourages—qualities like honesty, openness, intimacy, compassion, or cooperation. Yet these are the aspects of the social potential that are absolutely essential to forming and deepening the more important relationships in our lives, relationships with spouses and children and parents, with friends and lovers, with all those who truly matter to us. As professionals, we are constantly seeing the result of this inability to form and maintain relationships. It shows up in chemical dependency, divorce, depression, violence, and a host of other problems, all of which seem to be statistically on the increase.

But the picture is not totally black. In the last twenty years there has been a growing awareness among many people, particularly the young, that we must learn to live together more humanly if we are to survive—and that there is no time to lose. With the wise guidance of people like Virginia Satir, we *are* beginning to learn.

As the social potential is exercised, it brings rapidly accelerating results. Each contact and each relationship is supported by not one but two people, both with social potentials; meeting one new friend will open the door to meeting another; developing three skills successfully will invite increased contacts and with them the opportunity to develop three more. The social potential seems to spiral as a person begins to "blossom."

When this potential is neglected, however, as it is in alcoholic families, it also spirals—downward. Then the friendship and support of others who care, needed now more than ever, deteriorate rapidly until they all but disappear. Once lost, the social potential can be recovered only slowly, for of all the human potentials it is the most dependent on the others and must await some degree of recovery in them before it can be regained.

THE MENTAL POTENTIAL

Since Socrates, and probably long before, man has stood in awe of his own mind. It has often been exalted as the single gift that separates us from other animals. Even in societies that pay lip service to equality —whether democratic or communistic—the most lavish rewards are bestowed on those with the greatest mental potential. Knowing how unequally this potential is distributed at birth, we may understandably question whether placing so much external value on mental ability is fair. We cannot, however, disagree with the fact that the mind has immense internal value in helping the individual become a whole person.

Don Wegscheider, in his recent book *If Only My Family Understood Me,* [1] has given a vivid description of the mental potential—or perhaps I should say "potentials," for it embodies several separate abilities. He calls it the "mental power."

[1]Don Wegscheider, *If Only My Family Understood Me.* Minneapolis: CompCare Publications, 1979.

The mental power has three aspects. *One aspect is in the past, in the memory.* A person's memory contains many hidden crannies, which may come to light as a new experience triggers a whole string of remembrances. A memory is useful not only for obvious reasons—like being at the right places at the right times and for remembering birthdays and anniversaries. . . . Memories also can be a valuable teacher since memory, coupled with feeling, is experience, and experience is the best teacher of all.

The mental power also focuses on the present through ideas. A person makes connections with past facts and makes new learnings. The idea functions of the brain are still the marvel of electrochemical engineering. A person is able to formulate ideas, lay out plans, investigate alternatives, and organize priorities. That is much more complex than simply maintaining a file of information.

The third aspect of the mental power is in the future, in fantasy and imagination. The imagination, a world unto itself populated with all the creatures of one's dreams, enables a person to consider all alternatives, even the most bizarre. Fantasies enable a person to try on new behaviors. The imagination enables a person to try out new activities and explore possible consequences, to "rehearse" actions. The imagination lends color to logic, freedom to order.

The mental potential thus provides a bridge from past to future, making both real in the present. Our memories speak of the past, but they still live now, today. Our fantasies speak of the future, but those too we experience here and now, today. In this way our mind enables both past and future to contribute to the important work of living, all of which must be done in the present.

In the whole person the mind interacts constantly with the other potentials—receiving the messages the body delivers and returning its own messages to the outer world; directing the emotions into safe and satisfying channels while enriching itself with their energy and spice; moderating social interactions that they may be based in reality and conducted with wisdom; offering the spirit an entrance to the world and thereby extending itself where it otherwise could not go; giving the will a sound platform of fact and reason on which to stand and thus transforming thought into action.

THE SPIRITUAL POTENTIAL

Perhaps I should make clear at the outset what I mean by *spiritual*. Through the years the word has become so confused with *religious* that the two are often used as synonymous. I do not see them so. Webster's dictionary can help us begin to make a distinction: *"Religious:* relating to or manifesting faithful devotion to an acknowledged ultimate reality or deity."[2] Every bona fide religion is strongly spiritual, but not all that is spiritual is religious. The dictionary gives less help in defining *spiritual,* so I will explain my usage of the word.

For me, spirituality has its roots deep in our universal human need to understand the meaning of life. Where have we come from? Why are we here? Where does the journey lead? Does it continue after death? And is Someone orchestrating it all?

These questions have been burning in mankind's consciousness since long before he ever recorded his thoughts. They have spawned a thousand religions and cults, inspired poets and philosophers, and contributed to the inquisitive itch that has pushed science deeper and deeper into the physical mysteries of the universe. However an individual may ultimately answer them, the very questioning is spiritual.

In a fully developed person the spiritual potential can find expression in a wide variety of both inner and outer activities: meditation, prayer, discipline, organized religion, development of the higher Self, humanitarian service, commitment to causes fostering justice, health, human dignity, and respect for other parts of our planetary community —to name but a few. The possibilities for joy and satisfaction in such pursuits transcend anything else that the human potentials can offer.

But the spiritual potential does not forever drift among the clouds. It is also a very practical matter, for it is the source of our values. Every thought, experience, or action of our daily lives is shaped by the value system we hold. When that system is illuminated by a lively spiritual awareness, it can give even the most mundane aspects of our lives meaning, beauty, and nobility.

When the spiritual potential is not activated, the person sees little reason to exist. He tries one superficial satisfaction after another in his attempt to find a happiness that continues to elude him, because it is not there. Disillusioned, he develops symptoms that range from a vague restlessness and boredom, through fatigue, irritability, psychosomatic ailments, depression. Eventually, finding no reason for living, he may end it, either suddenly by suicide or gradually by addiction to work, food, or chemicals. The steady increase in all these slow forms of self-destruction warns us that spiritual malaise is reaching epidemic proportions in our time.

---

[2] *Webster's New Collegiate Dictionary.* Springfield, MA: G. & C. Merriam Co., 1974.

Those of us who work with alcoholics and their families are painfully aware of this problem. For them, spiritual anemia can be cause, effect, or both, interplaying with their primary disease to hasten the downward spiral. Much as we may wish to, there is no way a counselor can give them the spiritual richness they have lost or never had. But we can at least tell them, in words and in our own way of being, that it *can* be had; that spiritual energy springs from within, and as long as we are alive, at least a tiny spark of it remains buried there somewhere, waiting to be fanned. The wise men of all spiritual traditions assure us that everyone who sincerely tries to find it will succeed.

THE VOLITIONAL POTENTIAL

The volitional potential is the capacity for making choices. When it is informed and active, it can be a passport to freedom, our best hope for making our dreams come true. Centered in the will, it mobilizes the data, experience, values, and energy generated by all the other potentials and puts them to work in the service of the whole person.

The healthy will effectively sets goals, ranks priorities, makes decisions, perseveres in the face of difficulty, and sustains effort until its goals are reached—or changed. I realize that the term *willpower* immediately makes many people feel guilty because of the moralistic meaning it was given in their childhood, but it is hard to deny that a strong will can be our greatest ally in living life as *we* would have it be.

By strong, I do not mean rigid. A healthy will is flexible, always open to new input from the rest of the personality, ready to adapt and change as the situation changes. This is the quality that those voices from childhood did not allow for. (Refusing to conform without question to their unbending outside definition of what was good for us may well have been the sign of a *healthy* will.)

It is less risky, of course, to let someone else set the goals and make the decisions, and simply to follow their prescriptions. Many people do. But they do so at the cost of being a whole person, for the will that is not exercised in all its functions is not fully developed. "Prefabricated" choices tend to be dictated by abstract principles, performance standards, or someone else's wishes, rather than the goals of the individual for whom they are recommended. By contrast, the choices which a healthy will makes for itself are person-centered, made for one's own well-being as well as that of others.

Avoiding responsibility for our choices might be called *volition by default*—acting without deciding. There is also such a thing as *volition by acceptance*—deciding without acting. This can be a wise choice in certain circumstances. Sometimes, as in terminal illness, loss of a loved one, war, and other adversities, the events of life may leave us truly powerless to act in any way that would bring about an outcome we would want. At such times we might rage against our fate, turn off our feelings so we do not have to endure the sorrow, or simply give up and stop living, figuratively if not literally. But any of these courses would only prolong our pain. The choice we have that can eventually end it is to make the decision for acceptance; to admit the reality of our situation, our help-lessness in the face of it, and our determination to make the best of it anyway and find some renewed meaning in life. The wisdom of accept-ance has long been appreciated in AA. It is reflected in both the Twelve Steps and the Serenity Prayer: "Grant me the serenity to accept what I cannot change, the courage to change what I can, and the wisdom to know the difference."

WHOLENESS: THE ROOT OF SELF-WORTH

Each of the personal potentials, then, as it is developed, brings its own rewards in both inner satisfaction and effective behavior. But that is not all. When all six are healthily developed, the individual not only is whole, he *feels* whole. There is no dark corner of his personality where he feels inadequate, nothing that he feels he must build a protective wall of defenses to hide. Thus, as a synergistic bonus, he enjoys strong feelings of self-worth.

Self-worth is an essential ingredient—perhaps *the* essential ingredi-ent—in personal well-being and interpersonal harmony. The diagrams shown here make clear why. When a person has a feeling of healthy self-worth, when he has no touchy areas of underdevelopment that he must shield from exposure to the outside world, he can be open. He can receive all messages from others and from his environment without blocking them, and he can respond honestly and spontaneously with messages of his own.

This does not mean, of course, that he is at the mercy of whatever winds may blow his way. He maintains some healthy defenses to protect his legitimate needs against unhealthy demands and assaults from with-out. The difference is that they are used to protect his integrity, not his weakness, and they are called into action only occasionally as the need presents itself, not erected as permanent walls.

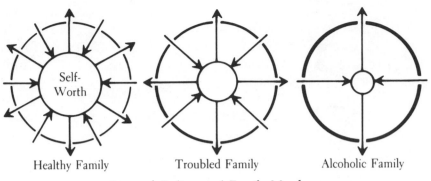

| Healthy Family | Troubled Family | Alcoholic Family |

Personal Defenses of Family Members

And so we see that strong self-worth, the hallmark of the whole person, does not make him egocentric, as one might mistakenly think. On the contrary, it frees him from preoccupation with himself and enables him to enter into a satisfying relationship with the rest of the universe.

When some of a person's potentials are damaged or under-developed, he cannot find within himself much justification for feelings of self-worth. To protect what fragile dignity he has left, he erects a wall of defenses against the critical attitude and hostile actions that he ex-pects from the outside world—an expectation based a little on actuality and a lot on projecting onto others his own harsh view of himself. It is very hard for such a person to experience honest, intimate relationships with others. Their overtures have trouble reaching the real person be-hind the defenses, and what messages they get back from him seem indirect and carefully screened.

The situation of the chemically dependent person, and eventually the members of his family as well, is even worse. They feel so vulnerable that honest interchange is almost completely closed off; it is hard to find any openings in the wall at all. Here lies the first challenge to an alcoholism or family counselor: to penetrate that wall of defenses and help the stunted or eroded feeling of self-worth to grow enough so that the wall can be dismantled, block by block, and communication reestab-lished with the larger world.

The Anatomy
of a Family

WHETHER we, either counselors or clients, have succeeded in becoming whole persons depends a good deal on the families
in which we grew up. Whether we can remain whole and continue to
develop our potentials will depend on the families (or other intimate
living networks) that we have created ourselves.

Some families function in a way that encourages health and wholeness; others, however well-meaning, seem to create stress and pain. An
experienced family therapist does not have to be in the room with a
family very long to know which kind of family it is. Virginia Satir has
given us a vivid and compassionate picture of them both in her book
Peoplemaking:

> The atmosphere in a troubled family is easy to feel. Whenever I am
> with such a family, I quickly sense that I am uncomfortable. . . . My
> stomach feels queasy; my back and shoulders soon ache, and so does my
> head. . . . After having this kind of experience over and over again, I began
> to understand why so many of the members of troubled families were beset
> with physical ills. Their bodies were simply reacting humanly to a very
> inhuman atmosphere.
>
> In troubled families the bodies and faces tell of their plight. Bodies
> are either stiff and tight, or slouchy. Faces look sullen, or sad, or blank like
> masks. Eyes look down and past people. Ears obviously don't hear. Voices
> are either harsh and strident, or barely audible.
>
> There is little evidence of friendship among individual family mem-
> bers, little joy in one another. . . . When I would see whole families in

my office who were trying to live together in such an atmosphere, I used to wonder how they managed to survive. I discovered that in some, people simply avoided one another; they became so involved in work and other outside activities that they rarely had much real contact with the family.

It is a sad experience for me to be with these families. I see the hopelessness, the helplessness, the loneliness. I see the bravery of people trying to cover up—a bravery that can eventually kill them. There are those who are still clinging to a little hope, who can still bellow or nag or whine at each other. Others no longer care. These people go on year after year, enduring misery themselves or, in their desperation, inflicting it on others.[1]

These are the families we see every day as therapists, feeling their pain with them as Virginia did. Sometimes we may wonder if there are any happy, healthy families at all. Reassuringly, she goes on to describe the healthy families she has known, offering an ideal toward which every family can begin to grow:

How different it is to be with a nurturing family! Immediately, I can sense the aliveness, the genuineness, honesty, and love. I feel the heart and soul present as well as the head.

I feel that if I lived in such a family, I would be listened to and would be interested in listening to others; I would be considered and would wish to consider others; I could openly show my affection as well as my pain and disapproval; I wouldn't be afraid to take risks because everyone in my family would realize that some mistakes are bound to come with my risk-taking—that my mistakes are a sign that I am growing. I would feel like a person in my own right—noticed, valued, loved, and clearly asked to notice, value, and love others.

One can actually see and hear the vitality in such a family. The bodies are graceful, the facial expressions relaxed. People look *at* one another, not *through* one another or at the floor; and they speak in rich, clear voices. There is a flow and harmony in their relations with one another. . . .

Members of a nurturing family feel free to tell each other how they feel. *Anything* can be talked about—the disappointments, fears, hurts, angers, criticisms as well as the joys and achievements. . . .

Nurturing families show evidence of planning, but if something interferes with the plan, they can readily make adjustments. This way they are able to handle more of life's problems without panicking. . . .

In a nurturing family it is easy to pick up the message that

[1]Satir, *Peoplemaking.* Palo Alto, CA: Science and Behavior Books, 1973; pp. 10–12.

human life and human feelings are more important than anything else. These parents see themselves as leaders, not bosses, and they see their job as primarily one of teaching their child how to be truly human in all situations.[2]

What makes healthy and unhealthy families look and feel so different, both to their own members and to an outsider? To find an answer, we must first look at just what a family is and what makes it tick.

FAMILY SYSTEMS

If we picture the individual person as a wheel, then we can see the family as a whole machine, in which several wheels operate together for some larger purpose that none of them could accomplish alone. Or, we might compare it to a body, made up of several organs each of which is comprised of many cells, functions in its own way, yet affects and is affected by the whole.

Like machines, organizations, oak trees, and bodies, families are *systems*.[3] Every system is (1) made up of component parts that are (2) linked together in a particular way (3) to accomplish a common purpose.

In a family the components are, of course, the members. While the classic family group includes a mother, a father, and one or more children, not all families fit that pattern. Today more and more families have only one parent as an active component, and fewer families have a grandparent, aunt, or other member of the extended family living in the home. Where they are present, however, they must be considered part of the system. The same is true of stepparents and stepchildren, full-time nurses, or any other persons who are intimately involved in the day-to-day life of the family. Blood ties are not required. Even an absent or deceased person may continue to be a "member" if he still exerts a strong effect on the functioning of the family—for example, as author of the rules, silent critic, or model of what to be or not to be.

All the component members are linked together by *family rules*. These rules determine the functions of each person, the relationship between persons, the goals toward which they are all heading, how

---

[2]Ibid., pp. 13–16.

[3]For readers unfamiliar with the systems approach, let me explain that the term *system* refers here to structure while *dynamics* refers to functioning. This distinction can be seen in the field of medicine, for example, where anatomy might be considered the study of body systems, and physiology the study of body dynamics.

they intend to get there, and what will be required and forbidden along the way.

Since no two individuals are alike, no two families can be alike. Their parts are unique, so their rules must be, too. Any family's rules are flavored strongly by the personalities of the parents—the rule-makers— as well as by the life situations the rules were intended to meet.

Rules perform four broad functions for the family system:

1. to establish attitudes, expectations, values, and goals for the family.
2. to determine who will hold the power and authority, how they will be used, and how members are expected to respond to them.
3. to anticipate how the family will deal with change—in itself as a unit, in its members, and in the outside world.
4. to dictate how members may communicate with one another and what they may communicate about.

An analogy I like to use when I'm working with a family is that of a mobile (borrowed in part from Virginia Satir). Let us say that you have a mobile with five or six beautiful butterflies, all of different sizes, suspended by strings from three sticks. The butterflies can represent the family members, and the string and sticks the family rules. The whole thing has been very carefully designed to keep its equilibrium. If a puff of wind hits it, it responds immediately by rocking and twisting wildly, but then slowly it brings itself back into quiet balance. This is the beauty of a mobile, ever moving yet ever returning to equilibrium.

Similarly, when the winds of life put pressure on any part of the family, the first response is usually severe distress. Then the whole family system gradually regains its stability, held together by its accustomed rules and patterns of responding.

As we begin to understand how family systems function, it is not so surprising that the problems in an alcoholic family do not end magically when the alcoholic stops drinking. Sobriety, no matter how the spouse and children may have longed for it, *is* a change. Stress follows. Furthermore, since the rest of the system was designed to maintain its equilibrium with the alcoholic in his old role, his old place on the mobile, it will subtly work to put him back into that role (although no one in the family is likely to be aware of what is happening). This is why I feel so strongly that sobriety for the alcoholic is not enough. If it is to last and if the family as a whole is to find happiness, major changes have to be made in the family system.

The mobile is a source of hope for me, for it suggests that we have many points of leverage at which to initiate change. If one member of a family is resistant, we can work with another; if one aspect of family functioning is heavily defended, we can begin somewhere else.

THE UNWRITTEN RULES

When a new member is born into the family or enters it in some other way, he finds that the family rules are there ahead of him. Others have already worked out what things they value, who will make the decisions, how they will treat one another, all the questions that families face. These rules are rarely written. Sometimes they are not even recognized consciously. But they exist all the same and are passed along to the new family member by word and action. If eight-year-old Michael gets slapped every time he talks angrily to Mother, no one has to tell three-year-old Tommy that there is a family rule against angry talk. He learns quickly just from watching and listening.

As Tommy grows up in his family, some of its rules make sense to him. They protect him from being hurt and from hurting others. They help him shape a value system. They save energy and provide short-cuts; he doesn't have to wonder how to act every time a familiar situation arises.

But there are other rules which, no matter how hard he tries, he finds difficult to obey. Even when he succeeds, they leave him feeling tight, uncomfortable, and unhappy. They are "shoulds"—the expectations of others that never really seem to be part of him.

Now all these rules, helpful and otherwise, come from people who are very important to Tommy. He cannot risk being rejected by them or punished. So he complies with the rules anyway—at least for a while. When a particular rule makes him unhappy, he doesn't tell anyone.

Like Tommy's, every family has some rules that are healthy—that is, health-promoting—and some that are not so healthy. But the healthy families that I have known have had mostly healthy rules, while the families where there was alcoholism or other stress have had many unhealthy rules.

How can we tell whether a particular set of rules will increase or decrease the well-being of a family and its members? I have three tests, based on how those rules deal with the four functions mentioned earlier:

	Healthy rules	Unhealthy rules
1. Establish attitudes, expectations, values, and goals 2. Regulate the use of authority	Human	Inhuman
3. Deal with change	Flexible	Rigid
4. Set up communication patterns	Encourage open system	Enforce closed system

Human versus Inhuman Rules

The first essential of family rules is that they be *human*. This may seem too obvious even to mention, but at a practical level I find that some of the most universal rules in our society are inhuman when we examine them:

"Be nice to everyone."
"Always look at the bright side of things."
"Control your feelings."
"Don't say anything if you can't say something nice."

Familiar? Yes, we have all heard those old saws since we were children. There's an almost endless list of such rules, or notions and assumptions that have assumed the force of rules for us. On the surface they sound wise and wholesome, but when we try to follow them, they leave us feeling confused and often worthless.

"Father knows best."
    (Then why am I, a father, so often wrong?)
"A mother's place is in the home."
    (But if I stay home, how can I support my children?)
"Children should be seen and not heard."
    (Don't grown-ups care what *I* am thinking?)
"Don't interrupt."
    (But Aunt Lucy never stops talking!)
"Good mothers bake the cookies themselves."
    (But how can I find the time—give up our bedtime stories?)

Most of us have never stopped to challenge these bits of so-called wisdom, but the truth is they have all the earmarks of inhuman rules.

Inhuman rules

• are made for someone else's benefit or to uphold some impersonal principle or institution, not for the good of the person who must keep them.

- are often unrealistic and impossible to keep.
- encourage one to be dishonest and manipulative with others to avoid punishment or rejection.
- encourage one to be dishonest with oneself to avoid feelings of guilt.

Human rules, on the other hand, have not been picked up ready-made from the past. They are tailored to fit a particular family and have an honest, reasonable ring to them.

"You may not hit anyone in the family."
"You are expected to leave the bathtub clean for the next person who will use it."
"You are expected to be home by midnight, or call."
"You are responsible for developing a value system."

These rules have been made with people's well-being as their purpose; keeping them promotes self-worth in the individual and harmony in the family. How Tommy feels about school is more important than grades. How Dad feels about work is more important than dollars. How Mom feels about making a home is more important than being there full time.

Human rules

- are made for the benefit of the whole family, not just the rule-maker.
- accept each person for who he is—human, possessed of feelings, well-meaning but sometimes fallible.
- validate the worth of everyone involved.

Flexible versus Rigid Rules

A second requirement of healthy family rules is that they be *flexible.* Part of the inhumanity of some of the rules we've been examining is their rigidity. They are often applied like military justice, without room for individual personalities or extenuating circumstances.

Rigid rules

- make no allowance for differences in people or circumstances.
- discourage change, seeing it as a potential threat to the status quo (especially that of the rule-maker).

Flexible rules, on the other hand, make the whole family system adaptable—to new jobs, new neighborhoods, new interests, new definitions of roles as men and women, husbands and wives, all the inevitable changes that living in the world can bring. A few years ago as small a change as longer hair styles caused an unbelievable amount of hurt, anger, and conflict in families whose rules did not permit change.

Flexible rules

- are applied with appreciation for the inevitable differences in circumstances and in the needs and capabilities of people.
- accept and even encourage change as a potential source of growth for the individual and the family unit.

Open and Closed Systems

The third dimension of family rules concerns communication. Certain of the rules in every family lay down what may be talked about and what must be ignored or kept secret. In a lot of families there are certain subjects that have to be treated as if they simply did not exist. Sex, illegitimacy, how much money Dad earns or how he earns it, quarreling between the parents, religious doubts, and certainly abuse of alcohol or drugs are all taboo subjects in many families. In others it may be silently forbidden to imply that Dad (or Mom, if she is the authority figure) ever makes a mistake.

Whatever subjects may be off limits, the family in which certain areas of life are closed to communication is likely also to discourage expressing one's feelings. This is particularly true if the feelings are "bad"—anger, frustration, disapproval, sadness, helplessness, fear, any feelings that the rule-maker would rather not hear. If Tommy finds he pays a high price for sharing his unpleasant feelings—the ones he may most need to share—he soon stops sharing the pleasant ones, too. With everyone in a family doing this, they in time become virtual strangers to one another.

A family in which communication is limited by the rules is a *closed* system. The parts of the system—the family members—are walled off from one another so that they cannot interact. Information and feelings stay bottled up inside each one to be handled alone. And since no one has a full and reliable picture of the situation in the family at any given moment, he must speak, act, and make his decisions out of ignorance.

The closed system usually does not admit much communication from outside either. Thus the family remains effectively sealed off from change, learning, and growth.

By contrast, the family whose rules allow an *open* system appreciates that a free flow of communication is as important as a free flow of breath to everyone in the family. Each person can feel free to negotiate for his personal needs and wants without paying a price. Just as important, he can be sure of being heard.

Everything is out in the open. Everyone knows where everyone else stands and how everyone else feels. There is no need for secrets or dishonesty. The rules may require that certain subjects or feelings be handled with special delicacy out of consideration for others, but the very fact that unwelcome information is shared as it arises can keep small problems and dissatisfactions from being magnified to really painful proportions.

SELF-WORTH IN THE FAMILY SYSTEM

Family rules are intimately bound up with the self-worth of each individual in the family. They grow out of the self-worth, or lack of it, of the rule-makers, and they determine in large measure the self-worth of the rule-keepers.

If a parent enjoys a high level of self-worth, his expectations of himself will be human, realistic, and flexible. He is honest with himself and knows himself as he is, owning all his strengths and weaknesses, all his actions and feelings. He can tolerate imperfection, in himself and in others. It is quite natural, then, that the rules he sets up will have these same qualities.

A parent with low self-worth, on the other hand, places rigid, perfectionistic expectations on himself, trying in vain to earn the worth he needs so badly. He sets impossibly high standards for himself and others, especially in matters of performance, which may be subject to evaluation by the outside world. Having already established unhealthy rules for his own living, he simply extends them to the whole family. Unfortunately, where one parent's personal rules are healthier than the other's, those of the less healthy one all too often dominate.

Rule-making is only one place where the effects of parents' self-worth can be felt. The person who feels good about himself tends to radiate good feelings throughout the network of people close to him. In strengthening that network and nurturing the self-worth of the others in it, he reinforces and enhances his own worth.

The person who feels inadequate transmits his feelings, too—destructively. He may create an illusion of ties with others, but since he cannot risk true intimacy ("Someone may discover how worthless I am!") no closeness really exists. Feeling so empty himself, he is in no position to nurture the self-worth of his spouse or children—he has nothing to give. More likely, he will erode or even overtly attack what worth they do have in a desperate effort to get a little for himself.

How much self-worth our little friend Tommy develops as he grows will depend heavily on how much his parents have. It can be passed from parent to child just as surely as if it were hereditary. It does not take a very sophisticated understanding of family dynamics to imagine Tommy's young personality flowering in the warm, nourishing presence of parents who are secure in their own feelings of worth. Their set of rules is there to provide protection and gentle direction for his growth, flexing as he and the situation change. They help him develop the qualities and skills that will give him a realistic basis for self-esteem, and they offer an appreciative word for each new sprout of development.

But what if Tommy finds himself born into a family that lives at the poverty level when it comes to self-worth?

Every infant is born with a deep need to belong. It seems to be nearly as strong as the instinct for survival, and it becomes fixed almost immediately on the mother, expanding within weeks to include the father and the entire immediate family. Out of this need Tommy will try very hard to live up to his family's rules, at least at first.

If the rules are unhealthy, he will often find himself faced with the dilemma that in order to obey them, he must do something totally out of tune with the real-life situation or with his personal needs and desires. He faces a devil's choice of violating his own judgment and integrity by complying, or being punished or rejected for refusing to comply—or possibly avoiding either by being manipulative or dishonest.

For a while avoidance may seem like his best choice. He forgets to do things; he goes through the formalities of complying but in slow, slow motion. With experience he learns quite a few ploys. Outsmarting the rule-makers at their own game may even seem like fun—for a while.

But the truth is that Tommy must sell more and more of himself to play. Cheating, it turns out, confronts him with the same hard choice he has been trying to avoid. He still risks being found out, perhaps to be punished even more severely for his contempt of the family court; if he goes unpunished, his guilt is all the greater. All along he has been feeling angry, resentful, spiteful—all labeled "bad" emotions. Now he must add selfish and dishonest. He feels increasingly worthless.

As a young child Tommy related to his family with a sense of "I belong." He was important because he was part of this family, lived in this house, had certain responsibilities and privileges. Gradually he begins to feel, "*I* belong. I am important just for myself." This signals the birth of personal self-worth if it happens in an environment where it is allowed, appreciated, and encouraged.

If Tommy's budding sense of worth is seen as threatening by the rule-makers in his family, though, it is more likely to be greeted with hostility. Once again his natural thrust toward personhood finds itself thwarted by the family system. He may rebel and defy the rules, actions he has come to label as "bad," or he may surrender to the rule-makers and end up labeling himself "weak" or even "crazy." Whatever his choice, the effect on his self-image is negative.

And so it goes. People with low self-worth make rules that shape new little people with low self-worth. One day they will make the same kind of rules unless something happens to break the chain.

THE ALCOHOLIC FAMILY

Not every family in stress is alcoholic, but every alcoholic family is in stress—severe stress. They evidence all the characteristics of the unhealthy family that we have observed in this chapter, but usually to a more extreme degree than families with other problems. In addition, in nearly ten years of working with alcoholic families, I have come to realize that they have certain other distinguishing marks as well.

Let us look at two typical families, one alcoholic and one suffering from stress of some other kind.

FAMILIES IN STRESS

Non-Alcoholic	Alcoholic
Their Problem	
Identifiable. Family members often know the source of their distress when they come for help, or at least admit it when it is brought to their attention.	Denied. Family members show sincere delusion: "We're in trouble, but alcohol has nothing to do with it."
Their Feelings	
Painful, unexpressed, and to some extent repressed.	Acutely painful and generally totally out of awareness—part of a larger pattern of denial and delusion.

Non-Alcoholic	Alcoholic

Their Defenses

Highly developed to protect individual members from even greater pain and lower self-worth.	So highly developed that they are rigid and compulsive. Repressed feelings have become locked in as attitudes: anger has become resentment; fear has become withdrawal; guilt has become avoidance.

Their Self-Worth

Low.	Even lower, because all the worth-destroying factors in the family are more intense.

Their Behavior

Fixed in predictable patterns. Family members assume an array of defensive roles in an unconscious effort to survive, both individually and as a family unit.	Rigidly fixed and compulsive. The defensive roles are the same, but family members have become locked into them because of the denial and compulsion in the system.

Their Communication

Severely restricted by family rules.	Similarly restricted by family rules, but also blocked totally in many areas by denial and delusion.

Their Recovery Program

Educational efforts can be effective. In spite of impaired communication, pain often motivates the family to be open enough to accept information from an outside source and so move toward change.	Education alone ineffective; more formal treatment required. New information cannot penetrate a defense system with so much resistance, denial, and delusion. Members deny both their personal contribution to the family's pain and the fact that alcohol is at the bottom of it.

And so it seems that we have learned a good deal about families in stress that will be useful to us in helping families whose stress is caused by chemicals. But because their problems are not only the same but also different, that knowledge must be combined with a deep understanding of the eventually total devastation that chemical dependency wreaks, both on its immediate victim and on the family members who share his tragedy.

CHAPTER 4

The Addiction Spiral

Tragedy: a serious drama typically describing a
conflict between the protagonist and a superior force
and having a sorrowful or disastrous conclusion[1]

THOUGH I have worked with hundreds of alcoholics in my
years as a counselor, it is still a sad undertaking for me to describe the long
and relentless disintegration of the human being that chemical dependency brings about. Unless someone intervenes to change the scenario,
the alcoholic's story is, in the fullest sense of the word, a tragedy.

Since the deteriorating condition and behavior of a chemically
dependent person are so closely intertwined with what happens to everyone else in the family, we need to understand exactly what is taking place
at various stages of the disease and the symptoms by which these changes
can be recognized. Just as important, if we are to act compassionately,
is to know what the disease feels like to its victim.

So in this chapter we will trace the process of chemical dependency
from the first experimental use to total physical addiction. For our
protagonist we will use an alcoholic, a middle-class American family man
—the type of Dependent seen most often in treatment facilities. But let
me say once again that dependency does not respect age, class, gender,
or life-style. And it matters little whether the drug is alcohol, heroin,
amphetamines, prescription drugs, or another of the dangerous chemicals with which people in pain try to change their moods. Although we
will focus on adult alcoholism here for convenience, the growing dependence of a youngster on some other drug follows a similar pattern and
certainly is no less tragic.

[1] *Webster's New Collegiate Dictionary.* Springfield, MA: G. & C. Merriam Company, 1974.

My description is a composite from many separate observers: research pharmacologists in the laboratory, survey-takers who have questioned alcoholics for science, recovering alcoholics who have published their own descriptions, and first-hand reports from the hundreds of alcoholics and their families whom I have come to know in the last ten years.

No doubt, the scenes of this unfolding drama will be quite familiar to a few of my readers, those who are daily involved in alcoholism counseling; but for many others, not only lay persons but also those who work with alcoholics in less specialized professional ways, this description may complete what has been only a fragmentary picture.

THE PROCESS OF CHEMICAL DEPENDENCY

Social Drinking

All drinking starts out as social drinking. Except for members of certain subcultures, most people in our society drink alcoholic beverages at least occasionally. Young people are usually introduced to their first experience with alcohol in the teen years—sometimes earlier. For many, drinking becomes a regular part of social activities while they are still in high school.

What sort of experience a youngster has in his first experiments with chemicals depends on the circumstances—the type of chemical, its purity, and the quantity ingested; the situation in which it is used, whether at a party, in a crisis, or while alone; and the emotional state of the person at the time, whether excited, happy, depressed, or in pain. If the experience is positive, it leads to an important discovery: chemicals can change how you feel. If Cindy finds that alcohol makes her feel more confident and outgoing, if Tim finds it helps him forget that he's flunking math or losing his girlfriend, then an indelible lesson has been learned. The greater the mood swing, the more clearly the lesson is imprinted.

The next time those young people want a change of mood, the answer seems obvious—have a drink! A positive experience with one chemical sometimes encourages them to try others. They may decide that alcohol is more effective for certain situations and certain kinds of mood changes, other drugs for others, so they use either or both according to the effect they desire.

For most people this early learning about alcohol is the beginning of a lifetime pattern of "social drinking." (That rather imprecise phrase generally refers to drinking in moderate amounts at meals or on social

occasions.) But for every ten or fifteen experimenting youngsters who can look forward to years of uneventful enjoyment of alcoholic beverages, at least one other has taken the first step toward alcoholism.

Of course, that ill-fated young drinker has no idea what lies ahead for him. Even a physician, psychiatrist, or alcoholism counselor could not predict with any reliability which members of this year's graduating class might end up in trouble with alcohol. Research to uncover an alcoholism-prone personality type or other factors that might enable us to detect high-risk drinkers early has consistently ended in disappointment. One day such clues may be discovered. In the meantime, we can only assume that the person with the greatest perceived stress in his life and the fewest effective ways to cope with it is the most vulnerable; if his initial experience of easing that stress with alcohol is favorable, he is even more so.

The young drinker probably would, if asked, be aware of having learned that chemicals ease pain. But the learning seems to take place at another level, below awareness, as well. It is as though the body learns autonomically that a given chemical it has experienced relieves certain unpleasant sensations. That kind of learning is hard to erase. It is like learning to use a typewriter or ride a bicycle; it lasts for life.

In time many people move from *learning* the effects of alcohol to *seeking* them whenever they want a change of mood. This is still considered social drinking and a common occurrence in today's high-pressure living. "What a day! Let's have a drink!" Now and then that one drink may turn into three or four, or six or seven if the problem is big enough or the occasion special. The evening ends in intoxication, and morning brings a hangover. Yet, it may somehow seem to have been worth it. "After all, it was New Year's Eve!" Or, "A guy doesn't get a raise every day." Many people who drink can stay at this stage all their lives without complications.

But some drinkers will find that as months or years pass, they are gradually consuming larger quantities and more often. Their drinking may not yet be excessive enough to attract attention, especially if heavy alcohol use is common in their social groups. But chemicals affect more than one's mood. While the mind is enjoying euphoria, the body is slowly adapting its chemistry to this stranger that seems to have moved in to stay. At some point the drinker notices that he has to drink more to get the same "buzz." Two or three drinks used to wipe out the day's worries; now it takes five or six.

Exactly how and why the body acquires this increased tolerance for alcohol is still a subject of pharmacological research. It is known, however, that the tolerance crosses over to certain other drugs as well. Years ago, surgeons noticed that patients who drank heavily required larger amounts of ether or chloroform to become anaesthetized. And more recently, infants of mothers who were heavy drug users have shown the symptoms of alcohol addiction at birth.

Whatever the chemical explanation, one thing is certain: *acquired increased tolerance* is an early warning to the heavy social drinker that serious trouble lies ahead.

Blackouts

If that warning goes unheeded—as it most likely will in the incipient alcoholic—and larger quantities are ingested to get the old relief, sooner or later another warning sign appears. He has his first *blackout.* This is a chemically induced form of amnesia that occurs with regular, heavy use of alcohol or other mood-altering drugs. At first, blackouts may last only a minute or two, but as dependency develops, entire evenings and longer can be lost. Blackouts can even occur to a Dependent when he has not been drinking, and they continue for a long time after he has stopped and is detoxified.

The onset of blackouts is a frightening development. It can cause personal and job problems that are costly and hard to explain because neither his companions nor the victim himself has any clue that the blackout is happening. He talks and acts normally, does not lose consciousness, and may not even show any signs of intoxication, but for the period of the blackout nothing gets written on his memory. He can make promises, hear class assignments, negotiate business deals, incur debts, and have no idea afterward that he has done so.

There is not total agreement in the field of alcoholism studies as to exactly when the social drinker crosses the invisible threshold of harmful dependency. However, blackouts are a phenomenon unique to the prolonged, heavy intake of mood-altering chemicals. In my opinion, the occurrence of the first blackout is evidence that the user has become "hooked." During this first phase, however, the dependency is considered to be psychological. It will have wrought great devastation to the Dependent's life and person before it meets the rigid criteria for complete physical addiction.

Up to this point, the emphasis has been gradually shifting from *"social* drinking" to "social *drinking."* Once dependency sets in, alcohol is no longer consumed as a beverage but as a drug. Where drinking was once a matter of conviviality and pleasure, it is now a matter of need. The Dependent begins to become preoccupied with alcohol. "Will they serve something more than just a glass or two of wine tonight? Maybe I'll have a couple before we go. . . . Hmm. I'll toss this one down and get a refill before they serve dinner. . . . It's eleven o'clock and nobody's mentioned a nightcap. Wonder if there's anything left in that bottle I stashed in the trunk of the car."

He begins to sneak drinks, aware that he is drinking more than the people around him. "They don't understand—I *need* it." But all the same, he feels guilty. Much of the time and money he once devoted to his family is now going to alcohol. From time to time his drinking causes trouble with his wife or friends or employer. All this increases the load of guilt, and his self-worth begins to erode.

Early in his drinking career the Dependent drank to change his mood from normal to euphoric. Now his emotional pain is so great that the best he can hope for is a change from bad to normal. Euphoria is gone. When a person no longer gets "high," when he drinks for relief rather than pleasure, it is a sure sign that he is in trouble with alcohol.

Meanwhile, his blackouts are becoming longer and more frequent.

One cannot have a long blackout and simply return to normal the next day—the life complications are just too great. Nothing is more pitiful than to hear an alcoholic describe how it felt to wake up in the morning to find the front end of his car smashed—and have no idea where or how it happened.

As the disease progresses, blackouts can last for two or three weeks. I recall one man who came to our center for help after his boss had confronted him about his drinking. He seemed to sincerely want treatment to help him stop. He took the information we gave him about hospitals and left, presumably to be admitted to one of them. But he never arrived. Nearly three weeks later he walked into our office again, and once again he asked for information—just as though he had never been in before. As far as he was aware, he hadn't; he had been in a blackout since before the first visit. On being questioned, he told us that the last thing he remembered was leaving home one morning to find help. How long ago that was and where he had been ever since, he had no idea, and he would not have until the credit card bills came in. He later discovered he had been all over the country, staying in motels, spending money, and he knew not what else. That not-knowing is one of the terrors of the blackout.

Inevitably, episodes like this increase the alcoholic's already heavy burden of guilt and feelings of worthlessness. He needs relief more than ever, and for him relief is spelled *alcohol.* But now even relief is elusive and costly, because he must consume much more alcohol to get it.

Loss of control

Sometime before the average alcoholic's blackouts become as bizarre as in the story just related, the next critical event occurs—*loss of control.* Until now, despite the clear signs of a growing dependency, the drinker could still stop drinking when he chose to. Once loss of control sets in, that ability is lost. He can still make a choice whether to take the first drink of a bout, but after one or two, he no longer has that option. In the words of E. M. Jellinek, pioneer investigator of alcoholism as a disease, "Loss of control means that any drinking of alcohol starts a chain reaction which is felt by the drinker as a physical demand for alcohol. . . . [The bout] lasts until the drinker is too intoxicated or too sick to ingest more."[2]

Why this sudden, quantum plunge? In *The Disease Concept of*

[2]Jellinek, "Phases of Alcohol Addiction," *Quarterly Journal of Studies of Alcohol,* 13 (1952): 673–84.

Alcoholism, Jellinek attributes it to the same process that eventually will bring about profound withdrawal symptoms:

> The withdrawal symptoms as they occur within a drinking bout, in the presence of loss of control, are tremors of the fingers and lips, slight twitchings, some motor restlessness, and sometimes delusions (not hallucinations). These symptoms are promptly relieved by more alcohol, but the relief is of short duration and the symptoms recur after a short interval, whereupon the drinker again takes recourse to more alcohol. This process goes on and on until the drinker either cannot ingest more alcohol, or the drinking is stopped through extra-

neous circumstances. . . . In the bout with loss of control the elements of jocularity and philosophizing are absent and only anxiety, some degree of panic, the ebbs and tides of withdrawal symptoms, and the demand for more alcohol are conspicuous.[3]

In charting the progressive phases of alcoholism more than a quarter of a century ago, Jellinek saw loss of control as marking the critical transition into the "addictive phases." However, he was careful to make clear that even at this stage the alcoholic was not a completely helpless victim of his disease. "The drinker," he said, "has lost the ability to control the quantity once he has started, but he still can control whether he will drink on any given occasion."[4]

With his behavior so often literally out of control, the Dependent begins to encounter a lot more pressure from the people around him. They become concerned and warn him; they become angry and threaten him; they become hurt and weep. For a while their attempts to end his drinking seem to be meeting with some success, for many alcoholics "go on the wagon" at this stage. But the ride is usually short. The pain in their lives has become so great by this time that it cries out for relief. So the alcoholic steps into a bar, sincerely intending to have "only a couple," but he ends up drinking until after midnight. It will be a long while yet before he realizes, and admits to himself, that he can never again take "a couple of drinks." This is why complete, permanent abstinence is so important to recovery.

All of us face times when the pressures of life get almost too heavy, when we are filled with painful feelings and our self-worth is low. At such times the natural human tendency is to fall back on certain universal psychological defenses to protect us from further attack, by those around us and by ourselves. The alcoholic is no exception.

As soon as his drinking began to cause complications in his everyday life, he called out the time-honored defenses of denying, avoiding, blaming, making excuses, and all the rest. But those early difficulties were nothing compared to the pain, problems, and personal criticism that follow loss of control. He feels shame at his frequent episodes of complete drunkenness and the continuing failure of his best efforts to stay sober; he feels guilt at his neglect of his wife and family; he feels hurt and lonely as friends become fewer and fewer; he feels frightened as his

[3]Jellinek, *The Disease Concept of Alcoholism.* New Haven, CT: College and University Press, 1960; pp.145–146.
[4]"Phases of Alcohol Addiction."

job situation becomes precarious and debts mount. To admit his predicament would bring more pain than he could handle. (This is one of the reasons for the high suicide rate among chemically dependent people.)

So psychological defenses of one sort or another come to dominate all his interactions with others. This defensive behavior is so predictable and consistent among alcoholics that a counselor can quickly recognize it:

> *He alibis.* "I didn't drink too much last night. It was just those enchiladas that made me sick."
>
> *He blames.* "If I had a wife who cared about me, I wouldn't have to go out with the boys at night."
>
> *He threatens.* "Don't try to tell *me* what time I ought to be home for dinner—I'll come home when I get good and ready!"
>
> *He charms.* "Aw, come on, honey. Let's forget about it and start over. It'll be different this time."
>
> *He boasts.* "I'm the only guy in that whole shop that's worth a nickel. Why, you ought to see the mess there when I don't make it to work for a couple of days!"
>
> *He avoids.* "If they're so stiff a fella can't have a couple of drinks, I don't want to go there any more."

Such tactics may temporarily silence the accusers without, but not the harsher accuser within. The Dependent's last resort is repression. In order to survive, he turns off his painful feelings, keeps them turned off with more alcohol, and buries them somewhere deep in his subconscious. Unfortunately, positive feelings like love and compassion—the feelings on which relationships are built—get buried along with the negative ones. And in order to lay his feelings to rest, much of the objective truth about his situation must be repressed, too. As a result, he gets farther and farther out of touch with reality.

This growing delusion is reflected in his defensive maneuvers. The alibis are but a statement to others of the *rationalizations* that he is telling himself. The blaming is simply a reassignment of his own guilt, which he has transferred to someone else by *projection.* The boasting is a voicing of the *grandiose delusions* with which he has unconsciously filled the vacuum that was once his self-esteem.

Sometimes, though, even these bulwarks fail, and misery overruns his most elaborate defenses. Then he sinks into black remorse, followed by renewed periods of abstinence. Or, still denying his by now evident loss of control, he may set up rules to govern the time, place, and circumstances of his drinking, vowing to be faithful to them.

Such resolutions are, of course, predestined to fail, and the Dependent finds himself back where he started but a little worse off. Such is the downward spiral of dependency. His life now revolves more and more around alcohol. He hoards and hides bottles. If he has not already lost most of his friends, he drops them—except for drinking companions. He loses any remaining interest in outside activities. If he has not already lost his job, he may decide to quit it. He will give any of a thousand reasons, but the truth is that he could not handle it and his drinking, too. And the drinking is no longer a matter of choice.

In fact, less and less of his life is a matter of choice. He is trapped in a pattern of compulsive behavior that is controlled by his physiological dependence and his psychological defenses—both completely out of his awareness.

Through the long ordeal of his growing dependency his family may have stood beside him, protecting him and picking up the responsibilities that he was gradually abandoning. In fact, they have probably done so with a pathology to match his own (as we will see in forthcoming chapters). But sooner or later, even these ties wear thin. His spouse and children are likely to leave him literally or simply to close ranks for mutual support and survival, leaving him emotionally alone. This is also a point at which they may be motivated to seek outside professional help.

As the alcoholic's isolation thus deepens, he becomes increasingly egocentric. He is touchy, takes offense unreasonably at the slightest provocation, and indulges in extravagant self-pity, perhaps the only conscious emotion of which he is still capable.

The prolonged heavy intake of alcohol that has brought the Dependent to this desperate emotional state has taken its toll on his body, too. Now the damage begins to make itself known. He is likely to have his first hospitalization for a condition related to drinking.

Withdrawal Symptoms

Hospitalization means, of course, abrupt and complete separation from the one thing that he is sure he cannot do without. And the next few days may prove him right. When his alcoholism has progressed beyond a certain point, suddenly allowing the concentration of alcohol in the blood to drop from its usual high level will precipitate a crisis. The *withdrawal symptoms* that follow—convulsions, hallucinations, delirium, delusions, and tremors—arc collectively, in Jellinek's words, "the only criterion for the development of physical dependence upon alcohol."[5]

With withdrawal symptoms, the body is making a clear and dramatic statement that *physical addiction is now complete.* In order to live with the continuing presence of large quantities of alcohol, the cells have slowly adapted by incorporating the chemical into their metabolic script. Where once they could not function normally with alcohol in the blood, now they cannot function without it.

A life-threatening experience like withdrawal may reactivate all the alcoholic's old resolutions about sobriety. It may even be the crisis needed for him to be willing to accept treatment. But unless he does get treatment, effective treatment, and unless he is highly motivated to change, the weeks or months following hospitalization will be only a brief pause in the long downward journey.

Just before or just after the alcoholic gets clear evidence that he has become physically addicted, his drinking behavior takes a new turn. He begins looking for a *morning drink* to steady his nerves and numb his physical and emotional discomfort—that "hair of the dog" without which he cannot face the day, perhaps cannot even get out of bed.

Until this point, drinking, however heavy and uncontrolled, was probably limited to evening use or an occasional weekend afternoon. Now the morning drink must be followed by reinforcements at intervals during the day—perhaps at coffee breaks and lunch.

While the alcoholic at this stage is continually looking for a drink to maintain the blood-alcohol level to which his body has become habituated, he is still putting up a final effort to maintain the facade of his former life. He may still be employed, still trying to fulfill some of his functions as a husband and father, still trying to hide from public view the full extent of his dependency.

But before long he comes to one morning to discover he has had his first prolonged intoxication lasting for several days. What was formerly *continual* drinking has become *continuous* drinking, a distinction first made by Jellinek. His description is graphic:

> The increasingly dominating role of alcohol, and the struggle against the "demand" set up by [morning] drinking, at last break down the resistance of the addict, and he finds himself for the first time intoxicated in the daytime and on a weekday, and continues in that state for several

[5] *The Disease Concept of Alcoholism*, p. 130.

days until he is entirely incapacitated. This is the onset of prolonged intoxications, referred to in the vernacular as "benders."[6]

Morning drinks, daytime "nipping," now weekend benders—life as usual is no longer possible. Maintaining a full-blown addiction becomes a full-time job. Thus Jellinek believed that the bender heralds the end of what he called the "crucial" period of alcoholism and the beginning of the "chronic."

Chronic Alcoholism

In this last, chronic stage, as in high tragedy, the whole complex of dire developments that have been taking place over time now descend on the central figure with their full impact. Again, for a concise description we can do no better than Jellinek, whose restrained clinical language only accentuates the harsh reality of what it is telling us:

> This latter drinking behavior meets with such unanimous social rejection that it involves a grave social risk. Only an originally psychopathic personality or a person who has later in life undergone a psychopathological process [such as alcoholism] would expose himself to that risk.
>
> These long-drawn-out bouts commonly bring about *marked ethical deterioration* and *impairment of thinking* which, however, are not irreversible. True *alcoholic psychosis* may occur at this time, but in not more than 10 percent of all alcoholics.
>
> The loss of morale is so heightened that the addict *drinks with persons far below his social level* in preference to his usual associates— perhaps as an opportunity to appear superior—and, if nothing else is available, he will take *recourse to "technical products"* such as bay rum or rubbing alcohol.
>
> A *loss of alcohol tolerance* is commonly noted at this time [reversing the increased tolerance acquired earlier]. Half of the previously required amount of alcohol may be sufficient to bring about a stuporous state.
>
> *Indefinable fears* and *tremors* become persistent. Sporadically, these symptoms occur also during the crucial phase, but in the chronic phase they are present as soon as alcohol disappears from the organism. In consequence the addict "controls" the symptoms through alcohol. The same is true of *psychomotor inhibition,* the inability to initiate a simple mechanical act—such as winding a watch—in the absence of alcohol.
>
> The need to control these symptoms of drinking exceeds the need of relieving the original underlying symptoms of personality conflict [emotional pain], and the *drinking takes on an obsessive character.*

[6]"Phases of Alcohol Addiction."

In many addicts, approximately 60 percent, some *vague religious desires* develop as the rationalizations become weaker. Finally, in the course of the frequently prolonged intoxications, the rationalizations become so frequently and mercilessly tested against reality that the entire *rationalization system fails* and the addict admits defeat.[7]

The tragedy is complete. The Dependent has lost everything, even his alibi. He is left with nothing but his pain.

THE LOST PERSON

Let us pause here a moment to consider the magnitude of the alcoholic's loss.

When he first began to use alcohol socially, we can assume that even though he may have been immature, he was nevertheless a fairly whole person. (I say "fairly" because most people in our society today seem to be less than truly whole, and thus vulnerable to a whole range of emotional and physical problems—depression, obesity, work addiction, compulsive pleasure-seeking, psychosomatic ailments, chemical dependency.)

From that initial state of relative wholeness, his personal potentials began to erode. The loss became visible earlier in some areas than others, and we shall inventory the various potentials, not in the order in which they were introduced in chapter 2, but in the order in which healthy functioning appears to be lost. But I want to add a word of caution: any system of ordering these changes can be misleading, because the loss is actually taking place in many parts of the alcoholic's being simultaneously. Within the physical potential, for instance, it is hard to say whether personal appearance or sexual satisfaction deteriorates first. A sloppy appearance certainly is not going to enhance one's opportunity for sexual satisfaction; on the other hand, decreased sexual desire can reduce one's motivation to look appealing to a sexual partner.

The erosion of personal potentials seems to begin with the feelings.

The Emotional Potential

Whatever the personal pain that first made social drinking attractive to him, the chances are the alcoholic once felt good about himself

7Ibid.

and his life at least part of the time. While drinking, he could enjoy himself and feel "high." He was still clearly in touch with his feelings, pleasant or unpleasant. But as social drinking slipped into harmful dependency, the good feelings became fewer, and there were onslaughts of uncomfortable feelings that made his original discomfort, for which he started using alcohol in the first place, seem mild indeed. In time he experiences the whole catalog of painful human emotions:

- *Anger:* He feels angry at his wife, family, employer, friends, everyone; angry because they do not understand him, make unfair demands, won't leave him alone, think he cannot take care of himself; angry most of all at himself. The anger becomes chronic and diffused as *hostility* and *resentment* that alienate those around him.
- *Fear:* He is afraid that he will be discovered, that his family will leave him, that he will lose his job, that his health is deteriorating; afraid that his supply will be cut off so he cannot continue drinking, and afraid that he cannot stop. The fears become chronic and diffused as *anxiety* and *tension* that make him restless and unable either to focus his attention well or to relax and sleep.
- *Shame, guilt, feelings of worthlessness, and remorse:* He is ashamed of the drunken behavior he remembers the morning after, and ashamed of the behavior he does not remember because of blackouts; ashamed of his inability to control his drinking once he starts; ashamed of the mounting financial troubles, social rejection, and other problems caused by his drinking. He feels guilty about neglecting his job and family, squandering money in bars, telling lies and breaking promises. Shame and guilt pile up into feelings of worthlessness and remorse in the face of a growing addiction that he feels responsible for starting but cannot seem to stop.
- *Depression:* As his negative emotions multiply and fuse, they aggravate one another and feed a deepening depression, evidenced by lack of appetite, listlessness, and inability to sleep.

When the burden of painful emotions reaches a point he can no longer tolerate it, he begins to repress them—to turn them off. Gradually he is not so aware of the fear and guilt. But blocking out the bad does not bring back the good. Instead, he is left with no feelings at all—numb, "turned off," no longer able to relate to other people or events as a human, feeling being. Then, in the late stages of his addiction, he loses even the ability to repress, and the realization of his true situation descends on him in a flood of desperation and despair.

The Physical Potential

The body once offered the alcoholic a number of avenues for enjoying his life and wholeness. One by one they are destroyed:

- *Physical skills:* Sports, dancing, playing an instrument, arts and crafts, technical skills, all require some combination of strength, energy, and muscular control. At first, the alcoholic may simply find himself playing tennis less often—he has a headache this morning; he'll watch the tennis matches on TV this afternoon (with a beer). As he gets out of practice, he is even less inclined to make the effort. He is drifting away from his friends, so partners are harder to find, too. As addiction eventually sets in, the hand that could once put a ball just out of his opponent's reach or control a power tool with hair-breadth accuracy can no longer hold a cup of coffee without spilling.
- *Personal appearance:* As exercise and nutrition are neglected, his body begins to feel and look sluggish. He pays less attention to his dress and grows careless about his grooming. As his self-worth deteriorates, so does the personal appearance that may once have been both a source and an expression of that worth. After a certain stage of dependency, just a snapshot can tell much about the toll his disease has taken.
- *Sexual desire and satisfaction:* The Dependent's sexuality weakens early, partly from lack of energy and partly from lack of feeling, partly because his partner no longer finds him very appealing and partly because he no longer finds her as appealing as alcohol. This lessening of sexuality often causes a man to think that he has grown impotent, a woman to think that she is frigid—fears that may be projected onto the partner. Doubts about sexual adequacy are particularly difficult for an adolescent, who may not yet have established a healthy self-image as a sexual being.
- *Health:* The first effects of growing dependency on health occur by omission. Regular exercise is neglected, then abandoned. Nutrition suffers as more and more of the day's calories come from alcohol. Appetite wanes as hangovers become heavier and more frequent, and the digestive system begins to rebel. Stomach ulcers often develop, and the liver and pancreas begin to show symptoms of disorders that may one day be fatal. As alcoholism advances, the skin, heart, blood vessels, neurological system, even the brain cells can be severely damaged.

The Mental Potential

At first glance, the incipient alcoholic seems to have his mental powers honed to a fine edge. He alibis, "cons," charms, bluffs, covers all the bases; he plans ahead, maintains a supply, finds money to pay for it, keeps it hidden yet always in reach; he manages to keep his job and maintain a facade in the community long after he is far down the road to dependency.

But his cleverness is an illusion. As we have seen, the defenses that he has called into action to protect him from criticism and from his own painful feelings end up giving him a highly distorted picture of reality. Rationalization and denial keep him from seeing the truth about any person or situation, while projection, grandiose notions about himself, and other delusions let him substitute "truths" of his own making.

Blackouts are a profound insult to the mental potential, in effect destroying it for limited but growing periods of time. And the resulting gaps in memory remain as a permanent deficit. In the advanced stages of addiction, the victim suffers hallucinations, brain cells deteriorate, and there is a possibility of alcoholic psychosis.

The Social Potential

Before addiction, alcoholics run the gamut from withdrawn intro-verts to brassy extraverts. Thus at least many of them have known both close relationships with family and friends, and satisfying contacts with more casual acquaintances. In fact, social drinking may at first seem to make a positive contribution to interaction with other people.

But any gains are brief and seductive. As the alcoholic begins to drink more heavily and frequently than the others in his social group, the friendly connection becomes strained. If they do not ostracize him, he starts to find them "boring" or to resent their well-meaning advice about his drinking. As the disease begins to transform his personality and the hale fellow becomes increasingly hostile, all but his closest friends learn to avoid him. Meanwhile, he turns to new companions who fit more comfortably into a life-style that is being focused more and more on alcohol.

At home his relationship with wife and children is cold, stormy, tearful, or intermittently all three. Those close to an alcoholic must endure watching this person they love turn into a series of different and difficult strangers as his disease advances through its progressive stages. At first he may come home cheerful and "high" after "a couple of

Scotches with the boys from work"; with heavier drinking he becomes angry and hostile toward them; then he begins to dump much of his self-hate onto them, projecting and blaming; finally he seems to have no feeling for them at all, though he is exceedingly touchy himself.

No matter how strong their bond of affection once was, it wears thin. His marriage and home remain intact, if they do, through his wife's sense of duty, her inability to make a change, or—most often —her own participation in all the symptoms of his disease except the pharmacological.

The Volitional Potential

The free will and its power of choice are not the first to go in this slow disintegration of the person, but they may eventually be the aspect of the person that is most nearly destroyed.

The alcoholic loses his power of choice by slow increments. Long before dependency is present, he has become so accustomed to numbing any unpleasant feelings immediately with a drink that he loses his tolerance for emotional tension. The dice of decision-making are soon loaded against any choice that might involve a little personal discomfort, no matter what other value the choice might have.

As dependency sets in, loss of control literally deprives the drinker of choice over one very important thing in his life; how much he will drink and when he will stop. Later, when dependency has evolved into total physical addiction, there is no choice at all; continuing to drink is a matter of life and death. Indeed, the life-style of the chronic alcoholic, as we have seen, offers few choices about anything.

The Spiritual Potential

Deciding what does and does not have value is normally a function of the spiritual side of our nature, but in a Dependent it is usurped by the chemical. A person who finds relief in social drinking sees alcohol as a resource with value. But if he becomes dependent on it, the chemical moves from something that *has* value to something that *is* a value in itself—in time, the central value in his life. All else begins to revolve around it, and preserving his relationship with it is his first priority.

If the Dependent has formerly belonged to an organized religious group, his ties to it are likely to be one of the early social connections broken; he feels uncomfortable with the members now, both angered and shamed by their criticism (whether silent or spoken, real or a figment of his own projection). If he had an inner personal relationship with a

Higher Power, he has probably turned away from it in his growing sense of unworthiness.

It is interesting to me, however, that from the depth of their despair in the late chronic phases of their disease so many alcoholics have been reported to display again "vague religious desires." Even the feelings of guilt and unworthiness that have persisted throughout the long decline reveal that the spiritual potential is never entirely extinguished. Much of the effectiveness of AA may lie in its call to whatever remains of the alcoholic's spiritual self. The Twelve Steps emphasize establishing or renewing his relationship with a Higher Power, thus fanning the spiritual coals until they slowly reignite the rest of the personal potentials.

There was a time when it was thought that an alcoholic could not accept help until his disease had run its full course to the chronic phase —until he had "struck bottom." This pessimistic view seemed logical enough. How could anyone reach him earlier? By the time he was willing to admit psychologically that drinking was causing more pain than it relieved, he was hooked physically.

But the cost of the long delay was high, nothing less than total bankruptcy of the person. For that reason alcoholism counselors and others have tried to find ways to stop the destruction sooner. Working closely with those who care most about the alcoholic, they have succeeded in bringing an increasing number of drinkers to treatment and sobriety earlier. By intervening, they create a crisis (AA members call it a "high bottom") in which the alcoholic is helped to face his situation and his alternatives honestly before all is lost.

CHAPTER **5**

The Family Disease

F E W   A L C O H O L I C S play out their drama alone. Like the embattled protagonist of a Shakespearean tragedy, blind and unknowing, they take a whole cast of supporting characters down to disaster with them.

Everyone whose life touches the alcoholic's is in one way or another affected by his disease, but its direct consequences fall on the members of his immediate family, those who in a most literal sense share his life and eventually his illness. His boss can dismiss him. His employees can quit. His friends can drift away. But his family cannot so easily turn their backs on him and his problem. To do so would mean totally disrupting their own lives as well as deserting someone they love (or at least once loved) just when he needs them most.

So they choose instead the only alternative they can see—to stay and adapt to his illness. (Children, of course, have no opportunity for choice at all.) At first this decision may offer the satisfaction of knowing they are doing the "right," the human, thing. But it has one fundamental and fatal flaw: *there is no healthy way to adapt to alcoholism.*

In our last chapter the alcoholic himself occupied center stage, pursuing his long downward journey. Now the scene changes, and we will observe what is happening to the other players, his family, as they try to adapt to the increasing pressures and problems that his deteriorating condition brings.

During the early years, when the Dependent's drinking is still social drinking, the family may experience occasional episodes of embarrassing drunkenness or quarrels over too frequent nights out "with the boys." But since many people abuse alcohol this way without becoming dependent on it, neither the incipient alcoholic nor his family seriously anticipates the peril that lies ahead.

Sooner or later, however, they discover that seeking relief in alcohol has turned into psychological dependence on it and a preoccupation with making sure that relief is available whenever it is needed. The now dependent drinker spends less time at home, and his family begins to feel its first pressures. He neglects some of his responsibilities as a husband and parent. There are fewer good times together. He is rarely in the mood for an outing with the kids, and he complains that the friends and activities that he and his wife used to share are now "boring." He has substituted new friends and new activities that involve drinking, but for his wife and children the gap is harder to fill.

By now the Dependent's body has grown so accustomed to a heavy intake of alcohol that he must consume more than before to get the same relief. As a result, he spends more of the family budget for liquor—a source of friction in most families and downright hardship in many.

One of the early signs of dependency—blackouts—probably appears some months before the family becomes aware of it, because at first the episodes may be brief. But eventually some chance occurrence brings them to light. Perhaps the Dependent does not show up for dinner on a night when he "knew" guests were invited. Or he has no memory of where he parked the car before the movie. Or he promises to take the children fishing next weekend, only to announce on Saturday morning that he's going to the ball game with Joe.

To his wife and children, such incidents often seem to be a display of simply not caring. They feel lied to and abandoned, never realizing that he has absolutely no recollection of that dinner invitation or that promise to go fishing. They also feel frightened, because they can find no way to make sense of what is happening. Occasions like these occur more often and more bizarrely as dependency deepens. Trust and communication suffer.

As the inevitable pattern unfolds, loss of control sets in. Now even the promises he can remember are broken. After the first drink or two the alcoholic—the term can now be applied—could not stop even if a whole sea of children's tears waited at home. He drinks until someone eventually brings him home totally intoxicated. Meanwhile, his family are left to deal with their feelings—a bitter mixture of anger, hurt, disgust, frustration, and even some guilt for having such "bad" feelings about their husband or father. If he does not find his way home until the next day, when he has sobered up, they will also have had to worry whether he had been arrested, injured, or worse.

After a long bout or a particularly difficult family scene, the alcoholic may earnestly resolve to "go on the wagon." And he may succeed in avoiding that fateful first drink—for a while. The family enjoys a brief taste of the good old days, when things were different and life together held some joy. But it is only a matter of time until a problem at work, a quarrel at home, perhaps even a happy occasion like an anniversary will lead the alcoholic to take the one drink that in his present stage of dependency is inevitably followed by more. When that happens, his family's earlier pain is dwarfed by what they feel now—helplessness, frustration, and fear both for themselves and for the drinker, whose true condition they are finding it harder and harder to deny.

The crises that blackouts and loss of control bring are dramatic, but they are not any more damaging to health and self-worth than the sanity-eroding effects of living day to day with a chemically dependent person. The price of adapting to his erratic behavior is becoming very, very high. He threatens, and the family members feel afraid. He blames, and they feel hurt or guilty. He boasts, and they feel contempt or, if others are present, embarrassment. He alibis, and they feel distrust. He charms, and they give in—only to feel anger and self-contempt when he later betrays their trust.

As we have seen, the alcoholic's true emotions are by now so painful that he cannot bear to feel them. So he represses them and, instead of responding honestly to those around him, calls up a bewildering repertoire of psychological defenses. Let us watch a typical scene.

It is Monday morning, and Ralph is nursing a fearsome hangover. As he looks out of the window at the grass he didn't mow and the weeds he didn't pull, he feels a momentary shadow of guilt, then irritation. At an earlier stage of his illness he would have felt a *lot* of guilt. He might have alibied to his wife, or made contrite promises to clean up the yard the first chance he could find, or simply acted touchy when anyone mentioned it. But he no longer does any of these things. Instead, he blames his two sons and orders them to do the job after school. They try to explain that they have to go to baseball practice, but he walks out without listening. When he comes home to find the work still undone, he shifts the blame to his wife, shouting and accusing her of not raising the children to be obedient. Feeling hurt and unfairly treated, she starts to cry. Her tears once would have prompted compassion, or at least guilt, but now they are more than his beleaguered spirit can handle. He tells her with disgust, "Oh, stop acting like a baby!"

Thus Ralph not only denies his own underlying feelings of guilt, covering them with self-righteous anger and blaming, but he demands that his wife deny her feelings, too. As such scenes are repeated over and over again, she will indeed begin to deny them, for the same reason he does: they are too painful to bear. So it is that the psychological symptoms of alcoholism spread contagiously to every member of the family.

As painful emotions get repressed one by one, the alcoholic finally reaches a point where he is completely "turned off." He no longer shows any signs of caring about his family. He seems incapable of feeling anything at all. Remembering that feeling is the lifeblood of the family, we can begin to understand how devastating this situation is for his wife and children. It no longer matters much whether he is away from home or present; he has effectively cut himself off from them.

With the alcoholic no longer functioning either emotionally or practically as part of the family, the other members feel a great void. At some point they realize that in order to survive, they must close ranks and take on their own shoulders the responsibilities he has abandoned.

Ralph's wife, Mary, is already working, but now she looks for a second job to help pay the bills. Seventeen-year-old Jenny takes over most of the housework and helps out at the variety store on Saturdays to earn money for college. Fourteen-year-old Jim gets a newspaper route and tries to keep the family's aging car and household appliances running. Ten-year-old Kenny cares for the yard and does odd jobs for the neighbors. No one has much time for fun.

To friends it looks as though this little family was handling its difficult lot with great strength, courage, and wisdom. Professional people in the community, however, are beginning to see the family more often. The family doctor knows that Mary has been in to see him several times, complaining of pain in her back, headaches, and a developing ulcer. The police have picked Jim up twice on minor charges, and Kenny's teacher sent a note home last week saying that his noisy clowning was disturbing the rest of the class. The chances are, however, that like the blind men and the elephant in the old, familiar story, each of these professionals sees only one small piece of the puzzle; none is aware of the larger family disorder that is the root of the symptom with which he is trying to deal.

Sometimes visible problems like these lead one member of the family into counseling of one kind or another. When that happens, the larger picture may begin to take shape. Seeing does not necessarily mean understanding, though. There is so much denial and delusion surrounding chemical dependency—on the part of the entire family, not just the Dependent—that any picture presented in the consulting room is likely to be highly distorted. Further, that picture rarely fits the usual psychological models or responds to the usual therapeutic techniques. So members of alcoholic families can be very discouraging clients—*unless* the counselor fully understands the nature of their family disease.

In the hands of a counselor who does have that understanding, however, the disease is proving to be both identifiable and treatable. The same array of emotional and behavioral symptoms occurs with remarkable consistency among families and responds encouragingly to the specialized treatments that are being developed.

As a family disease, alcoholism is both *personal* and *systemic;* it affects each family member as an individual and the family system as a whole. This is simply a clinical way of saying that any butterfly can affect the balance of the mobile as a whole, and that once that balance is disturbed, it affects every other butterfly. As these others are set in motion, they, in turn, exert further pressures on the whole, pressures which eventually travel back through the system to the butterfly who started the whole chain reaction.

This model has been immensely useful to me in understanding the action-reaction patterns I observe repeatedly in alcoholic families. Each member is constantly having to react to what another member has done and to do so in a way that offers some promise of stability for himself. The more charming and irresponsible A becomes, the more serious and responsible B becomes. The more aggressive and blaming A is, the more passive and guilt-ridden is B. Family members' behavior can be understood only when it is seen realistically, as *an equal and opposite reaction to the dysfunctional attitudes and actions of the Dependent.*

RULES IN THE ALCOHOLIC FAMILY

Let us now look at what goes on in an alcoholic family in the light of the system principles presented in chapter 3. As you will recall, we described a system as "(1) made up of component parts that are (2) linked together in a particular way (3) to accomplish a common purpose."

We have only to consider the very first of those elements, the components, to realize that the alcoholic family is in for trouble. One member is hooked on an outside force and cannot move freely to maintain the system's balance. Because of that fact, he sends first ripples, then tidal waves of disturbance through the family system. Other members must adjust to this situation, and in time they become so damaged by the pressure and the postures they must assume to withstand it that they, too, start sending out waves of disturbance.

From this perspective, the alcoholic appears to be a very powerful person. And yet, did we not see him only a few pages ago trapped and helpless, tossed on the ever stormier sea of his addiction? Here lies the paradox: *as the alcoholic gradually loses power over his own life and behavior, he wields more and more power over those of the people close to him.* Though he is increasingly dependent on them for support— emotional, social, and financial—he plays the dictator to get it. He controls what they say, what they do, what they think, even what they feel. The control is so constant, all-pervasive, and often subtle that they may not even be aware of it.

As we established in chapter 3, the person who holds the power makes the rules. He literally designs the system, and he designs it in his own image. The problem is that in a dysfunctional family the most powerful person in terms of rule-making is also the most dysfunctional. In an alcoholic family that person is, of course, the Dependent. It should not surprise us, then, that the family takes on a group identity which mirrors that of the alcoholic, and soon everyone is displaying the psychological symptoms of his disease.

Predictably, alcoholic families are governed by rules that are inhuman, rigid, and designed to keep the system closed—unhealthy rules. They grow out of the alcoholic's personal goals, which are to maintain his access to alcohol, avoid pain, protect his defenses, and finally deny that any of these goals exists. Here are a few of the rules that I encounter again and again in my work with these families:

Rule: The Dependent's use of alcohol is the most important thing in the family's life. For example, he is obsessed with maintaining his supply, and the rest of the family is just as obsessed with cutting it off. While he hides bottles, they search for them. While he stockpiles, they pour liquor down the drain. Like two football teams, their goals lie in opposite directions, but they are all playing the same game. They all plan their days around the Dependent's drinking hours—he to be sure that nothing interferes, they to frustrate his plans, or to arrange to be home in order to meet his demands, or to arrange *not* to be home in order to avoid his fury or possible embarrassment in front of their friends. The Dependent's use of alcohol is the overriding family concern around which everything else revolves.

Rule: Alcohol is not the cause of the family's problem. At first, the drinker and his family deny that he is abusing alcohol. Later they deny that he is dependent on it. Finally, when dependency is glaringly evident, they insist that it is only a complicating factor, not the root of whatever difficulties have led them to seek help.

Rule: Someone or something else caused the alcoholic's dependency; he is not responsible. Here the Dependent's increasing tendency to project his guilt and to blame someone else for his situation gets crystallized into a rule and imposed on the rest of the family. The scapegoat may be his wife or a child in trouble or a job he does not like—anything. Curiously, the scapegoat often goes along with the delusion and is overwhelmed with guilt and feelings of worthlessness.

Rule: The status quo must be maintained at all cost. It is easier to understand the extremely rigid way an alcoholic family responds to change by looking once more to our model of a mobile. If the largest butterfly were to become snagged on some outside object, the string with which it is attached would pull taut and the supporting sticks would become rigid. Something similar happens when one family member gets snagged on a chemical. What's more, he is afraid to get unsnagged, for he feels that without it he cannot survive. So as rule-maker he makes sure that the sticks and strings of the family system stay rigid enough to protect him from change.

Rule: Everyone in the family must be an "enabler." When you ask members of an alcoholic family how they feel about the Dependent's drinking, they are of course quick to say that they would do anything to get him to stop. But all the while they are unconsciously helping him to continue—"enabling" him, a process that we will examine more closely in the next chapter. One person in the family plays the role of chief Enabler, but according to this unwritten rule, everyone else must do his part, too, to protect the Dependent and his dependency. They alibi for him, cover up, take over his responsibilities, accept his rules and quirks docilely rather than rock the boat. These actions may be defended on grounds of love or loyalty or family honor, but their effect is to preserve the status quo.

Rule: No one may discuss what is really going on in the family, either with one another or with outsiders. This is exactly the sort of rule we would expect in a system as unhealthy and closed as an alcoholic family. Feeling threatened, the rule-maker tries to avoid, first, letting people outside know about family affairs—specifically, the degree of his dependency and the magnitude of its impact on his wife and children—and second, letting family members have access to new information and advice from outside that might undermine their willingness to enable.

Rule: No one may say what he is really feeling. This is a standard rule in severely dysfunctional families. The rule-maker is in so much emotional pain himself that he simply cannot handle the painful feelings of his family, which make his own even sharper. So he requires that everyone's true feelings be hidden. As a result, communication among family members is severely hampered. What there is tends to be rigid, distorted, and incomplete, the messages bearing little resemblance to the real facts and feelings that exist.

Eventually, as his disease advances, the alcoholic completely represses his own feelings and, like Ralph, unconsciously puts in their place false emotions that are less painful. These are the feelings that seem on the surface to prompt his actions. But to those who know him well, his performance is not quite convincing. They may respond as though they took his behavior at face value, but at some level they sense a second, subliminal message coming from the real self that he has repressed.

They are thus confronted with contradictory messages coming from different parts of the Dependent. One they hear with their rational

Dependent's true feeling ⟶	*Dependent's behavior* ⟶	*Family members' feelings*
Guilt, self-hatred	Self-righteousness, blaming	Guilt, self-hatred
Fear	Aggressiveness, anger	Fear
Helplessness	Controlling (of others)	Helplessness
Hurt	Abusiveness	Hurt
Loneliness, rejection	Rejecting	Loneliness, rejection
Low self-worth	Grandiosity, criticalness	Low self-worth

minds, the other with intuition. They feel confused because the two messages are saying such totally different things:

"If these kids would show a little responsibility about money, I wouldn't have to be so hard on them."

(I'm worried that I'm going to lose my job because I've called in sick so many Monday mornings.)

"If you were more affectionate, I wouldn't stay out late at night."

(I know I'm not satisfying you—I don't know what's happened to me lately.)

"Why should I go to church? That new minister is only interested in money."

(I'm no damned good. I can't face the minister, or the congregation either.)

Most often the false emotion expressed in his behavior is the opposite of the true emotion that lies underneath. Aggressiveness masks fear; blaming masks guilt; controlling masks helplessness. But, ironically, his behavior evokes the same painful feelings in family members that the Dependent is feeling underneath. In the table on page 83 we can see the dynamics of contagion by which family members gradually come to manifest the psychological symptoms of alcoholism.

A CHOICE OF ROLES

Trapped (or at least thinking they are trapped) in this highly disordered system, how do family members adjust? The only healthy response would be not to adjust to it but to open it up by voicing honestly their practical problems, their mental confusion, and their emotional pain and frustration. This course would protect their own psychological well-being and offer the best hope of bringing the Dependent to treatment as well. But few family members choose it, for they risk losing the whole matrix of their lives. Instead, they opt for preserving the family system at whatever cost.

Left with only unhealthy alternatives, they choose—and by now this should not surprise us—the same defense as the Dependent: they hide their true feelings behind an artificial behavior pattern, a supporting role in the alcoholic drama, which seems to promise some kind of reward in a system that offers few.

In ten years of working with alcoholic families, I have watched the same five basic roles being played out in virtually every family. I have labeled them the *Enabler,* the *Hero,* the *Scapegoat,* the *Lost Child,* and the *Mascot.* In a small family there may be more than one role for each person; in a large family, there may be more than one person for a single role. But in all families all roles are played by someone, and everyone plays a role.

Role-playing and the adoption of a particular role are not calculated behavior, of course. They happen subconsciously, and the family member is likely to deny vigorously that the masquerade exists. The destructiveness of these roles for the person who plays them does not lie in the nature of the role but in the fact of role-playing at all. The family member who plays a role cannot be honest with either himself or others. Instead, he must send double messages, an overt one from the role self and a covert one from the real, hurting self. These can be just as unhealthy coming from a family member as from the Dependent.

None of us ever becomes so whole that he is not tempted to fall into a role. The reader will no doubt recognize some of these roles from his own experience. They occur in all troubled families, even occasionally in healthy families in times of stress—and stress is a part of our everyday reality. But in alcoholic families the roles are more rigidly fixed and are played with greater intensity, compulsion, and delusion.

Let me make it clear that we are talking here about behavior, not people. Occasionally, when circumstances change or one role becomes too uncomfortable, a person may try another. This often means that whoever has been playing the newly chosen role will also have to switch, relinquishing the old role and adopting the one that was vacated. The most common role-trading is between the Hero and the Scapegoat. During most of my childhood and adolescence I was my family's Hero. But when the time came that I felt a need to leave home, they did not understand, and I suddenly found myself the Scapegoat. Though the family I have created enjoys healthier functioning than the one in which I grew up because there is no one who is chemically dependent, I nevertheless find myself sometimes tempted to play the Enabler for the three children I love so much.

In an alcoholic family, however, switching roles for any reason is not really common. We must remember that this family mobile is not moving freely. The individual gets trapped into one role, and his personal potentials are gradually deformed to fit its demands. He slowly *becomes* the role.

Each role grows out of its own kind of pain, has its own symptoms, offers its own payoffs for both the individual and the family, and ulti-

SYSTEM DYNAMICS OF THE ALCOHOLIC FAMILY

Role	Motivating feeling	Identifying symptoms	Payoff		Possible price
			For individual	For family	
DEPENDENT	Shame	Chemical use	Relief of pain	None	Addiction
ENABLER	Anger	Powerlessness	Importance; self-righteousness	Responsibility	Illness; "martyrdom"
HERO	Inadequacy; guilt	Overachievement	Attention (positive)	Self-worth	Compulsive drive
SCAPEGOAT	Hurt	Delinquency	Attention (negative)	Focus away from Dependent	Self-destruction; addiction
LOST CHILD	Loneliness	Solitariness; shyness	Escape	Relief	Social isolation
MASCOT	Fear	Clowning; hyperactivity	Attention (amused)	Fun	Immaturity; emotional illness

mately exacts its own price. The table on page 86 presents the identifying features of each.

Which role is played by which person is more related to his position in the family than to personality factors. To understand how roles are adopted, let us go back for a moment to Ralph and his family. As his drinking developed into dependency and he became less responsible, Mary felt she had little choice but to step into the breach. She tried to preserve family income, reputation, relationships—all the things that were being jeopardized by Ralph's drinking. It was taxing, but it rewarded her with feelings of righteousness and importance. However, in order to protect the family, she also had to protect Ralph. She became an Enabler.

By the time their daughter, Jenny, was eight years old, she knew that all was not well in the household. She did not fully understand the things she saw and heard, but she did sense that the family desperately needed someone to give it the sense of worth it had all but lost. At the same time she needed a way to get some attention from her preoccupied parents. So she worked hard and became a Hero.

Jimmy was only five then. He needed attention, too, but there was no way he could out-hero Jenny. So he decided to get attention the only other way he knew—by being naughty. He became the Scapegoat.

From infancy Kenny knew only a family that was deeply troubled. By the time he was old enough to take part in the family exchanges, three of the roles were already filled. So he escaped the pain of interacting by spending a lot of time alone in his room, playing quietly or just daydreaming. However, there were times when he felt confused and frightened by the incomprehensible—and, he had concluded, unmentionable —things that were happening in his family, his only source of security. Then it was impossible to sit quietly. He felt he would explode. By chance he discovered he could let off tension by clowning. It even brought the family a little fun, and him some unaccustomed attention. So Kenny became a Mascot. But when things are particularly difficult, he still leaves the scene—thus playing the Lost Child as well.

This family illustrates the most usual sequence of roles, with the spouse (either husband or wife) playing the Enabler; the oldest child, the Hero; the second child, the Scapegoat; the youngest child, the Lost Child, Mascot, or both. If there had been a fourth child, the two roles probably would have been separated. The Lost Child, however, is the role most likely to turn up randomly in the age progression, and appears to be more influenced than the other roles by the temperament of the individual. (In families where the chemically dependent person is a child, of course, the arrangement of the cast is somewhat different.)

A particularly sad situation, to me, is the plight of the only child in an alcoholic family. My experience with these children, confirmed by the findings of the Booz-Allen Report,[1] is that they take on parts of all the roles. They may play them simultaneously or alternately, but either way their pain and confusion are overwhelming.

The longer a person plays a role, the more rigidly fixed in it he becomes. We have noticed that families who are fortunate enough to get help early in the progression of their disease shed their roles more easily. In the later stages of alcoholism, however, the roles seem to have taken over the people. One might say that *family members eventually become addicted to their roles,* seeing them as essential to survival and playing them with the same compulsion, delusion, and denial as the Dependent plays his role of drinker. Eventually someone "hits bottom" and reaches out for help. If the professional who provides it is wise in the ways of alcoholism, this may provide an opportunity for intervention with the whole family.

The following chapters will describe these roles in detail. My characterizations are admittedly broad, almost caricatures, to make the distinguishing features of each role stand out; and no individual will fit a given role in every particular, for it is only a composite of probabilities. Those things said, let us now take a closer look at each of the roles— its identifying behavior, its special pain, its potential dangers, and its implications for the counselor who would penetrate it to help the helpless player cast it off. (In good theatrical tradition, the cast will be listed in order of appearance on the family stage.)

---

[1]Booz-Allen and Hamilton Report. Prepared for the National Institute on Alcohol Abuse and Alcoholism, 1974. (Available from the National Technical Information Service, U.S. Department of Commerce, Springfield, VA 22161.)

CHAPTER 6

The Enabler

$\mathbf{I}$т is no accident that every alcoholic has a supporting cast—literally supporting—as he plays out his drama. Without them he would have had to face the consequences of his actions long before his dependency on drinking could have developed into full-blown alcoholism.

Even at a relatively early stage, the Dependent's behavior is already becoming unhealthy, irresponsible, and so antisocial that its natural consequences constantly threaten to overwhelm him—if he should have to face them. But he rarely does. The people around him, especially those who love him or whose well-being is intimately bound up with his, step in to protect him from those consequences. As his disease progresses, they step in more often and with more elaborate protection. The effect is to deflect the hand of fate and soften its blow.

I call this process *enabling*.

All these efforts do not, of course, succeed in saving the Dependent from feeling intense emotional pain. But they do avert for a time many of the social and financial difficulties the family would otherwise experience, and thus they delay the day of reckoning.

The physical grip of dependency, however, continues to tighten. And so, by preventing the crises that might bring the alcoholic to treatment, his well-meaning family actually prolong the disease.

Almost everyone who has any relationship with the Dependent— child, parent, employer, co-worker, friend—enables, at least occasionally. He is surrounded by people who pinch-hit for him, hide his mistakes, alibi or lie for him even to themselves.

But among them there is always one who is the chief Enabler. Predictably, this is the person emotionally closest to the Dependent, usually the spouse. For simplicity, just as we referred to our "typical" Dependent as *he,* we will now refer to the Enabler as *she.* But we must remember that, while less visible, millions of women are closet alcoholics —they may equal or even surpass the number of men—and for every dependent wife there is an enabling husband.

Where the Dependent is unmarried, divorced, or widowed, the Enabler may be a roommate, lover, or perhaps an oldest child. Where the Dependent is a youngster, the parents, one or both, play the Enabler. (We will take a closer look at parent Enablers later in this chapter.)

Why, we may ask, would anyone knowingly choose to help a loved one destroy himself with chemicals? The answer is, of course, that they don't. The small daily choices that add up to enabling are made individually, under stress, and without any clear understanding of their real effect on the course of the Dependent's disease.

An enabling wife often acts out of a sincere, if misguided, sense of love and loyalty. Sometimes she may also act out of shame, to protect her own and the family's self-respect. And unquestionably she is motivated by fear, the realistic fear that she and her children may have to share the unfortunate consequences of the Dependent's alcoholic behavior. Most Enablers I have known do not even see their actions as choices; they honestly feel they have no alternatives. "If I didn't take over, who would?"

When Julie and Bob were married, they were each very proud of the other. Julie was bright and attractive; Bob was personable and already launched on a promising career with his company. They shared a wide variety of interests and enjoyed teaching each other new things. Julie loved to cook, so they started a gourmet dinner club among their friends. Bob fancied himself something of a wine connoisseur and introduced Julie to the fine points of labels and tasting.

Then in the second year of their marriage, Bob was promoted to regional manager, a position that required him to travel a good deal. About the same time Julie discovered she was pregnant. In some ways the prospect of parenthood brought them closer than ever, but there was a new distance, too. Julie was, after all, enjoying an experience that was exclusively female—motherhood. Fatherhood was different. Where once they had shared so much, now each had a separate project, Bob his business, Julie the coming baby.

Bob did feel some natural pride and happiness at the thought of starting a family, but also loneliness, a heavy sense of new responsibilities, and a nostalgia for the days only last year when there was time for things like tennis and concerts. He needed someone to talk to, some way to pick himself up—"for Julie's sake."

The evening the baby was born, Bob celebrated by going out and getting, as he put it, "gloriously drunk." He had been drinking a lot more lately. In fact, it seemed to Julie that everything they did socially involved having a drink. But she put down her concern, thinking, "Oh, he needs a chance to relax and have a little fun. I guess I shouldn't make a big deal of it. Now that I'm no longer pregnant, things will go back to normal. He won't feel the need to drink so much."

But things did *not* go back to "normal." Julie wanted to be a good mother, and that took more time than she had expected. Sometimes she felt irritated that Bob never volunteered to help with the baby. Yet, she realized that he was having to take second place most of the time. She really wanted to be more available to him as a companion and friend and lover, but what could she do? She felt torn between her husband and her child, both of whom needed her.

"Maybe I could become more efficient so I'd have more time for him. . . . Maybe I could pretend I really am interested in hearing about that new machine they're installing. . . . Maybe I shouldn't let him know how tired I feel when I have had to be up at night with the baby. . . ."

Bob's drinking did not go back to "normal" either. It was getting heavier. Julie's attempts to hide her own problems and pretend interest in his only seemed to increase his growing moodiness. His behavior began to embarrass her, and often he made her the butt of cruel jokes in front of their friends. Still, she quietly tolerated whatever he did, hoping to smooth things over. She—whom Bob had originally been attracted to for her honesty and willingness to express her feelings—now found herself carefully guarding every word and action.

The years passed. Julie went on putting up with her life, but she was far from happy. There were so many things she had to do that she hated, and the list continued to grow. She hated having to alibi for Bob to his boss, to their friends, even to the children (by now there were four). She hated having to secretly check up to make sure he had paid the bills. She hated taking care of him when he got sick from too much alcohol. She hated always having to give in and say *she* was sorry, just to keep peace.

Yet things could be worse. When Bob was sober, she still loved him very much. After their blow-ups he would repent and tell her over and over that he didn't intend to hurt her. He would vow to change and for a while would behave just as he had in the good times years ago, sensitive and loving. There were candy and flowers, evenings out and intimate conversations. Dare she believe his promises?

For a while she did, but always he disappointed her. His drinking, his undependability, his mood swings became all too predictable. Yet Julie felt that as a wife her role in life was to support her husband and help him as best she could. If a husband can't count on his wife, whom can he count on?

So she developed a whole repertoire of ways to cope with the many problems Bob's now compulsive drinking presented. It seemed there was nothing she could not do. People complimented her on being so organized yet so flexible, so able to deal with any crisis that came up. But Julie herself simply felt tired, very tired. Too tired to be hurt, too tired to be angry, too tired even to be a good mother.

"Tired" certainly did describe the way Julie looked the day she first walked into my office, weighed down by all the physical and emotional fatigue that had been accumulating during the thirteen hard years of her marriage. She wore a dogged smile chiseled on her lips, but her eyes told me a different story, of grief, bitterness, and near despair.

As Julie proceeded to tell me about her life, she recounted a series of crises as melodramatic as any television soap opera. I knew it was all true, for I had heard it many times before. I also knew, however, that she was telling me only about 10 percent of what the family had actually been doing and feeling. That was all she was aware of! I could make some fairly accurate guesses about the other 90 percent, based on my experience with other alcoholic families. My job, however, was to help Julie gradually let down all the screens and defenses she had built up through the years and discover the truth for herself.

Enabling, like chemical dependency, begins imperceptibly. As the Dependent's social drinking more and more frequently ends in intoxication, the Enabler finds herself trying to make explanations to the children or smooth over embarrassing incidents with friends. For a long while she excuses the Dependent or at least resists admitting that he has a real drinking problem. "With a high-pressure job like Hal's, I suppose he needs to unwind on weekends." Or, "The crew Ed works with always want to stop for a beer on the way home, so he hasn't much choice."

As his pathology increases and takes on the dimensions of a disease, so does hers. In the beginning her constant defense of him might have been discounted as gullibility or simple wishful thinking, but now, in the face of his steadily worsening behavior, it must be recognized for what it is—denial, a characteristic symptom of alcoholism in the Dependent! In time her behavior, like his, will assume a classic, compulsive pattern and follow a predictable course.

The Enabler steps into her role in earnest when she first decides to take over some of her husband's responsibilities. Though she may

not yet realize the seriousness of his illness, she does know that he is getting less and less reliable; if the household is going to function at all, she had better take charge. Before long, she finds herself playing father as well as mother and, on top of her usual duties, is making most of the family decisions, controlling the finances, and probably earning extra money as well.

All the while she goes on carefully protecting the Dependent. On Monday morning she calls his boss to say he has "the flu" (read: "hangover")—and thus saves him from being reprimanded or fired. On Thursday afternoon she turns down the Hadleys' invitation to dinner—and prevents their watching him get drunk long before the food is served. She skimps, budgets, does without—and so relieves him of financial responsibility. She looks after the children, the car, the yard, the household repairs—and saves him from both the burden of attending to these chores and the guilt of seeing them neglected.

To friends, relatives, neighbors, even professional people if they are naive in the ways of alcoholic families, she appears to be trying hard to discourage the Dependent's drinking. She pleads with him and berates him; she destroys his supply and cuts off his drinking money. But all the while her super-responsible posture is actually making it possible for him to go on drinking. *She is preventing the crises that offer the Dependent's —and the family's—one hope for change.*

While the Enabler's load is heavy, it is not without its rewards. The household now runs more smoothly, and she is its de facto head. She may be having an opportunity to show, as never before, how capable she really is. These are powerful payoffs, and they reinforce her role as Enabler.

Nevertheless, her life is hardly enviable. Her days are long and exhausting. She spends little time in fun and a lot in worry. For all her efforts, the things that make life worth living seem to be getting scarcer and scarcer. She feels deeply resentful, and her feelings begin to show.

THE PRICE THE ENABLER PAYS

In spite of her competence and indispensability to the family, the Enabler suffers constant assaults on her self-worth. The Dependent's erratic and sometimes outrageous behavior leaves her embarrassed to face family, friends, creditors, the larger community, even her own children.

As his dependency grows, he relieves his own pain by dumping (projecting) his guilt and self-hatred onto her. He criticizes her for her appearance, her sexuality, her disposition, her mothering of the children, her housekeeping, her spending habits, her friends—indeed on every conceivable count, including problems that are a direct result of his own alcoholic life-style.

All these charges are hurled at an exhausted target that is already feeling a great deal of self-doubt. After all, she has been putting all her imagination, skills, time, and energy—more energy than she ever thought she had—into trying to make things right with the family. But things are not right; instead they seem to get worse and worse. Why? Maybe she *is* a poor wife, a poor homemaker, a poor mother. Maybe she's just an all-around failure as a woman . . .

And so the most painful attacks of all come from within. She, too, begins to feel guilt and self-hatred. To endure them and go on functioning under the load she has assumed, she does exactly what the Dependent has done—she turns off her feelings. In time she goes on to follow his next step as well—projection. She heaps the blame back onto him, along with a generous measure of the anger that she has been holding back for so long.

It is in this stage of her "disease" that a counselor is likely first to encounter her. No wonder so many counselors see Enablers as "bitching," nagging, sarcastic, unpleasant to work with. But I would remind these professional people that what they observe are not traits of the person before them but rather symptoms of this family illness as typically manifested in whichever member assumes the enabling role.

The Enabler, like the Dependent, is engaged in a single-minded pursuit of what she sees as her very survival. She, too, suffers from the generally deteriorating relationships and life situation of the family; time, energy, joy, hope, and often money are in chronically short supply. Inevitably, this constant stress from within and without takes an increasing toll of the Enabler's personal potentials.

The Physical Potential

Stress wreaks much of the same havoc with the Enabler's health that alcohol does with the Dependent's. Only the symptoms differ. She experiences one or several of the familiar stress-related conditions— digestive problems, ulcers, colitis; headaches and backache; high blood pressure and possible heart episodes; nervousness, irritability, depression.

If her symptoms are mild, her doctor may write them off as neurotic or menopausal. But for the alert practitioner, the Enabler's physical complaints can offer the first crack in the family's wall of silence, the first opportunity for a professional to intervene.

Her health is often further undermined by poor nutrition, over-weight, too little exercise, too much smoking, and possibly too much intake of alcohol, tranquilizers, or other drugs herself. As an unhealthy life-style saps her energy and sense of well-being, she exercises even less and eats, drinks, smokes even more. She is trapped in the same downward spiral as the Dependent.

Ill health may offer an Enabler her only opportunity to receive a little nurturing herself. Friends show concern; her family assumes some of her responsibilities for a while and cares for her physically. Such by-products of ill health are seductive, undermining her will to get well and stay well. Many spouses of alcoholics end up with some chronic illness, if only hypochondria.

The Enabler is not only feeling the strain of her situation, by now she is likely showing it. Her eyes and complexion, once bright with a zest for living, grow dull. If she is inclined to be thin, she gets thinner; worry robs her appetite, and it seems there is always something more important to do than eat. If she is inclined to be heavy, she adds pounds; eating is one of the few satisfactions she has left, and she has neither the time nor the energy to exercise away the bulges.

Grooming no longer seems important unless her job requires it. "Why bother? We never go any place anymore." And with the family budget squeezed, she makes do with the old coat for another year.

Her neglected body doesn't give her pleasure from dancing or sports as it once did. Even that universal physical pleasure, sex, deserts her. Just as a guilt-ridden, hung-over Dependent finds it hard to play the dashing lover, so does his exhausted, frumpy-feeling wife find it hard to think of herself as a sex symbol. Inside she feels hurt, cast aside in favor of his new love, alcohol. And always there is the gnawing anger.

Shamed by the loss of his own potency, her spouse is quick to shift the blame and confirm her doubts that she can any longer either give or enjoy sexual fulfillment. She fulfills instead his expectations and retreats into non-orgasmic response—safe at least from advances she no longer welcomes. (This scenario is the same whether the Dependent is a man or a woman.)

As their sexual relationship withers, the Enabler loses far more than physical pleasure. Gone too are the warmth and closeness, the satisfaction of being loved and satisfying another whom she loves. She looks in the mirror and wonders, "Is it my fault?"

The Emotional Potential

In most of the alcoholic families I have known, *anger is the characteristic feeling of the Enabler.*

Anger is an emotional prelude to and trigger for physical or verbal attack. At earlier stages of our evolution it served us well. Even today the healthiest response to feelings of anger, frustration, and resentment is to express them honestly (but not accusingly) to the person who has aroused them. When that person is a practicing alcoholic, however—as many of my readers know so well—the chances of getting any satisfaction or improving the situation are slim.

Not knowing what else to do, the Enabler keeps all her angry feelings bottled up inside. Each day of living with the Dependent seems to add new irritations until she can scarcely contain them. Often she can't, and at unexpected moments they burst forth, a telling clue for the aware professional.

Like every member of an alcoholic family, the Enabler also feels fear. Certainly there is much in her life situation to summon it. Will the Dependent lose his job? Can they pay the rent this month? Will the car run for another year? Will he stop drinking? What if he doesn't? How will all this affect the children? How long can she herself hold up under these pressures?

Some of her fear is focused realistically on practical problems, of which the family has many. But part of it seems to wrap itself around her in a cloud of anxiety, vague and oppressive. Sometimes she cannot even name what she fears most—everything seems to carry the possibility of disaster.

Holding in the anger and holding off the fears, playing both father and mother, breadwinner and homemaker, deteriorating physically, enjoying little fun or relief and little prospect of any to come, the Enabler feels very tired. This is in part a genuine bodily fatigue, but it is more —a bone-tiredness of spirit. It comes so close to despair that she cannot afford to feel it. As a result, though it is always present, the counselor may or may not find it evident on the surface.

The Mental Potential

The Enabler who takes a job or goes back to her earlier profession, who takes over management of the family finances and learns to repair the sewing machine as well as using it, would seem to be actually stretching and enhancing her mental potential. But the gains are shallow if any. There is always so little time and so much to do that she can never give her mind fully to anything, never follow an idea or a project through to realize its full possibilities. As a result, she never really enjoys the satisfaction of creative thinking, good planning, or astute decision-making.

Mental pursuits like these are peripheral anyway. The ultimate value of the mind is to help each of us find the knowledge and develop the intuition to live our lives wisely. In this central chore, the Enabler's mental potential is not serving her well at all. The system of denial that she has built up through years of protecting the Dependent acts as a screen to prevent her from seeing the realities of her situation—the nature of the Dependent's disease, the inevitability of its outcome if not arrested, the parallel disease in herself and other members of the family, and their blind complicity in the whole process.

As a result, she misinterprets both the causes and the effects of the thousands of little events and interactions that make up their daily lives. The real data never get fed into her mental computer. Working with wrong data, she comes up with wrong conclusions. In other words, *she is suffering from the second characteristic symptom of alcoholism—delusion.*

The most tragic miscalculation of all is the Enabler's failure to see the very real power she has to change things, if only she would claim it.

The Social Potential

The Dependent has found new companions, most likely others who frequent his drinking spas. When he does agree to spend an evening with friends or relatives, his behavior is almost certain to cause the Enabler grief or embarrassment, so she soon is as willing as he to turn down any invitations.

For a time, she may find friends and activities of her own to fill the gap. But the demands of her life leave little time or energy for socializing, and as her pain, fear, and shame mount, she finds it harder and harder to maintain a cheery facade. She begins to withdraw from those who have offered support and companionship in the past. They, sensing her pain and feeling helpless to relieve it, allow her to go.

Outside the home her contacts are kept to a "safe" superficial level; at home her relationship with the Dependent becomes a cold war of silence and avoidance, or bickering and sometimes bitter quarrels. Even her relationship to her children loses its joy as she tries to meet their natural needs with ever dwindling resources (inner and outer), trapped between love and exhaustion.

By the time the Dependent reaches the later stages of alcoholism, little remains of the Enabler's social potential. She, too, is isolated. This loss is felt directly in her emotional self, for much of its renewal comes from meaningful contact with others. As she continues to spend herself without replenishing her resources, she is heading for emotional as well as social bankruptcy.

The Spiritual Potential

The embattled Enabler has little time to ponder ultimate realities. And her list of values has been narrowed down to one: survival.

But in an alcoholic family even survival seems daily to be threatened, and in her desperation she may turn to some Higher Power (which she may or may not call God). As so many members of Al-anon have learned, this can be a constructive and consoling step if it is done with a clear perception of the family's situation and a courageous willingness to cooperate with Providence.

Too often, however, I find that Enablers misuse the spiritual resources available to them and simply hide behind their faith. It is so much easier to sit and wait for a miracle than to risk looking honestly at their plight and taking steps to change it.

The Volitional Potential

Volition—making choices—presupposes that a person has options and knows what they are, that he is free to choose among them and has the power to act on his choice. It is clear that the Enabler's volitional potential is not functioning well, but the counselor needs to know why.

An old saying has it that there are three views of any situation: your view, my view, and the truth. Something similar might be said of the Enabler. To the world at large this dependable, competent woman looks like a tower of strength, but in the privacy of her own fears she feels absolutely powerless. In actuality she is neither. Or perhaps we might better say that she is both, because in fact *her power lies in facing and accepting her powerlessness.*

Feeling weak, the Enabler typically compensates by trying to control the situation—by trying to make the Dependent stop drinking, trying to change his other behavior as well, trying to hold off the inevitable consequences for him and for the family single-handedly. Attempting the impossible, she fails and so feels weaker than ever. The spiral of her debilitation is curiously like that of the Dependent.

But what can an Enabler do? What choices can she possibly have?

Paradoxically, she must first look squarely at her own helplessness and admit it. She must accept the fact that no one can make another person stop drinking. Further, she must realize that the Dependent himself is equally helpless to stop the inexorable progress of his disease without outside help. And until the disease is arrested, all its complications for the family will worsen despite anything she can do.

Next, she must summon her strength to take whatever risks are necessary to confront the Dependent with his true situation and to get the whole family the help it needs. Such a confrontation is, of course, a frightening prospect to the Enabler, one that threatens to rock her whole world. It may indeed call for all the courage she can muster. But the Enabler who takes the risk will for the first time realize her true power—power to help the Dependent or, if he refuses, at least power to help herself and her children.

In my experience, her chances for success in bringing the Dependent to treatment and sobriety are excellent. After all, he needs her desperately—she is the only cement holding his fractured life together.

IMPLICATIONS FOR THE COUNSELOR

The chief Enabler is clearly the first avenue of intervention with the alcoholic. But I would urge counselors to remember that she, too, is the victim of a disease process. She needs help, yet like the Dependent she may resist seeking it unless someone from outside the family intervenes.

The chances for this intervention, however, are much better, because the Enabler is so much more accessible. In her many roles as parent, patient, bread-winner, she is likely to be in regular contact with a variety of professional workers in the community. Any one of them could be the critical force that would reverse the family's destructive course and put it on the road to health and happy living again.

It is my dream that one day soon every physician, psychotherapist, lawyer, law-enforcement officer, teacher—everyone who meets people with problems in the course of the day's work—will learn to recognize the symptoms peculiar to each role in the alcoholic family, particularly those of the Enabler.

To each of these professionals I would say, watch for the following telltale characteristics in the people who pass your way:

Super-responsibility. "If I don't take care of things, they just won't get done."

Pseudo-fragility. "I don't know how much more of this I can take!"

Hypochondria. "I hardly get over one cold when I catch another."

Powerlessness. "I've tried everything to get him to stop."

Self-blame. "I should have planned for that."

These are all defensive postures by which an Enabler avoids looking honestly at her position and doing something about it. This is not to say that every hypochondriac, for example, is married to an alcoholic; but where several of these symptoms are present, alcoholism in the family should be suspected.

Counselors have long observed that an Enabler whose relationship to an alcoholic is ended by death or divorce has a strong tendency to choose another dependency-prone person when she marries again. We know now that she has to—there is no other way she can maintain her balance in the overextended role she has become locked into.

And locked she is. Unless the Enabler gets professional help, she will continue to play that old role indefinitely.

PARENT ENABLERS

One has only to read the newspapers to be aware of how widespread drug use has become among American youngsters of high-school and even elementary-school age. In many schools those who have not used, or at least experimented with, drugs are a minority. And surveys are showing that, as the psychedelic sixties fade farther into history, alcohol is increasingly the drug of their choice.

Whatever the chemical that is being used, its impact on the family is similar. If a youngster becomes dependent on it—as a disturbing number are—the classic roles and scenario of chemical dependency begin to appear in his or her family. (We are seeing about equal numbers of boys and girls in treatment programs.)

Recalling that it is the person emotionally closest to the Dependent who becomes the Enabler, we can predict that for a youngster that person will be one of the parents. Often it is both.

To have a chemically dependent child is even more threatening to a parent's self-esteem than to have a dependent spouse. When a husband is alcoholic, society holds *him* responsible; when a child is alcoholic, society blames the parents. Thus societal pressures, along with the Dependent's immaturity, tend to intensify the parents' efforts to deny, conceal, protect, take over—in a word, to enable.

Exaggerating their natural role of protecting and caring for their child, they start controlling his comings and goings, and make decisions for him that he should be making for himself. They deny the seriousness of the problem, cover for him, excuse or even defend his actions against the criticism of others. They try to shield the child, and the family with him, from the painful consequences of his behavior.

In some families, only one of the parents is an Enabler because the other flatly refuses to play the role. If so, the "uncooperative" parent may find himself cast as Scapegoat. Or one of the parents may himself be chemically dependent. Then one person serves as Enabler for both Dependents, spouse and child. This is a situation that we see often in counseling.

Statistically, research shows that youngsters who have an alcoholic parent are four times as likely to become chemically dependent themselves. To one unfamiliar with alcoholism such figures may seem strangely coincidental, but in my work with these families the underlying dynamic has become quite clear: the drug-abusing child is playing a typical Scapegoat role, creating enough problems to keep the focus of family and community attention off the dependent parent. (We will look more closely at this role in chapter 8.)

Treating a child under these circumstances is very discouraging because his dependency is so firmly locked into the larger family pathology. Everyone involved has a stake in keeping him in his role as second-generation Dependent. It is therefore doubly important that school and law enforcement personnel be able to recognize this pattern and intervene to get help for the whole family.

Lacking professional intervention, the problems for the parent Enablers eventually reach a point where denial is no longer possible. All their suppressed anger suddenly wells up—anger at their child, their spouse, themselves. In their rage they may punish the youngster severely or throw him out of the house.

Once their anger is released, however, they usually make a last-ditch effort to control the situation. They may bring in the authorities or try to get the child committed to a treatment center involuntarily. Only when these efforts, too, fail to stop the drinking or drug use (as they probably will), do the distressed parents at last face the reality that *there is no effective way to force anyone to recover,* even when that person is a child.

Recognizing and admitting this powerlessness is—for parents as for other Enablers—a first, giant step toward change. They have come to realize that their child is not just stubborn or wayward, but ill. Freed now from their painful frustration, anger, and guilt, they can stop trying to control his behavior, recover their own strength, and rekindle their love and concern for him.

CHAPTER **7**

The Hero

EVERY DRAMA has its hero, and the one we are watching is no exception. If he is not onstage with the Dependent and the Enabler when the alcoholism begins, he makes his entrance soon afterward, for where dependency occurs in a classic family structure (two parents and their mutual children), the oldest son or daughter usually plays the Hero. Of all the children's roles in the alcoholic family, this one is most often determined by birth order.

The Hero is helpful inside the family circle and successful outside. He provides those moments of hope and pride that even the most desperate families experience from time to time, furnishing a source of worth for the family when all other sources have run dry. Indeed, the Hero sometimes seems "to have it made," to be so "together" that he bears no scars of the emotional strife at home. But his facade of good nature and success is an illusion. Behind it he, too, feels miserable. Ironically, his very success may make him the most difficult member of the family to reach with treatment.

Until his appearance, the Hero's parents have been a couple—a relatively simple, stable, straight-line kind of relationship. But baby makes three. Now the family takes on that unstable, potentially stormy configuration, the triangle. Family therapists have written at length of the triangular interactions that go on in families.

From the moment of his conception the oldest child is embedded in this family triangle. During the prenatal months he may affect it more than it affects him, but from the day he is born, this triangle forms the backdrop for the infant's dawning sense of himself. He is an integral part of it; whatever happens to either of its other members, or between them, is of vital concern to him. He is in a unique position, one that no later child in the family can ever occupy.

This position has a number of practical considerations for the Hero. Unless he is one of those unfortunate children who was never really wanted, he grows up feeling special. Parents and grandparents, aunts and uncles all dote on him. He receives more parental time and extended-family attention than any of his siblings is ever likely to enjoy. This acceptance, nurturing, and support during his early developmental years provide the base of self-worth that makes possible his high performance later.

On the other hand, by virtue of his charter membership in the family triangle, he is subjected to stresses unlike any that his siblings will face. (I am speaking here of the nature of the stress, not the level of pain —everyone in an alcoholic family hurts!) He is locked into a system where the Dependent is overreacting to a chemical, the Enabler is overreacting to the Dependent, and both are either overreacting or underreacting to him, their child, because of their other problems. If we think of the people as the points of the family triangle and their interactions as its sides, we could say that the only healthy thing about this triangle is the child. And even that statement is academic, for in such a situation he cannot remain healthy for long.

Being part of such a tight system also leaves the Hero feeling obliged to do something to correct its imbalances, make up for its weaknesses, heal its pain in order to heal his own. It is to this impossible dream that the Hero dedicates his life.

To pursue our geometric model a little further, we might see our original family threesome as an isosceles triangle, with the Dependent typically more distant from both the Enabler and the Hero than they are from each other. Their shared problem tends to draw them together, and in the normal course of growing up, the Hero learns much from the Enabler: how to tie his shoes, how to share his toys—and how to enable. We might well have named this role the "Little Enabler." Thus the Hero's early impulse to make up for the family deficits is reinforced steadily as he grows.

What is it like to be a Hero? Steve could tell us.

Steve's dad is an alcoholic. He began drinking regularly on weekends before he graduated from high school, and by the time he married,

he was handling six or eight drinks in an evening without getting notice-
ably drunk. He used to joke that he had practiced so much that he could
"drink anyone under the table."

With the added pressure of having a wife to support and a
baby on the way, he worked harder and drank harder. On the night
Stevie was born he went out to celebrate the event and experienced
his first blackout.

As little Stevie becomes aware of the people around him, he
watches and listens and learns. He begins to notice that Daddy's moods
change a lot; sometimes he's laughing and noisy, sometimes angry and
silent. Sometimes Stevie hears quarreling. Mommie sounds upset and
keeps trying to please Daddy. Those are the times that Stevie feels
scared. Will one of them go away and never come back? What will
become of *him?*

He doesn't understand what's happening, but he doesn't ask. He
has already learned that children aren't supposed to ask questions. It
makes parents cross.

He has also learned that the best way to stay out of trouble is to
be very, very good. Sometimes, then, Mommie hugs him and tells him
what a good little boy he is. And sometimes Daddy brags to Grandma
about him.

The family's rules for how to be good get clearer as he gets older.
No one really tells him, but he learns:

- to keep negative feelings to himself
   (they are sure to make someone angry).
- to express a lot of positive feelings
   (they can win you approval).
- to give people what they want
   (you can control the situation that way and get rewarded).
- not to talk to outsiders about what happens in the family
   (no one would like you if they knew the truth).
- not to talk about Dad's drinking, even to other family members
   (well, that's just something we don't talk about).

When our Hero starts going to school, he finds a whole new world
of ways to "be good." He can be good at his schoolwork and bring home
A's. He can be good at music or sports and make the family proud. As
a bonus he discovers that kids who are good at things are popular with
teachers and other kids, too. At some level he says to himself, "I'll show
the world this family is okay. A family *has* to be okay to have a kid who

can do things better than other people, doesn't it?" And when he does well, *he* feels okay, too.

So young Steve pitches his team to the Little League championship; the editor of the *Times-Democrat* asks him to write a column of school news for the paper; he's elected treasurer of the eighth-grade class. Mom and Dad seem proud. Each time he achieves something new, things feel happier at home for a few days.

But even his biggest triumphs don't change things for long. Dad's drinking gets worse. Mom works harder and worries more. Steve feels more and more helpless to make things better, yet guilty because he cannot. To his teachers and coaches and friends he's a real winner, but in his heart he feels he's losing the only game that really matters.

In time Steve realizes that Dad's drinking has a lot to do with the troubles at home. But he's still confused. Everyone in the family seems to be saying one thing and feeling another, though he can't know for sure what any of them is feeling because, of course, nobody tells. He's confused about his own feelings, too. He does love Dad, but sometimes he sort of hates him, too. At least, he hates the drinking. And he hates to see Mom hurt. She really looks after Dad.

Puzzled, discouraged, but not knowing what else to do, Steve goes on being a Hero—good, considerate, successful. By now those qualities form the very basis of his character. The praise and popularity they have brought, both to him and vicariously to the rest of the family, provide some feelings of worth that they all need badly.

In the alcoholic drama, the Hero usually makes his exit early, not openly deserting the family but leaving in glory for some more distant enterprise. Steve, for instance, has carried a heavy schedule all through high school. By taking a couple of extra courses in summer school, he is able to graduate a year early, and before his seventeenth birthday he leaves home for college—never to return as a full-time member of the family.

THE PRICE OF HERO-ISM

For the Hero, as for everyone in an alcoholic family, the price of role-playing is high. Superficially this may not appear to be true of him, for some of his visible potentials are allowed to develop to a greater degree than his siblings' are. But the goal of his achievements never is to satisfy his own needs but rather to make up for

the self-worth deficit that his parents as individuals and the family as a whole are suffering. All the wages for his effort and the dividends on his talents are deposited to these accounts. Yet so great is the deficit that nothing he can do is enough. And thus his ultimate goal —the one he must reach to acknowledge his *own* worth—remains forever beyond him.

Heroes will differ in the specific potentials from which the highest toll is exacted, depending on their natural endowments, but a toll there will be. Where achievement is prized too highly, most of the effort will be channeled to those parts of the self that promise rewards. Weaknesses will grow weaker while strengths are developed.

The Physical Potential

The Hero who has natural ability in physical skills like sports, dance, playing an instrument, drawing, or crafts will most likely develop that part of his potential energetically, though at the expense of other capacities (including other physical ones). The child whose talents lie in other directions, however, such as intellectual pursuits, may sacrifice the physical activity needed to develop his young body and coordination normally, feeling it takes too much time away from his studies.

With the example of the Enabler constantly before him, the Hero is ever in danger of overextending himself. When he does, like her, he pays with his health. At first, his symptoms may not be dramatic—recurring colds, frequent stomach upsets, allergies, susceptibility to childhood diseases. In later years, however, the effects of prolonged striving can threaten his life.

His biological vulnerability is greatly intensified by psychological factors, especially his unconscious feelings of guilt (which we will examine momentarily). Any feelings that one does not allow into consciousness will manifest themselves some other way—often in physical illness. When the repressed feeling is guilt, the picture gets even more complicated. The Hero may develop a phobia about illness or succumb readily upon exposure; he may even bring accidents or psychosomatic illnesses upon himself—all because his unconscious guilt tells him he deserves to be punished.

Eventually, the Hero grows up and leaves the alcoholic family of his childhood, but he does not walk away from his role. His goal-oriented striving and all the health hazards that accompany it continue into adult life. Heroes are prone to stomach ulcers, migraine, dependency on tranquilizers, and—as classic "type A" workaholics—to heart attacks and strokes.

The Emotional Potential

The characteristic feelings of the family Hero are inadequacy and guilt. Though most of the people who have known him, even members of the family, would see this youngster as anything but inadequate, he knows better. He knows that although he is good in many ways, nothing he does is ever good enough to make things right with the family; he is inadequate to heal their pain. The Dependent and the Enabler, growing more rigid and perfectionistic as they start to project their own feelings of inadequacy, do little to allay his self-doubts.

This supposed inadequacy makes the Hero feel guilty: he is not doing what he should be doing, namely, healing the family pain. Even his successes make him feel guilty because, however briefly and incompletely, they do bring him some glory and satisfaction, while his parents are miserable. Meanwhile, those parents, unconsciously projecting their own guilt, play upon his.

As we have seen, the predominant emotion of the Enabler is anger, so it is natural that the Little Enabler feel some anger, too. Anger at having to strive so hard and be so good; anger at living in a family that needs so much and gives so little back; anger at parents who are so often critical and irritable when he is trying so hard; anger at himself for constantly discounting his own needs and selling out to other people's demands. But "good" sons and daughters don't show anger toward their parents, so he immediately buries the feeling in his unconscious, where it further feeds his guilt.

The Social Potential

The Hero can be one of the most admired and popular youngsters in his group—as he often is—and still feel very lonely. Whatever other skills he may have, genuine relationship is not likely to be one of them. For one thing, he did not learn to relate to others openly and trustingly in his formative years; in his family, intimacy was not encouraged. In school and other activities, he has always been so intent on goals that he has not had much time or concern for deep friendships. And the high standards he has held for himself have made him hypercritical of others, so they rarely measure up to his ideal of the kind of person a friend should be. Too, whether or not he is aware of it, he knows that it is safer not to get too close to anyone. There is so much to hide—Dad's embarrassing behavior, family quarrels, financial and other problems, and of course all his own suppressed feelings that could slip out at any time if he were to let his guard down with anyone.

The Mental Potential

As with physical skills, if intellectual activities are not the Hero's greatest gift, he probably will neglect developing what mental potential he does have in order to pursue achievements where the chance of success is greater. If his talents do lie in his mental potential, of course, one can be sure he will develop it to the utmost. The problem is that he can never enjoy the full satisfaction that normally accompanies realizing one's potential. Good, very good, superior—nothing is ever quite good enough.

Alcoholics often develop very rigid, perfectionistic value systems. Their expectations, especially of this first, "special" child, are too high for even a Hero to meet. In counseling I have had Heroes who have become super-successful tell me, "You know, I used to bring my report card home with four A's and a B, feeling pretty good about it, and Dad would say, 'What's that B all about? Any kid who can get four A's can get five!'"

So the Hero goes through life always feeling that, no matter how good he is, he must be a little better before he has a right to take satisfaction in his achievements. He exhibits the same perfectionism as the Dependent—one of the symptoms of family alcoholism that consistently shows up in the child who plays this role.

Even the Hero who reaps many academic honors only partially realizes his true mental potential. His intellect may be highly developed, but his mind—that higher faculty where our wisdom is lodged—is severely crippled. He has, let us remember, bought into the family delusion. His behavior is governed, not by truth and good judgment, but by false perceptions and an overriding compulsion to pursue a goal that is forever out of reach.

The Spiritual Potential

The super-achieving Hero is ever busy pursuing prizes and, though he may be the pride of his Sunday school, has little time to search for the deeper meaning of life. Indeed, he may avoid such a search, for it would necessarily bring him face to face with much that he has repressed, either to deny personal pain or to obey the family taboos.

The child whose Hero-ism manifests itself less in stellar performance than in appeasement, helpfulness, and nurturing of his parents may appear to family friends like a veritable saint. But something is still out of tune. His goodness has a compulsive quality—he *has to* be good. He *must* set his own needs aside, placate the Dependent, lighten the Enabler's load, or some dire consequence (which he may or may not consciously envision) will follow.

A person with truly mature spirituality, unlike the Hero or any other member of the alcoholic family, acts out of his own personally built value system. He is free to be helpful or troublesome, nurturing or neglectful. He voluntarily chooses the behavior we call "good" because it is consistent with his picture of himself and the rest of the universe. Humanitarian actions flow naturally from him with none of the driven quality that we see in Heroes. His goodness has nothing to do with family or other rules, or with some goal he has set, or with fear of what may happen if he acts otherwise. It is rooted deeply in his own spiritual center.

In spite of all his sincere efforts to be a really good child to his needy parents, the poor Hero reaps little spiritual reward. For the truly spiritual person, virtue is indeed its own reward—an open, loving, joy-filled pouring out of one's essence into the world. But for the Hero, because he lacks the tap root that would bring him a continual supply of renewing energy from deep within, being generous only leaves him tired, frustrated, depleted.

The Volitional Potential

By now it must be clear that the Hero—like most heroes perhaps —is not a Hero by choice. His part was written into the family script, and he was born to it. He plays it because he must, coerced first by subtle family expectations, and later by the compulsion that results when he internalizes those expectations and makes them his own—forever unless something intervenes to erase them.

A PERSONAL RECOLLECTION

Writing this book, and particularly this chapter on the Hero, has been a moving experience for me. My observations are of course based, not subjectively, but objectively on what I have seen and heard in all the consulting rooms and group sessions where I have shared the anguish of alcoholic families. But each time I watch a Hero faithfully playing out his role, something deep inside me reverberates, a memory of the old pain and futile compulsiveness that I once experienced myself.

You see, I was my family's Hero.

Most of the time my childhood home was a happy place, and I felt like the most loved little girl in the world. I knew my parents cared about me and about each other. This was joyously evident when they worked together in the garden, or when we had company and played music, or when the whole family went on trips together. Most of all I remember the hugs and kisses and arms around me.

Mom used to hide extra dimes and quarters in a little Band-Aid box in the kitchen cupboard and would count a few out for me whenever I needed something. Even though we had very little money, I felt rich. Later, when I would go out at night, Dad would be waiting for me to come home so that he could fix me a cup of tea and a fried egg sandwich. Just the two of us.

But then, out of nowhere, would come arguments, loud accusations, and hurt. At night I could hear my parents fighting and arguing. When I was small, I would put my hands over my ears and cry myself to sleep. The next day they would act as if nothing had happened; no one ever talked about the arguing, but I remembered it. These times were painful and frightening.

To make things better, I began to play the Hero. I worked hard at home to be useful to my parents, and I studied hard at school to get good grades that would make them proud of me. Later on, in high school, I won parts in school plays, was chosen as homecoming royalty, made lots of friends, and tried to be liked by everyone. I worked part time for my dad as a bookkeeper, kept my room spotless, and never got into trouble.

During these growing-up years, I never connected alcohol with the episodes of pain and bitterness. In our family, alcohol had always meant good things—Sunday, friends coming over, some special event to cele-brate. For a very long time I did not notice that these were not the only occasions when my father was drinking. By the time I was in high school, however, his addiction was growing, and I was aware that strife was plaguing my parents' marriage. I also sensed a growing distance between Dad and me.

I felt tense and confused. I often saw my mother crying, and some-times I even saw tears in my father's eyes, though they rarely fell. Things got worse. Mom became ill, and Dad was sad, jumpy, and suspicious.

I thought to myself, if only other people knew how wonderful my parents really are, someone would help us; if they realized that Dad was abandoned by his own parents, then they would sympathize with him and love him as I did; and if enough people loved him, then maybe he wouldn't drink to feel important. That would give Mom and Dad a fresh start.

So I decided to write to Ralph Edwards, host of the old television show "This Is Your Life," and ask him to do a show about my father, bringing in all the people who had cared about him through the years. I could imagine Dad's face when he saw them—that old happy smile that we seldom saw anymore. It was a brave try, but sad to say, I never received a reply.

My chief feelings toward Mom at this stage in our lives were anger and guilt—anger because I thought that she picked on my father, that she actually enjoyed her martyr role, and that she had very little time for or interest in me; guilt because I felt angry at her when, after all, she did take good care of me and try hard to protect me from the family pain.

As soon as I graduated from high school, I moved away, married, and began my own family. I felt such tremendous relief at escaping from the stress that I went home less and less often—I who had been the soul of responsibility all those years. I felt ashamed of my neglect, but my concern about the old pain in that family was simply not as great as the relief I found in building a home and a new family of my own.

Dad's alcoholism advanced, and a few years later he sank into deep despair and committed suicide.

Besides my grief and shock, I was engulfed by an overpowering guilt that lasted two or three years. I had neglected my family. I was their Hero and I had failed them.

(The story of this period and the later events that intervened to change my life are recounted in the Prologue and the Preface of this book.)

RESCUING THE HERO

Whatever the Hero's pain, it rarely shows. In fact, he appears to function unusually well. He will receive help for his own well-hidden pathology only if the whole family comes into treatment through the problems of some other member.

He is more likely to be seen later in his life. Even then he will probably seek help only for the medical complications of his lifelong habit of ignoring his own inner needs and often of a stressful, success-driven life-style as well. After all, dysfunctional as his approach to living is in many ways, it often does have enough cultural value or bring enough tangible personal reward that he does not perceive a need for change until threatened with dramatic illness or other serious consequences. Frequently one of those consequences is professional "burnout."

By the time a Hero begins his working life, he already has had many years of experience in taking care of others. Not surprisingly, many

Heroes enter the caretaking professions—medicine, nursing, psychiatry and psychology, social welfare work, the ministry. From time to time I do workshops for "recovering" family Heroes—those who through treatment of an alcoholic family member or in some other way become aware of the role they have been playing. It is always interesting to me to see what a large proportion of them have chosen helping careers.

In their work these people are driven by the same compulsion that kept them in the Hero's role all those years in their childhood families, and the characteristic quality of that role—caring for others' needs at the expense of one's own—is acknowledged to be the basic cause of the professional burnout syndrome.

The adult Hero may also find his way to treatment because of problems that manifest themselves in his spouse or children. Unconsciously, he is attracted to a mate with whom he can play the only role he knows, and by the only rules he knows. The Little Enabler has grown up to be a big Enabler, and thus the stage is set for a sequel to the original drama.

All those years of catering to other people's needs and wishes may have given him a good deal of practice in nurturing, but healthy marriage and parenthood also call for openness and honest assertiveness—requirements for which the Hero is ill prepared. He finds it particularly hard to set and maintain suitable limits for his children. No wonder that in counseling we see so many Enablers, of both spouses and children, who were the Heroes of their childhood families. Their enabling is reinforced by their characteristic feelings (as Heroes) of inadequacy and guilt, particularly if the Dependent is their child.

Long before alcoholism was recognized as a disease, folk wisdom noticed that drinking problems seemed to recur in second and even third generations of the same families. From time to time theories were put forth to try to explain this apparent "heredity" factor, but the phenomenon remained a mystery. At last, as we are coming to understand alcoholism as a disease of the whole family system, I believe we have found the key we have been looking for. The progression of the Hero into the later role of Enabler is one piece of the puzzle. We shall find more pieces as we examine the other family roles.

The Scapegoat

WHILE THE Hero's fate is determined by his position in the original family triangle, the Scapegoat's is determined by his position outside of it. He walks onto the family stage only to find that there are already three people there, and the action has started. He is too late—the Hero's part has already been cast. (Occasionally, if the first two children are of opposite sexes or have widely divergent talents, both may find viable roles as Heroes; usually, however, the second child in the family ends up playing the Scapegoat.)

The young newcomer notices that being good seems to bring praise and importance to the Hero, so for a time he may try the same tactic. But somehow it does not work for him. It is always the Hero who gets labeled "special," always the Hero who reaps the approval. Sooner or later it becomes clear to the second child that no matter how good or talented he is, he cannot compete. Not only is the Hero an insider, but he is also older and more mature; even with no greater genetic endowment, he will always seem better and brighter.

Yet the Scapegoat does not feel free to vent his frustration onto its source. The authors of the Booz-Allen report have noted the tendency of alcoholics' children not to fight the stress in the family directly.[1] They have learned that belligerence only arouses angry retaliation from their parents, especially the Dependent. Flight is easier.

[1]*Booz-Allen and Hamilton Report.* National Institute on Alcohol Abuse and Alcoholism, 1974; p. 36.

So the Scapegoat withdraws from the family. At first, withdrawal may be dramatic—a small child hides under the bed or in the attic, hoping the Dependent cannot find him; an older one runs away. When the child finds that neither of these options works, he withdraws by simply spending more and more of his time away from home, relying on his peers to fill his unsatisfied need for belonging. Eventually, if he is typical, he turns to another escape route, one the Dependent discovered years ago—chemicals.

Up to this point, our drama has had no "heavy." The Dependent has, of course, been causing great strain within the family, but both the Enabler and the Hero have been denying that reality and protecting him, so the heavy's role is still open. By now the Scapegoat is starved for some kind of attention from his parents—anything to tell him they know he exists—so unconsciously he puts on the black hat. True, a problem child will never hear the cheers of approval that he craves, but even a *boo* is better than no acknowledgment at all.

Because of his own bottled-up emotion, the Scapegoat finds himself attracted to other youngsters who are acting out their frustrations. They begin by merely getting into mischief, but the trouble-making escalates. He starts using alcohol or other drugs heavily. Before long he finds himself involved in a car accident, expelled from school, or picked up by the police for vandalism, shoplifting, or some other charge.

We can perhaps best understand the Scapegoat's behavior by viewing it as a reverse image of the Hero's. From the matrix of possible responses to the troubled family situation, the Hero has carved out a mask to fit his role; the Scapegoat has had to find *his* place in the space that was left when the Hero-ic possibilities were removed. Where the Hero is good and responsible, the Scapegoat behaves badly and irresponsibly. Where the Hero works hard and brings honor to himself and the family, the Scapegoat "goofs off," gets into trouble, and brings disgrace. Where the Hero shows concern for the family and its problems, the Scapegoat seems not to care. He does care, of course—desperately. To him, it is the family who does not care.

At this point let me introduce a couple of Scapegoats whose problems have indirectly brought their families to me for help. First, a boy whom I will call Duane.

Duane was the second of three children. His father was a successful engineer but drank heavily. By the time Duane was nine, the drinking had progressed to dependency.

Duane's older brother, Dennis, got good grades in school and showed some promise of having fallen heir to his father's mechanical ability. He also seemed to get along better with the parents and stay out of trouble. Duane admired Dennis, yet he felt jealous and irritated at all the attention Dennis got. Somehow, compared to his brother, Duane always felt like a troublemaker, though he did not intend to be.

The two boys spent many hours together, and Duane was impressed with what his brother could do. On weekends they would help their dad as he tinkered with the engine of his sports car. Sometimes a neighbor would come over, and the two men would drink beer and watch the boys at work. Dad always had a word of praise for Dennis and seemed to enjoy showing off his talented son.

When Dennis left home for college, Duane hoped that now he would have a turn in the limelight. He tried everything he knew to win his father's respect, but nothing worked. By that time his father's alcoholism had reached the stage where he was pulling away from the family. Unfortunately, Duane did not understand what was happening. He only knew that he could work for hours on a job that Dennis would have been praised highly for, and his father did not even notice. His efforts always seemed less clever, less exciting than Dennis's.

Duane's mother watched what was happening and felt sorry for him. She was an easy mark when he asked her to buy him something or give him extra money "for books." But Duane needed more than money, and since she had taken a job to help with Dennis's college expenses, she seldom had time to talk with him or give him the emotional support he could not get from his father.

As soon as he was old enough to drive, Duane spent his savings on an old car that he planned to fix up. His friends liked to come over to work on their cars with him until Duane's father announced that an expensive sports car was one thing but a front yard full of "greasy jalopies" was another. He told Duane his friends were going to have to find someplace else to do their tinkering. There was an angry scene, and Duane stormed out of the house. Deep inside he was less angry than hurt.

From then on, the crowd gathered at other boys' homes, Duane with them. They usually chose places where they were free to drink beer and "smoke dope" as they worked. Sometimes on weekend evenings they experimented with other drugs.

Then one night when he was in the eleventh grade, Duane had an accident and was charged with drunk driving. Since it was a first offense,

he was placed on probation, but his father was furious and blacked his eye. "No son of mine is going to be a drunken bum!"

A couple of months later Duane was picked up again, this time for stealing car parts. Through the juvenile court he and his family found their way to treatment.

A DAUGHTER IN DISTRESS

So far in this chapter I have referred to the Scapegoat as "he." In actuality, the role is just as likely to be played by a girl. She, too, may run away, fail in school, become promiscuous, steal, drink, or use drugs.

But she runs another risk—she may also become pregnant. In an unwanted pregnancy the boy may face some problems, too (if his identity is known), but the heavy physical and social consequences of unwed parenthood are borne by the girl.

The family institute that my husband has established operates a medical clinic which, among other services, offers tests for teenage pregnancy. The girls seen there range from thirteen to seventeen years old, and almost invariably they occupy the Scapegoat position in their families. Though the same constellation of roles can be observed in any troubled family, by far the majority of these girls turn out to be from alcoholic families.

Scapegoats get involved in sexual activity young, hoping to find there the love and intimacy that they could never find at home. One may wonder, in this day of ready availability of contraceptives, why a girl who wishes to be promiscuous finds herself pregnant. The answer is sometimes simply ignorance. But we must also realize all the deep, unconscious motivations of a troubled girl to become pregnant. Her condition is clear evidence that for a little while someone "loved" her, and it offers at least an illusory hope that she may establish a lasting relationship with someone, even if only her baby.

Let's meet one of these girls.

Karen was naturally a pretty child, outgoing and full of fun. While she was small, her father delighted in her. Sometimes he brought home a toy or a new dress just to please her. She adored him and looked forward to hearing his car pull into the driveway after work. Ted, her older brother, was quieter and studied a lot. Their mother often helped him with his school projects and was proud of the report cards he brought home.

About the time Karen started junior high school, her father began staying at the office late many evenings. He said he had to catch up on his work, but he smelled of liquor when he got home, and her mother acted upset. She and Karen often quarreled, too. It seemed to Karen that her mother had always resented the attention she got from her father. Now that he was at home so little, they competed more openly for his time and quarreled more bitterly.

Karen did her household chores grudgingly; she did not feel like helping a mother who she thought would probably just criticize anyway. Her mother complained that Karen was lazy and said that she could get better grades in school if she worked as hard as Ted did.

Ted's typical Hero behavior annoyed Karen. When her mother was not around, she called him "Ted Goody-Goody." If she had to spend all her time studying in order to get her mother's love, she'd just do without it!

Home had become a lonely place. Karen missed the attention and affection she once received, but before long she discovered that the boys she knew were more than ready to give it to her. She started dating young, and by the time she was fifteen was sleeping with several boys. At sixteen she discovered she was pregnant.

Her father was shocked and hurt that his "little girl would do such a thing." Her mother was humiliated and furious. They both blamed and shamed her, and argued far into the night what was to be done about the situation. One thing they could not do, however—they could no longer ignore her.

Karen had an abortion, but that did not end the matter. She immediately went into a suicidal depression that led her, and eventually the whole family, into treatment.

In treating hundreds of alcoholic families, I have observed a rather curious phenomenon: in spite of their diametrically opposite natures, the Hero and the Scapegoat are the two family roles most frequently exchanged.

This switch may occur if the Hero's early departure from home is interpreted by his parents as rejection or desertion. He suddenly finds himself plunged into the Scapegoat position, and the next child enjoys a long-denied opportunity to be the Hero.

Another possible scenario involves the Scapegoat who, as a result of treatment, makes such a dramatic change for the better that the family is overwhelmed with relief and gratitude. Then he may by his own efforts have earned the Hero's wreath, while the bewildered oldest child must content himself with second place. In his hurt and anger at this turn of events, the former Hero may become hostile or himself resort to alcohol or drugs. Such Scapegoat-like behavior then makes it easy for the rest of the family to lock him permanently into the role.

THE SCAPEGOAT'S BURDEN

The personal cost of playing a role is more obvious in the Scapegoat than in any other member of the alcoholic's family. The pathological forces already inherent in the family system are magnified and augmented by his own self-destructive behavior. Before he leaves the family, his worth, both in his own eyes and in the opinion of others, may be almost totally destroyed.

The Physical Potential

The gravest effects on the Scapegoat's physical body come as a result of his acting-out behavior. Drinking and using drugs—besides their immediate and powerful pharmacological consequences—can affect his nutrition, lead to hazardous exploits and accidents, and of course carry the very real possibility of addiction. Promiscuity, so often accompanied in youngsters by a lack of accurate sexual information, can lead to venereal infections and, for girls, to the alternative hazards of abortion or childbearing. And ever lurking in a Scapegoat's self-hatred is the possibility of the ultimate physical damage—suicide.

The Emotional Potential

As he sits in a counselor's office, the typical Scapegoat may act sullen and uncooperative, or openly rebellious and belligerent. Either way, he appears to be consumed with anger—anger at his parents for not caring about him (as he sincerely believes they do not), anger at the Dependent for drinking, anger at the Enabler and the Hero for what he sees as a conspiracy to belittle and manipulate the Dependent, anger at the world for "falling for his [the Hero's] act," and most of all, anger at the self that has brought him to his present plight. Since such intense anger eventually becomes frozen into a chronic attitude of hostility, it poses a real danger of being turned destructively against either the self or society.

But in working with Scapegoats, I have discovered that much of their anger is an unconscious mask for the more painful feelings of rejection and loneliness. Surprising though it may seem, beneath the shell or the bombast *the characteristic feeling of the Scapegoat is hurt.*

Most of these youngsters also feel guilty. Though a Scapegoat may break all society's rules for decent behavior, he has probably not truly rejected them. In his heart he accepts their validity and bears a heavy sense of guilt for his transgressions.

While burdened with this heavy load of negative feelings, the poor Scapegoat enjoys few positive ones to offset them. From early childhood he has learned that he can expect little affection, understanding, fun, peace, or joy within his family. Turning to his peers instead, he finds shallow companionship but rarely the deep, caring friendships that would satisfy his longing. He discovers his acting-out friends are all as needy as he is. Never having received much love or trust themselves, they have little to give.

The Social Potential

As we have seen, in his flight from the family, the Scapegoat's peer group becomes the primary institution in his life. He often learns to function quite effectively in it and so succeeds in getting the attention and acceptance that were denied him at home. But whatever social skills he acquires are at best shallow and self-centered, at worst manipulative and exploitive. They lack the honesty and genuine concern for others needed to build intimate, cooperative, loving relationships.

The Mental Potential

The role of scholar is likely to have been preempted by the Hero, and the Scapegoat (often realistically) sees it as useless to challenge him. As he watches the long hours of studying that the Hero puts in to earn A's, he decides they aren't worth the effort anyway. His anger and low self-esteem have left him with little motivation to try to achieve academically or in any other way.

A bright child who finds himself in the Scapegoat position is more likely to use his mental abilities to become leader of his peer group or to devise schemes that eventually end up in juvenile court.

The Spiritual Potential

What can we say about the spiritual potential of a youngster who seems bent on breaking every code and every rule? We must begin, I think, by restraining any impulse to pass judgment on him, even though we may at first experience him as surly, uncooperative, delinquent, even incorrigible. Those words may be accurate to describe the role he is playing, but as long as we are tempted to use them, we have not really met the child himself.

He is acting out of a value system that is not his own. Just as the Hero's apparent goodness does not flow from his own spirituality but is prescribed by his role, so it is with the Scapegoat's "badness." Neither child wrote the part he is playing, yet neither feels free to leave the stage. Legally, of course, the Scapegoat who breaks the law is accountable; he *is* aware of what he is doing. But morally, which is to say spiritually, the case is far more complicated. We may be grateful that as either jurors or professional workers we do not have to render moral verdicts.

Being cast in a role that requires its player to violate accepted standards of behavior—bringing on himself not only society's indictment and contempt but his own as well—is devastating to this youngster's spirit. Its development, retarded by the very fact of living in an alcoholic family, is blocked almost completely when he begins to perform in the manner prescribed by his Scapegoat role.

But a potential is always potential. The sudden realization that he can still find worth in himself and meaning in his life can provide strong motivation for the Scapegoat in treatment.

The Volitional Potential

If the Hero is not a Hero by choice, reluctance must be even more true of the Scapegoat. The Hero, however, may not be aware of the degree to which he is controlled by forces outside himself, for he can honorably own all his actions and indeed receives ample reinforcement from family and community to do so. The Scapegoat *knows*. In his heart he does not want to be a bad kid. He just feels carried along toward trouble by some momentum, some unseen force that he does not understand.

This situation offers further hope for the Scapegoat's recovery. He has more to gain from laying aside his role than the Hero has, and little to lose but his troubles.

SAVING THE SCAPEGOAT

Often the Scapegoat is the first person to suffer serious effects from an unhealthy family system. Certainly he is the first to become visible. Unlike the Hero, he may well have his need for help identified while he is still living in the family, because his behavior or its consequences attract attention outside the home. If a youngster abuses alcohol or drugs, has an auto accident, gets pregnant, or attempts suicide, the medical community is alerted. If he is failing in his studies, school authorities become involved. If he is picked up for reckless or drunken driving, stealing, vandalism, or possession of drugs, he ends up in the hands of the law. Any of these community resources can channel a child into counseling.

Such a disproportionate number of youngsters in trouble come from alcoholic families that it is urgent for everyone who works professionally with young people to recognize clues to the Scapegoat role. Some of the characteristic attitudes and behaviors can be seen in the following responses, which we hear over and over again in counseling:

Reliance on peers.	"My friends are the only ones who understand me."
Acting out.	"We just thought it would be fun to drive a Jag for an hour or two."
Rationalization.	"Aw, grown-ups don't know anything about grass. Everybody smokes it."
Irresponsibility.	"But I didn't mean to get pregnant."
Giving up easily.	"School's no fun. It's too hard."
Defiance.	"Just try to make me go."
Withdrawal.	"Leave me alone!"
Sullenness.	No reply at all.

If one looks only at his facade, the Scapegoat is not a very appealing client, but the more perceptive counselor can see in him a tragic picture of low self-worth. It is already causing him anguish at every level of his being, and unless something intervenes to change his direction, he will carry it with him for the rest of his life, continuing to play the same role in later dramas and even setting up systems that will perpetuate it. He is forever in danger that his chronic low self-worth and self-destructive tendencies may suddenly be acted out in suicide.

More frequently, however, a Scapegoat chooses a slower form of suicide—chemical dependency. He has learned early in his family about the pain-killing potential of alcohol and other drugs and has experimented with chemicals himself while still in high school, possibly even elementary school. He has found that drinking and drugs offer not only pain relief but also "kicks" and a chance to defy parental or other authority, all tempting payoffs. It should not surprise us then to learn that in clinical experience, just as Heroes grow up to be Enablers, Scapegoats grow up to be a new generation of Dependents.

In chapter 7 we watched the Hero follow a trial blazed by the Enabler; something similar, though more covert, seems to happen between the Scapegoat and the Dependent. Like the Dependent, the Scapegoat gets caught up in a chronic behavior pattern defined by society as deviant. Both feel shame and guilt; both believe that they cannot change their patterns so must pursue them in spite of themselves; both suffer heavy social consequences for their behavior, a deepening self-hate, and eventually, despair.

To be sure, any learning by the Scapegoat is more subtle and unconscious than the Hero's. And he does not enjoy the companionship and mutual support often found in the Enabler-Hero alliance. But in his very alienation from that righteous pair, he finds his sympathies aligned with the Dependent.

The cost of allowing Scapegoats to go on playing their roles without intervention is clearly exorbitant, to both the individual and society. But too often a youngster in trouble is placed in a hospital, juvenile facility, or foster home, and any attempt at treatment is on an individual basis. Few of the agencies involved are prepared to treat (or are probably even aware of) the larger family problem of which the Scapegoat's behavior is only a manifestation. As a result their efforts are likely to fail.

I cannot overemphasize that *intervention must be with the entire family.* Treatment of the Dependent alone does nothing to correct the negative self-image and destructive behavior pattern of the Scapegoat; treatment of the Scapegoat alone will be quickly undone by the very family system that gave rise to his problems.

We must keep constantly in mind that this child's delinquent, self-destructive behavior has been triggered by the alcoholic family system and is performing a needed function both for him and for the family as a whole. For him, it brings attention, importance, and some honest communication, painful though it may be; he has found no other way to get any of these. For the parents, it furnishes a welcome change of focus, away from the more central problem of alcoholism, which they are so busily denying. And they, too, find relief in this opportunity for an honest expression of feelings. *As long as we try to help one youngster without treating the rest of the family, they cannot afford to let him get well.*

In a suitable treatment program, however, the Scapegoat can, for all his negativity, respond to counseling. As he becomes aware that he is playing a role and behaving compulsively, he can begin to transform the energy and daring of his self-destructive behavior into productive, rather gutsy self-care. At the same time, his long experience with pain can make him sensitive to the pain of others, and the social drive that carried him into a pack of peers can help to make him a responsible member of the community.

CHAPTER **9**

The Lost Child

BY THE TIME the third child makes his appearance, the plot of the alcoholic drama has thickened, and the four characters already on stage are intensely involved in it. Like the Scapegoat before him, this child feels like an outsider. Unlike the Scapegoat, however, he does not try to force his way into the action or resort to some attention-getting tactic on another part of the stage. Instead, he simply retires to the wings.

Almost from infancy he senses the tensions of the drama being enacted around him, but he cannot comprehend the plot. He has arrived in the middle of the play, and no one volunteers to explain what has happened so far—family members are all too preoccupied to notice his confusion. Should he dare to ask questions, he risks being abruptly put down; frank discussion is against the rules in this family, as we have already discovered. Any answers he might receive would only compound his confusion anyway, for although the active participants have person-ally witnessed earlier family events and behavior, none of them really understands what is going on.

So the little newcomer finds his own way of adapting to the situa-tion—he "gets lost." He becomes a loner, looking after his needs himself and staying out of everyone's way, finding more comfort in the privacy of his own company than in the midst of the family chaos, where he is for all practical purposes alone anyway.

Everyone welcomes his choice. In this family where the Depen-dent's drinking, the Enabler's coping, the Hero's triumphs, and the

Scapegoat's escapades are all vying for attention, a child who makes no demands is a source of great relief.

The Lost Child's withdrawal can be considered functional for himself, too, insofar as it protects him from some of the direct, negative effects that the Hero and the Scapegoat are experiencing. But the same protective wall also isolates him from whatever positive interaction and communication still exist in the family.

In a family where communication among all the members is poor, he is the most out of touch. Not only did he miss the first part of the drama, but he is offstage so much of the time that he misses many of the ongoing developments, too, so he grows ever more confused. When he does occasionally move into the family circle closely enough to observe the current state of affairs, he finds himself increasingly a stranger in his own family.

Sometimes I call this role "the forgotten child." Interest in his undertakings, praise for his achievements, reassurance in his fears, companionship and affection in his loneliness—none of these necessities of childhood is forthcoming from those who would normally provide them. Because he is so often out of sight, he and his needs are also out of mind.

This neglect is rarely by intent, of course. But to the Lost Child it nevertheless carries a message that he is not important, that he does not have much personal worth. Characteristically, Lost Children blame themselves for not being able to fit into the family, rather than looking for the fault where it really lies—in the dysfunctional system itself.

As the child retreats behind his wall of isolation, he often builds a fantasy world of his own, where for a few years he seems to find peace and satisfaction. Here is a safe place, secure, predictable, within his control. Sometimes it seems more real to him than the bizarre "real" world of his family. So he spends a lot of time in his room, playing, reading, pursuing a hobby, or just daydreaming. While he is very young, he may develop imaginary friends with whom he feels more at ease than with live playmates; or he may choose a favorite doll or stuffed animal as his special companion, later transferring this affection to a pet. He finds what short-term pleasure he can in solitary indulgences like eating, watching television, or listening to his favorite music; later he may seek it more destructively in chemicals.

But he cannot remain in his private little world forever. As he moves out into the larger arenas of school and peer group, his defensive scheme begins to fail him. He finds himself an alien in the everyday world where children from healthy families have been learning to live since infancy. He has had little experience in either expressing his own feelings or handling such expressions from others; in cooperation or in negotiating disputes when cooperation breaks down; in sharing or in defending ownership; in assessing the real value of either material possessions or sensory pleasure. *He has had little experience in living.* In his confusion he makes many errors in judgment, with results that range from ineffectiveness to downright humiliation.

Since he has never experienced warm, human closeness, he is not prepared to make friends and engage in the social give and take of

day-to-day school contacts. Yet in the midst of the crowd, withdrawing into himself leaves him feeling lonely, different, and inept.

When my work takes me into schools, I long to reach out to all the Lost Children I see there. Though they are quiet and shy, almost fading into the woodwork, anyone familiar with family roles can pick them out quickly. I rarely find them in the band—Heroes join the band and march in the spotlight. Nor are they noticeable on the playground—the Scapegoat and his pals have usually taken it over. I am more likely to find them singing in a choir, or doing a long project for the teacher, or reading alone in an out-of-the-way corner.

As youngsters move on into the high-school years, social skills—complicated by the blossoming of sexuality—begin to assume great importance in their lives. Now the Lost Child finds himself more lost than ever.

Each human being learns what it means to be a man or a woman from the adults in his or her childhood family. The same-sex parent provides a lasting model of what he is to be, and the other parent an object for his first important relationship with a person of the opposite sex. These are powerful teachings, beginning many years before formal "sex education," even before a child is consciously aware of sex role differences. They are powerful, that is, *if they occur.*

The Lost Child, however, has never felt close to either of his parents; he has been too insulated from them to experience this kind of learning. Consequently, he reaches puberty with no clear sense of his own sexual identity or how to relate in a healthy way with those of the opposite sex. As adolescent sexuality increasingly colors all aspects of the daily world he occupies, he is engulfed by yet another kind of confusion. True to his pattern, he withdraws. He rarely dates and in his loneliness suffers growing doubts about his own sexual normalcy.

I remember a college student named Tim, who came to me several years ago after just this kind of childhood experience. At that time I was working with a wide variety of clients and had not yet identified all the roles in an alcoholic family. Today I realize that Tim was a Lost Child, grown up but still lost.

Tim was the third in a family of five children. He told me that he felt he never really knew either of his parents. When he approached his mother, she was always either preoccupied with something else or resting. Tim noticed that she took a lot of naps, but it was not until years later that he realized she had become dependent on prescription drugs.

His father, in the hours he was at home, was worried, impatient, busily trying to catch up on the household chores that his wife neglected.

Before Tim started school, his older sisters used to play house and pretend he was their baby. They would push him in his stroller and read him fairy tales. Afterward he spent hours playing "prince," riding his stick horse and acting out fantasies of his princely life.

As he got older, though, Tim no longer fitted into his sisters' play, and the younger children were not much fun for him. So he spent most of his time alone in his room, making models and listening to music. As the problems of his mother's dependency mounted, he was glad to have his headphones to block out the rest of the world. At school he was liked well enough but had no close friends, a pattern that continued into high school. Because of his shyness he rarely dated.

By his second year in college, Tim began to worry: he had never had a girlfriend. Our first meeting brought out the fact, however, that he was not close to young men either, nor did he feel attracted to them. Through counseling he came to realize that his problem was not his sexuality but his difficulty in forming relationships of any kind, whether sexual or just companionable. He was suffering a common handicap that Lost Children carry as a scar of their years in a sick family system. Counseling helped him begin to learn the skills of relating—a task he was able to continue on his own.

During the first several years of developing my model of the alcoholic family roles, I considered the Lost Child a Scapegoat who just happened to manifest his sense of rejection by the family in a particular way. But I have since realized that there are fundamental differences in the two roles. True, both children find themselves locked out of the original triangle of parents and Hero, but their responses to that primal frustration are at opposite poles—a difference that will reverberate through all their later responses to the recurring challenges of life.

Emotionally, both rejected youngsters suffer from low self-worth. However, the Scapegoat's is a slowly growing self-hate, rooted in unfavorable comparisons to the Hero and in his own antisocial behavior; the Lost Child's lack of self-worth simply results from years of being ignored and treated as though he did not exist. The Scapegoat, feeling unfairly excluded from the heart of the family, is hurt and angry; the Lost Child, on the other hand, accepts his exclusion as all he deserves, experiencing loneliness and worthlessness but little anger.

Behaviorally, their difference is a matter of stance. The Scapegoat attacks his situation aggressively, first by trying to get positive attention, then by negative acting-out; the Lost Child yields to his fate passively, retiring from the field. The Scapegoat plunges into the peer culture; the Lost Child becomes a loner. The Scapegoat courts trouble and thus attracts attention; the Lost Child avoids trouble and rarely gets any attention at all.

Earlier I said that second children tend to become Scapegoats rather than Lost Children. This has been my observation in counseling hundreds of families. I think, however, that given the sharp difference in the level of aggressiveness of the two, we have to allow for the possibility that individual temperament plays some part in the choice of roles.

In adult life the Scapegoat and the Lost Child face some of the same risks, but again they do so with differences. We will examine these long-term problems later in this chapter.

THE LOST CHILD'S LOSS

The damage that the alcoholic family inflicts on the Lost Child is not so much in what it does as in what it does not do. Family members come to expect good behavior and success from the Hero and trouble from the Scapegoat, but from the Lost Child they do not expect much of anything. As a result, he learns not to expect much of himself, either. In steadily living out everyone's low expectations, he fails to develop the potentials with which he was born.

The Physical Potential

Since the Lost Child's passive behavior pattern provides him with no way to release his negative feelings directly, he must repress them; they lie in the unconscious, waiting for some indirect (and thus undefended) avenue of expression. Physical symptoms offer one such avenue. There is, for example, a high incidence of allergy and asthma among Lost Children. They also have more than their share of accidents. Illness or injury offers one way to get nurturing without seeming to ask for it; simply riding to the doctor's office can mean a little exclusive time with Mother or Dad that the child would not otherwise have had.

Lost Children are often reported to be bed wetters, too. It is easy to see how much attention (albeit not always positive!) this behavior can generate.

Eating is a readily available gratification to which many Lost Children resort in their emotional emptiness, and at first it may seem innocuous; but pursued with the compulsiveness that drives everyone in an alcoholic family, it often leads to obesity. Too, the foods a child chooses as "goodies" are rarely those that nutritionally build a healthy young body.

Not long ago I gave a workshop for pediatricians in Baltimore. As I described the characteristic symptoms of the Lost Child, these physicians confirmed that they saw many such children in their practices. They said that they always felt helpless because, although they had not understood the dynamics of the troubled family, they sensed that the child's problems were rooted deeply in the functioning of the larger family system to which they did not have access. As they came to recognize what might be happening in that larger "patient," they became aware of new choices in finding help for everyone, including the original child patient.

The Emotional Potential

Unquestionably, *loneliness is the characteristic feeling of the Lost Child.* His aloneness, while protecting him from some of the family chaos and pain, keeps him from becoming an active part of the family system. He does not know quite where he fits into it, or indeed whether he belongs at all. While he is young, the safety of his solitude may be worth the cost, but as his personal world expands beyond the home, what once was a sanctuary becomes increasingly a prison. All around him he sees people involved in human relationships, yet he cannot seem to get past the bars of his own solitary habits and social inexperience to participate. Aloneness turns into a deep, aching loneliness, with its companion feelings of sadness, confusion, and fear.

The Social Potential

At this point it hardly need be said that the Lost Child's stunted development is felt more in the social potential than in any other aspect of his personality. Indeed, this handicap underlies much of the rest of his limitation and unhappiness.

He has failed to learn the rudiments of human interaction where they are traditionally learned, in the family. Instead of seeking out playmates during his early childhood years, he contents himself with solitary activities, or imaginary playmates or a pet. In school, if he has friends at all, it is probably only one at a time; even then, the relationship is likely to be shallow, for he has never experienced intimacy so can neither offer it nor feel comfortable in its presence.

Passing time only intensifies his social poverty. As youth turns to adulthood, his sexual doubts, added to his inability to achieve intimacy, make his chances for a satisfying and lasting love relationship slim.

The Mental Potential

The child who is fortunate enough to grow up in a family or community where a high value is placed on intellectual pursuits, or the one who is gifted with strong natural capabilities, may use his hours alone in reading, study, or creative activities that can actually enhance development of his mental potential. More often, in my experience, however, the combination of low expectations and low self-worth have such a dampening effect that most Lost Children grow up with deficits in their mental as well as their other personal potentials.

The Spiritual Potential

The same handicaps that the Lost Child experiences elsewhere among his peers carry over to Sunday school, church youth groups, and other organized religious activities. Unless he happens to be deeply touched by some empathetic adult or a powerful spiritual experience that he associates with his religion, he will be inclined to leave this scene, too, as quickly as he can.

His very solitude, however, provides a fertile setting for the development of a rich personal spirituality. The quiet and isolation, the active fantasy life, the very emptiness that offers no competing relationships or satisfactions to which he has become attached—these are all circumstances that have been recognized throughout human history as conducive to spiritual growth.

While the flowering of his spiritual potential appears possible, does the Lost Child in truth experience it? It is hard to say. A child who cannot tolerate intimacy is not likely to confide such intimate personal information in a family session, group therapy, or the limited number of individual sessions provided by most treatment programs for alcoholic families. We can, however, assume that he is at least familiar with the ground where spirituality can take root. That in itself has value. If the seed should ever be planted, it could thrive.

The Volitional Potential

As the Lost Child walks away from the family to become a loner, he seems to be not so much making a conscious choice as saying that there *are* no choices. But the choice to withdraw really is a choice, and one that is self-perpetuating. By opting out, he so curtails his personal development that he severely limits future choices in all aspects of his life. Forever after, in every decision, he must choose the solitary course.

Only to the extent that the Lost Child can appreciate where his problem lies and gradually acquire the physical, mental, and particularly the social skills that he lacks can he begin to enjoy his first genuinely free decision-making.

GUIDING THE LOST CHILD BACK

Although the Lost Child plays the least destructive of any of the family roles, he also has the least chance for personal satisfaction or fulfillment. If not identified and given professional help, he becomes a Lost Adult—struggling against huge odds to build a satisfactory life with the limited resources his restricted childhood has given him.

Never having developed communication skills or the ability to form close relationships, he can never know intimacy. He has few friends and rarely finds a suitable partner. He is likely either to marry several times, without success, or not to marry at all. For a while he may become promiscuous until he learns that sexual contact is no substitute for intimacy.

To compensate for his loneliness and low self-worth, he puts a high value on possessions and pleasures. He may take inordinate satisfaction and pride in a new car, an antique, a stereo system, an exotic vacation. These things give him something to brighten his lonely days and something to talk about when he finds himself, uncomfortably, in a social gathering.

As in childhood, he may overeat to fill his emptiness, and like the Scapegoat, he often abuses alcohol or drugs. His pattern of use, however, is different. The Lost Child is more likely to go on occasional binges, while the Scapegoat is in greater danger of becoming actually dependent. (I have worked with a few clients who originally played the Lost Child in their families, then for one reason or another found themselves the Scapegoat.)

Unless someone intervenes, the Lost Child will go on playing the same role for the rest of his life, suffering his private pain in silence.

Most of the Lost Children we see in counseling find their way to treatment fairly young, if at all. Some come as part of a family group. Others may be referred, either by pediatricians who have been treating them for asthma or allergies, or by school systems where they have been classified as slow learners or so shy as to be socially "retarded." Adolescents often come in on their own initiative because of sexual worries or difficulty in forming relationships.

As adults, however, relatively few of these lonely people seek out a counselor. They received so little help, advice, or even emotional support from anyone during the formative years of their lives that it seldom even occurs to them to turn to a professional for help except in the most acute crisis. I am convinced that if the community of professionals who see these clients at any age for any kind of human service could only recognize a Lost Child's syndrome for what it is and refer him for counseling or psychotherapy, many more of them—and often their entire families—could be helped to find themselves and their unrealized potential for happiness.

Here are some of the common characteristics to watch for:

- *Low profile.* Quiet, unobtrusive, often unimpressive, revealing neither his problems nor his potential.
- *Independence.* Willing and often able to look after himself, expecting little from others.
- *Aloneness.* Avoiding closeness, denying the need for it, and unable to form the relationships that would allow it.
- *Problems with sexual identity.* Confused about sex roles and sometimes about sexual preference.
- *Materialism.* Taking inordinate comfort and pride in possessions.
- *Overindulgence.* Overweight, given to binging on "goodies" and possibly on alcohol.

If the Lost Child's odds of reaching treatment are poor, his chance for success once he gets there is, in my experience, excellent. Some of the by-products of his role in the family are positive. Just as the Hero learned to achieve, the Lost Child learned to be independent and self-reliant. He is also free of the unrealistic expectations that cause many people unhappiness in life; and he has probably developed a number of interests and skills through years of solitude that can continue to give him satisfaction and enjoyment.

These qualities offer an underlying base of strength on which a counselor can help him build some solid self-worth and a useful, productive life.

CHAPTER **10**

The Mascot

THE CAST of our family drama is almost complete. We have watched as the Dependent slowly succumbs to the characteristic symptoms of alcoholism: *compulsion, denial,* and *delusion.* We have seen the Enabler beginning to manifest those same symptoms, as one person's dependency has gradually become a family disease. The children, too, manifest all three symptoms; for each, however, one seems to be dominant. The Hero and the Scapegoat are both propelled, in opposite directions, by an irresistible compulsion, while the Lost Child makes his entire existence one grand denial. Now it remains only for someone to express fully the family's delusion. That someone is the fifth and final supporting player—the Mascot.

The Mascot is usually a latecomer, most often the youngest child. By the time he (or as frequently she) arrives on the scene, the family's circumstances have deteriorated still further. Mother is preoccupied with Dad, and Dad is preoccupied with drinking. Brothers and sisters are busy playing their own survival roles. He feels alone and helpless. How can such a little fellow fit into such a threatening situation, which he does not understand at all? Yet how can he survive if he does *not* fit in? This family is all he has.

We may recall that the Lost Child experienced much the same kind of aloneness and confusion, but the plight of the Mascot is worse. People not only fail to explain to him what is going on; they consciously withhold information and may even tell him things that are misleading or untrue. Let's see why.

When a baby is born, his family sees how helpless and fragile he is, so they lovingly protect him while he grows. In time, as he matures and another child comes along, their protectiveness is phased out and shifted to the new baby. In the case of the youngest child, however, there is no later infant to remind the family that so much protecting is no longer necessary or appropriate. Every parent has sensed, I am sure, how much greater tendency there is to "baby" the youngest child. He always seems a little more fragile, less mature, unready to face the hard realities of life.

(Occasionally a family's protectiveness is focused on some older child who, because of a handicap, chronic illness, or other special circumstance, seems particularly vulnerable. An only daughter in the middle of a family of sons, or a son among daughters, may also be sheltered in this way.)

Parents and older siblings take great care to screen what they say to this child. They do not tell him about Susie's abortion or Tony's smoking dope or the fact that Mom and Dad do not sleep together any more. When he asks questions about what is going on in the family, he is answered, not with information, but with vague reassurances. All this protection is well intentioned, of course. The problem is, it doesn't work.

Often I hear a parent say, "My children weren't affected by my divorce [or hospitalization or whatever]. They were too young when it happened." That parent forgets that even a small child has eyes to see worried expressions or unusual behavior; ears to hear adult conversations, shouting, or the sound of crying behind a closed bedroom door; sensitivity to pick up subtle clues to hidden anger or hurt or fear in those he loves.

Working professionally with families, I have learned that children usually know much more of what is going on than parents think they do. Sometimes a tot of four or five can give me an astonishingly clear account of what is happening at home. He sees it all; the trouble is that in his immaturity he cannot make sense of it. His intuition merely tells him all is not well. Naturally, he becomes frightened; or perhaps *anxious* is a better word, for although he feels fear, he does not know what he is afraid of. Whatever it is, it seems to threaten the whole family system —the only security he knows.

In an alcoholic family, where there are so many secrets and so much pain to protect a child from, the tendency to overprotect is intensified.

Imagine how confusing it must be—all the child's senses are telling him that something is wrong, dangerously wrong, yet everyone he trusts

is telling him that things are just fine. Are they really fine? Doesn't anyone else see and hear and feel what he does? Is he going crazy?

Now his original, justified fear, for the family, is compounded by a second fear, which is not justified but inescapable under the circumstances—fear for his own sanity. All this fear has no place to go, no object to focus on, no way to be expressed because everyone else is denying there is anything to be afraid of. As the anxiety builds up inside him, it creates tensions, which find their outlet in the distinctive behavior of the Mascot role.

Many Mascots learn while only toddlers that showing off can bring rewards. They have only to start their antics and everyone laughs. They can release pent-up energy and get some positive attention in the bargain. That is a big payoff, especially in a family where there are few satisfactions for anyone. So the Mascot resorts to clowning every time life presents him with a difficult situation. He becomes the class cut-up and, as he gets older, the life of the party, the Pagliacci hiding his own pain behind a permanently painted grin.

The Mascot who creates fun wherever he goes has some things in common with the Hero. Both manage to get positive attention for themselves and at the same time bring good feelings to the family. When the other members laugh at him, it relieves their tensions, too. Everyone seems to forget, at least for a moment, how grim it all is. Mascots, however, also vent their hyperactivity in annoying habits and bursts of sudden, erratic behavior, so the attention they receive can be negative as well as positive.

Whether entertaining or merely agitated, the Mascot's behavior achieves its purposes: it puts him in control of the family scene for as long as he can hold the floor and so makes him feel more secure; it brings him attention of some kind, whether positive or negative; it moves family members to some rare honest expressions of feeling, whether laughter or scolding; and it temporarily takes the spotlight off the Dependent and the family crisis.

You do not have to be with a family more than a few minutes to know which child is playing this part. He may act cute and helpless, or show off, or joke around and refuse to take anything seriously, or squirm and interrupt and do "crazy" things. He may beguile you or bedevil you, but he is very hard to ignore.

In counseling sessions I have a good opportunity to see just how effective Mascots' behavior can be. They may realize that my office is not an appropriate place for outright clowning, but they fidget, they whine, they have to go to the bathroom, they may knock over a plant or an ashtray. When one of these interruptions occurs, the whole family seems to welcome the chance to shift their attention away from their problems and onto the Mascot.

To make the outlines of this role clearer, I would like to tell you about Beth. She was a classic Mascot—the fourth and youngest child in her family, who played only this one role.

Beth was in the third grade when I first met her. She had become such a behavior problem in class that her teacher had referred her to the school psychologist for testing. Finding no signs of abnormality in Beth, he suspected problems within the family and suggested they seek a counselor. At that time I was working with all kinds of family problems, so they called me for an appointment.

In one of our early sessions together, I noticed a certain quality in the relationship between the father and mother that I had seen many times before. Further questioning confirmed my hunch: he was in trouble with alcohol and she was protecting him. Beth was displaying symptoms that I later recognized as characteristic of the Mascot role.

After several weeks Beth felt safe enough to talk about what it was like to be the youngest child in that family. She said she never knew what anyone was thinking. She wondered what was going on inside of them—and inside of herself, too. She felt mixed up, afraid of something but she didn't know what. A few times she tried to tell her mother or her sister about it, but they just said there was nothing to be afraid of. That didn't help. In fact, it made her feel even more scared. Though they didn't say so, she thought maybe her mother and sister were scared, too.

One episode Beth described was a perfect example of the contradictory input that Mascots must try to make sense of. One Friday evening when Beth was only five years old, her father came home three hours late for supper, stumbling, noisy, and smelling of beer. Beth was already in her pajamas, so her mother rushed her into bed. In a few minutes she heard angry voices from her parents' bedroom; her father was shouting and her mother began to cry. Then she heard her father say, "You call me drunk once more and I'm gonna let you have it!"

Beth lay awake for hours, too frightened to go to sleep. (I remembered the nights like that in my own childhood and understood her fear.) She loved her mother—she couldn't get along without her! And yet she loved her father, too, except maybe when he came home like he did tonight, smelling of beer. Did she hear right? Would he really say such a thing? Would he *do* it?

The next morning Beth was still very upset when she went downstairs for breakfast. The rest of the family were sitting around the kitchen table silent and serious. No one said anything. (As Beth told this story, I asked everyone what they had actually been feeling that day. Her father admitted that he had felt overwhelmed with remorse; her mother, that she was very angry and hurt; her brothers and sisters, that they were all confused and scared, like Beth.)

The tension was more than Beth could handle. In her agitation she tipped over her glass of milk, and the meal ended in a confusion of sponges and scoldings. (As Beth reported this, the whole family agreed that Beth's "accident" had broken the tension at the time, and they had all felt relief.)

Later Beth asked her mother, "Is Daddy going to hurt you?" Her mother acted surprised. Why, where would Beth get such an idea? Daddy loved Mommy and Beth and the whole family very much. Beth should never think about such a thing again.

Beth did think about it, though—a lot. She couldn't help it, even though it made her feel sort of dizzy. Did she just imagine that whole conversation? Surely, Mother wouldn't say anything that wasn't so. . . .

This was only one of many such episodes in Beth's life. When she tried to make sense of them, she felt uncomfortable and jumpy, she said —"sorta crazy." Eventually she stopped trying.

By the time she reached third grade, she found it almost impossible to concentrate on her schoolwork or even to sit still at her desk. Sometimes she would kick the boy in front of her or hum until one of the other kids complained and the teacher made her stop. She honestly didn't want to be bad in school—she just found herself doing those things. It was so hard to sit still and be quiet!

Beth had trouble sitting still in my office, too. Her father would give her a stern look and say, "Beth, stop squirming!" or "Beth, sit down!" Each time, she complied and actually seemed to relax for a few minutes.

On one occasion she bumped a stack of file folders that were piled on my shelf, and they scattered all over the floor. Our discussion stopped abruptly, and everyone became very busy picking up papers. Though the whole family were full of apologies for Beth, they seemed to enjoy the interruption, relieved at not having to face their family pain for that few minutes.

In the months of treatment that followed, Beth came to understand why she was feeling and acting as she did, and made a start in the long process of learning to use her overabundance of energy in more constructive ways. As a result of our family discussions, her father also began to face the truth about himself and entered treatment for alcoholism.

BEHIND THE MASCOT'S COMIC MASK

Playing the irresponsible Mascot may look at first like a perfect defense, but like all the roles in an alcoholic family, it has its price. Any child who is singled out young as special carries a heavy burden of either demands or limitations, depending on whether that specialness implies a gift or a handicap. For the Hero, with his capacity for achievement, being special brings a burden. For the Mascot, whom everyone sees as (and keeps) immature, it brings limitation. So severe is this limitation, in fact, that it can retard development in every aspect of his being.

The Physical Potential

For years I have noticed that Mascots seem to have distinct physical characteristics. Most often they are wiry, with tense, tight muscles. They also tend to be smaller than their siblings, a fact that has always struck me as curious. Recently, however, I have read of research indicating that emotional pain can actually retard children's physical growth. The same investigators found that relieving that pain through treatment could trigger belated growth to catch up, even though treatment came as late as the thirties.[1]

Because of their tightly wound emotional springs, these youngsters may develop stress-related physical illnesses. An even greater hazard is that they may be diagnosed as hyperkinetic. I say "hazard" because the usual treatment for that condition is the drug Ritalen. Such a diagnosis will mean that one more member of the family will start depending on a chemical. Concerned about this situation, Dr. Ken Williams recently studied one pediatrician's files and discovered that 37 percent of the children who had been prescribed Ritalen had fathers who were practicing alcoholics.

In treatment centers we encounter a lot of what we call "chemically maintained families." Dad will be dependent on alcohol, Mom on tran-

---

[1] "Resolving of Emotional Pain May Trigger Physical Growth in Adults." *Brain/Mind Bulletin*, May 19, 1980, p. 1.

quilizers, the Scapegoat on street drugs, the Lost Child on sugar, and the Mascot on Ritalin. Only the Hero escapes, and perhaps even he is sustained by the adrenalin from his own successes.

The Emotional Potential

The Mascot suffers from the same sense of inadequacy, unimportance, guilt, and loneliness as his siblings, though for him these feelings may be even more intense because he is younger. What few good feelings there are to be had in this unhappy family are being grabbed by someone else. He is even more confused than the others, too.

Above all, he feels scared. *Fear is the characteristic emotion of the Mascot.* He feels that the very foundations of his existence—his parents, the family unit, his own sanity—are in danger. Yet it is a danger that he cannot see or name, one that is all the more frightening because it is invisible. A perceptive person can often detect a hyperactive Mascot's fear, but when he is clowning, the Mascot manages to hide it so well that even his friends and family would probably tell you, "Nothing worries Tommy—he just laughs things off!"

The problem in being a clown is that no one ever knows the real person he is behind the funny mask, the greasepaint. Whereas the Lost Child was lonely in the midst of a crowd, because of his shyness, the Mascot is lonely even while being the center of attention.

The Social Potential

The Mascot, though he may not be aware of it, is a manipulator. He uses diversionary tactics to control a situation and to elicit the response he wants. When fun is his tactic and laughter the desired response, he may fool us into thinking that he is socially very skillful. In a way he is. He is in close, if not meaningful, contact with other family members and with his peers as well, something the Lost Child is not.

But he is a singer who knows only one tune. He can be funny, period. Whatever the situation—a family argument, a poor report card, rejection by a girlfriend, an illness or accident—he has only one response in his social repertoire. His friends soon learn this. They may enjoy having him in the crowd, but they never take him very seriously. Inside he knows this, and the feelings of unimportance and inadequacy that began when he was a small child are reinforced.

The hapless child who finds himself a Mascot by circumstance but not a clown by nature is in a worse situation. He, too, manages to manipulate and to that degree engages with those around him. But the single tactic he knows for doing it is to irritate. While the clown sings only one tune, the hyperactive Mascot does not sing at all; he simply makes noise. He does accomplish his purpose, but he pays an even higher price than the clown. He gets, not approval, but negative feedback, not smiles but reprimands. His self-worth suffers accordingly.

The Mental Potential

Whether funny or frenetic, the Mascot's behavior has nothing to do with his intelligence. He may actually be more gifted than the Hero who is bringing home A's—or again he may not. The problem is the degree to which he is using and developing his natural endowment.

In medieval times the court jester—the clown of his day—was often called the fool. The common use of this word today to indicate a low level of, or at least a lack of applying, intelligence suggests the kind of danger the Mascot faces. In his preoccupation with capturing the attention of those around him, he cannot focus in any deep or sustained way on learning. In school the clown cuts up instead of listening to the teacher or doing his seat work; the hyperactive child is not *able* to sit quietly long enough to do either.

As the Mascot misses layer after layer of fundamentals, his deficit of knowledge and skills grows geometrically. His maturing peers, who once may have thought him great fun, now seek him out only for a party. When they get together for more serious pursuits, he is not included, so another avenue of learning is blocked. Even in his own self-image, there is no place for the role of scholar.

So much for book-learning. But what about common sense?

I cannot help comparing the behavior I have seen in Mascots with the communication "stance" that Virginia Satir calls the *distracter*. [2] She says, "Whatever the *distracter* does or says is irrelevant to what anyone else is saying or doing. He never makes a response to the point." Those words are certainly true of the Mascot.

To me, common sense means the ability to bring one's mind to bear effectively on the everyday questions and problems of living. In his schizy irrelevance, the Mascot is not able to do this.

The Spiritual Potential

I can think of no image more totally opposite to the Mascot than that of a monk or nun in deep contemplation—peaceful, silent, serious.

[2]*Peoplemaking.* Science & Behavior Books, Palo Alto, CA, 1973; p. 70.

Whether one calls it meditation, silent prayer, or something else, and whether it is practiced kneeling, sitting in the lotus position, or prone, some kind of quiet turning inward is accepted by all the major spiritual traditions as the surest path to inner development. For the Mascot, however, closing out distractions and focusing his mind are virtual impossibilities, even for a few minutes at a time. He cannot be still that long. He cannot be silent that long. He cannot in his anxiety tolerate an activity-vacuum that long. Most of all, he is *afraid* to look inside, afraid what kind of person he might find there.

Please let me make it clear that *this situation has nothing to do with a child's being good or bad.* It simply tells us that as long as he is playing his role, he stands a dim hope of developing spiritually based values to enrich the pragmatic one that he is so single-mindedly pursuing—survival. Survival, which to a Mascot means the endless and frenzied pursuit of attention.

The Volitional Potential

Like the Lost Child, the Mascot has limited his choices severely; the difference lies only in the nature of their choices. The Lost Child flees from attention and social contact; the Mascot needs them like air and water.

These basic choices set the style for so much of their total relating to the world that they have forfeited most of their other opportunities to make choices. Both pay a high price. Of the two, however, I believe that the Mascot is the more impoverished. The Lost Child may at least have developed his mental and spiritual potentials, and perhaps some physical skills as well, to a point where they can offer him satisfactions. The Mascot has not. He has developed only his social potential, and that in a shallow and distorted way. In his immaturity, the seeds of what he might be are still dormant, no matter what his age.

But his potentials are still potential, not damaged, and therein lies hope.

HELPING THE MASCOT GROW UP

As the Mascot grows older, it will become ever clearer to him that, special as he may have been in his family, the rest of the world does not see him so. His self-worth, already shaky, is due for some hard blows. And we can safely predict that he will meet these with the only tactics he knows, avoidance and distraction, fixing the defenses of his childhood into an ever-hardening pattern. Without counseling he faces some very real dangers.

One is that he will remain forever a child. We have all known the jokers, the incessant talkers, the people with annoying nervous mannerisms, or the fragile adults who are still being protected by their parents, their spouses, eventually their own children. The fragility of these people, though sincere, is often phoney; they are rarely as fragile as they and others think they are. The problem with the Mascot is that he has never learned to cope with stress. Not only did his family overprotect him; he overprotected himself. Instead of dealing with problems as they arose, he would run away from them by changing the subject or "going into his act." When those familiar ploys failed, as they often did, he felt helpless and decided that he just could not cope. His family agreed. Hadn't they thought that all along?

Such immaturity can be a great handicap in adult life. Some stress is inescapable in the give-and-take of relationships, the work world, even such casual encounters as making a purchase or sharing a traffic right-of-way. The person who has not learned to handle moderate amounts of unpleasantness and frustration will have trouble accepting other people's feelings and expressing his own.

But the Mascot's hypersensitivity to stress can lead to more serious consequences. As stress builds up, he may escape into either physical illness or, that familiar resort of his, delusion. His fears develop into phobias, which are often then misdiagnosed as paranoid schizophrenia. He may actually *feel* schizophrenic because of the irreconcilable split between the carefree facade he turns outward and the frightened person he is inside. If anyone in the alcoholic family is going to have serious psychiatric problems, it will be the Mascot. I have referred more persons for hospitalization from this role than from any other.

Another danger is that he will succumb to the family pattern of chemical dependency. Often, while still children, Mascots begin to use mood-altering drugs to help them deal with the day-to-day pressures of their lives. Prescribed these drugs by well-meaning physicians, they learn so early that chemicals can dull their pain and quiet their chronic fears that often they become dependent on prescription drugs.

Finally, if the Mascot does not receive help, there is always a possibility that his ever-present fears for his sanity will drive him to the one permanent painkiller—suicide. Recently I was talking to a group of high-school students about the effects of living with an alcoholic parent. After the session one girl lingered when the others had left, as though something were on her mind. I walked over to her and suddenly she collapsed into my arms in tears. I held her for a few minutes, until she recovered enough to talk. Then she told me how relieved she felt to discover that she was not the only person who had ever felt she was going crazy. With that she showed me her wrists—bandaged. Just a week earlier she had attempted suicide because she thought she would rather die quickly than go slowly crazy.

Grim as this outlook may be, there is one strong reason for optimism: the Mascot's problems, like the Scapegoat's, are likely to become visible while he is still relatively young. In any human disorder, the sooner a problem is recognized, the better the prospects for its cure, correction, or arrest, and that seems to me especially true for the Mascot. He needs help to grow up before his deficit of maturity gets any worse or his old way of coping more fixed.

These youngsters may come to the attention of professional people in the community in a number of ways. They may get into trouble for clowning or misbehaving in school; they may have emotional problems ranging from common fears of the dark to psychosis; they may get physically ill from their state of constant tension; or that tension may burst out in so much random activity that they are diagnosed as hyperkinetic.

The teacher or counselor, therapist or physician who tries to deal with any of these situations stands little chance of success unless he recognizes the problem for what it is—merely a symptom of a much larger disorder. Then, in addition to working with the symptom, he can use his leverage to motivate the whole family to get the help they need.

Whatever the symptom that brings a child to us for help, he is not likely to arrive in our offices wearing the label of Mascot. It is up to us to recognize his symptoms and know what they imply. The clues are usually clear, however, to anyone alert for them, because Mascot characteristics are so distinctive: immaturity, apparent fragility, hyperactivity, clowning, overdressing, super-sexiness, or other bids to attract attention. Whenever a child displays some combination of these characteristics, we can reasonably suspect a chemical problem somewhere in the family.

The next step is, of course, to check out our suspicions by some judicious questions and close observation of the way family members interact. Fortunately, many Mascots become visible while the family is still intact, and this kind of confirmation is possible.

In providing diagnosis and treatment, either medical or psychological, it is important for us to remember:

1. Mascot behavior can be misleading. These children may be irrelevant, but they are not necessarily schizophrenic. They are frightened, but not necessarily paranoid. They may do poorly in school, but that does not mean they are slow learners. They may be exasperating, but I find that like all children they really don't want to be bad.

2. Mood-altering drugs should be prescribed with great caution, if at all. I feel that at the very least they interfere with treatment; pain is one of the most powerful motivations for change and growth. And drugs, instead of truly helping, will simply *enable* the Mascot to go on playing his role. By preventing whatever family crisis he might precipitate, they enable continued dysfunction for all the other members as well, including the Dependent. (We will take up the question of professional Enablers in chapter 17.)

Sometimes a Mascot will arrive on one's professional doorstep while already being treated with drugs by someone else. In such a situation I try to arrange a conference to share our understanding of the client and explore the possibilities of discontinuing drug therapy.

3. Once he recognizes the Mascot's problem, the counselor's first task will be to allay the child's fear that he is going crazy. As he learns that the craziness is in the family system and not in himself, he can find both relief from his tension—without drugs—and motivation to grow out of his present limiting role.

4. Growth will take time, because the Mascot's role has so long prevented it. During the process, he will need a wise and patient counselor/guide and perhaps some continued professional or group support after formal treatment is completed. Given these things—and a recovering family—he can make up for lost time, learn new responses, and find the tranquility he has never known.

CHAPTER 11

Intervention

A ND SO THE drama grinds on, each member of the family evoking and reinforcing the alcoholic pathology in every other member and in the family system as a whole. For all the countless generations that have reenacted this familiar story, the ending has been the same. Even after death draws the curtain on the Dependent, the tragedy continues, for his children and his children's children.

This was true, that is, for all generations until our own. In the last half century the ancient script has been rewritten. In fact, it has been rewritten repeatedly, offering more hope each time as new knowledge, insights, and treatment techniques have been developed.

Until well into the present century, the victim of alcoholism was seen, not as sick, but as either weak or depraved. Then, in the years immediately preceding World War II, two important forces for change came into being: Alcoholics Anonymous, a loosely knit fellowship of alcoholics who wished to stop drinking, and the Yale Center of Alcohol Studies, dedicated to scientific research on the subject. The two were independent, unrelated, and in many ways polar opposites. But on one revolutionary idea they agreed: *alcoholism is a disease and as such can be arrested short of total tragedy—provided its victim gets suitable help soon enough.*

This seemed, however, to present a Catch-22 problem. It was generally agreed that the alcoholic had to "hit bottom" and voluntarily seek help before it could be effective, but that usually happened too late to salvage much of his life. For many drinkers, even Skid Row did not seem to provide a "bottom." Yet for a lucky few just the realization that they were risking their job or their marriage proved incentive enough to seek help (they were sometimes said to have hit a "high bottom").

In the last ten years, day-to-day experience with thousands of alcoholics in treatment and counseling programs has taught us a lot about what is and is not possible in chemical dependency. We now know, for instance, that it is unrealistic to expect that an alcoholic will seek help on his own (though a few do); the denial, delusion, and compulsion characteristic of the disease seldom *let* him do so. Fortunately, we have also discovered that *there is another way.*

Those who said that an alcoholic could not accept help until he sought it were describing accurately the situation that they saw. Virtually every alcoholic did indeed continue sliding down a steep path to self-destruction—losing his health, job, family, and whatever remained of his self-respect along the way—until he either died or "hit bottom" and asked for help. By that time, however, his physical, mental, and social potentials were often so damaged that they could never be fully restored.

The fallacy here lay in assuming that because no alternative was then known, none was possible. We have since learned that "hitting bottom" is just another way of saying that the alcoholic has found himself in a crisis so painful and so frightening that he will do anything to escape from it—even stop drinking. Further, we know that *such a crisis can often be created* by those who care about him and that it can be done before he has lost everything.

This process is called *intervention.* Does it work? Yes, if it is done lovingly, under the guidance of an experienced person, and is backed up by an effective support program for treatment[1] and recovery of the whole family. In the last few years thousands of alcoholics have achieved sobriety because their families, working with specially trained counselors, have orchestrated just such a crisis.

DIRECT INTERVENTION WITH THE DEPENDENT

Any one of the many crises that punctuate the lives of alcoholic families can be a starting point for intervention. It need only be serious

[1]Lest there be any misunderstanding, let me say clearly that in this book "treatment" means *treatment for the characteristic symptoms of alcoholism—denial, delusion, and compulsion*—not for the specific medical, psychological, or behavioral problems that may arise from it. They may, however, be relieved as a result of the treatment.

enough to cause someone close to the Dependent to seek help for him (or for himself, but we will speak of that later in the chapter).

The family member who issues the first call for help (the intervener) is one who is still in touch with some of his own feelings and cares enough about himself and the rest of the family to take a risk. Make no mistake, seeking help for an alcoholic without his knowledge or consent does seem like a terrible risk to the whole family. If they are not afraid of his anger, which they usually are, they at least feel that they are being disloyal to him and betraying family secrets. One of a counselor's first tasks is to assure them that intervening is the most loving thing they can do for all concerned.

The obvious person to intervene is the Enabler, who has taken responsibility for everything else in the family. If she is too immobilized by her own symptoms to act, the intervener can be one of the children, most likely the Hero, or even a family friend.

In more and more cases employers are intervening. Probably no one else is in such close contact with the Dependent without being caught up in the family pathology. Employers and supervisors can, of course, get involved in enabling, too (we will take a closer look at employer Enablers in chapter 17). But if they are informed about alcoholism and honest with themselves about its cost, both on the job and in a Dependent's personal life, they will try to bring him to treatment before his potentials as an employee and a person are eroded beyond repair.

Intervention begins when some concerned person picks up the telephone and calls the alcoholism counselor for an appointment. We will trace briefly here the careful preparatory work they undertake together to assure that the eventual crisis—the confrontation with the Dependent—achieves its goal.

At their first meeting the counselor and the intervener review the critical issues currently facing the Dependent (absenteeism or poor performance on the job, drunk driving charges or other legal problems, health complications, marital difficulties, school or delinquency problems of the children, etc.). They then make a list of all the people intimately involved with the Dependent who have personally witnessed his alcoholic behavior or its consequences and who might take part in a confrontation. There should be at least two persons and preferably more. Besides the spouse and children, an intervention team might include the employer or supervisor, pastor, family physician, attorney, or close friends.

The counselor arranges a joint meeting of all the persons on the list to explain the intervention process and enlist their cooperation. At this session he will present some basic information about alcoholism, stressing the fact that the Dependent is no longer able either to stop drinking on his own or to seek help for himself, that only their willingness to risk a confrontation will bring him to the treatment that he so desperately needs. This is also the time for the counselor to determine the extent to which members of the family display symptoms of the disease that may interfere with their participation in the intervention.

The amount of time that will elapse between this initial meeting and the confrontation with the Dependent depends on several factors: (1) how early in the disease the intervention occurs, and consequently how much the functioning of family members has been affected; (2) whether the major intervener is an involved family member or an outsider who is not a party to the family pathology; and (3) the general level of sophistication in the community about alcoholism and its treatment.

At an intervention center that has opened recently in Southern California, we have found that it takes six to eight weeks to train a family team. On the other hand, in places like Minnesota or New York, where intervention programs have been operating for a long time, the process is often faster. There is less stigma attached to alcoholism, so people seek help earlier. They simply come in and say, "We think our family's in trouble—we want help!" The whole intervention can sometimes be planned in a day or two.

On an average, nationwide, the time needed to train a family to intervene is four to six weeks. Several things must be accomplished:

1. They must be brought to the realization that alcoholism is not just one of their problems—it is their *primary* problem. When people have been enabling for a long time, they are likely to continue that pattern by telling the counselor in great detail of their many other difficulties, partly to avoid the pain of talking about the central problem and partly to offer alibis for it. Gently, the counselor must help them to see and admit the reality of the situation. John G. Hubbell, writing in the *Reader's Digest,* phrased it well: "Whatever the reasons he [the Dependent] started drinking, alcohol is no longer a *symptom* of other problems; it is now the cause."[2]

2. They must learn how the disease of alcoholism affects its victim at its various stages. As they come to recognize how typical is the bizarre and destructive behavior of the Dependent in their family, they find it

2"A Dynamic New Approach to the Alcoholic." *Reader's Digest,* May, 1976; p. 3.

harder to deny his true condition. This in turn will help them accept the counselor's stand that the Dependent is not able to seek help for himself, and their determination to take the initiative is strengthened.

3. They must learn that worrying about the Dependent, taking care of him, trying to control his drinking, assuming his responsibilities, and covering up for him—all the "helpful" things they have been doing—are worse than useless. They are actually making it possible for him to go on drinking without facing the consequences. The only thing they can do that is truly helpful is to use their combined influence to get him to accept treatment.

4. They must learn how alcoholism affects the rest of the family. It will not be easy for the Enabler—she who has endured so much—to admit that she has become part of the problem. But until each person recognizes his own role in the family dysfunction and is willing to accept help to lay it aside, he cannot fairly or convincingly ask the Dependent to do the same. If the alcoholism is in an advanced stage, the family members are likely mired in their own denial and delusion, and will probably require psychotherapy in order to have enough clarity and courage to confront the Dependent.

The therapist's major task will be to help them break out of the defensive behavior patterns into which they are each locked and to let their long-buried feelings emerge. (This usually requires primary care, which we will examine in the next chapter.) As negative feelings are released, positive ones like love and courage will begin to return. Gradually, the family's delusion of powerlessness will be replaced by a readiness to take the risk of intervening.

5. Now planning for the day of intervention can begin. The first step is for each person who will be present, including children, to make a written list of specific instances when the Dependent's behavior caused someone pain, danger, embarrassment, or other problems. Exact time, setting, and details of each episode should be included. These lists will probably turn out to be quite different. Individuals will have been present at different times, recalled different things, and perceived the same things in different ways, so comparing the lists can be very enlightening. Given the blocked communication in an alcoholic family, one person may not even know that the episodes on another's list occurred.

6. When the lists are complete, family members must next look at how their statements are phrased. The facts should be presented in a straightforward, objective way that does nothing to ease the blow of the painful truth. At the same time there must be no hint of hostility or

blaming that could put the Dependent on the defensive. To be able to reach him, the intervention team must catch him with his strong and ever-vigilant defenses down. The effectiveness of intervention lies in the emotional impact of heaping fact upon documented fact in a setting that allows little room for denial. Reasoning or arguing with the Dependent will accomplish nothing. By this time the only message he can hear— because he has no defense for it—is one of love and deep concern.

7. They must practice presenting their statements so they can do so calmly and courageously on the critical day. Usually it is best for each person to read from his list rather than speaking extemporaneously. This gives what he is saying an aura of factual evidence, not mere opinion; it prevents emotional ad-libbing in the tense atmosphere of the confrontation; it keeps the entire intervention effort predictable and under control; and it focuses the speaker's mind on his message, minimizing any fears that might be aroused by eye contact with the Dependent.

The counselor will coach each speaker as needed so that his voice will be consistent with the objective and loving tone of his words. There can be no play-acting here, however. Each person's caring must be clearly genuine, for in his present state of self-loathing and raw sensitivity, the Dependent will immediately detect any pretense.

8. Finally, they must determine exactly what action the Dependent will be asked to take. Together, the intervener and the counselor study the available sources of treatment in the area and select the one that best suits the Dependent's needs. If he requires hospitalization, they determine what benefits his health insurance provides and arrange for him to be admitted to an inpatient facility on the very day of intervention— while his motivation is at its peak.

In some cases they may also quietly notify the Dependent's employer of the plan so that someone else can take over his duties temporarily. This step should be taken with caution, though, for it could jeopardize his job if the employer is not enlightened. The counselor will usually know which employers in the locality make a policy of being cooperative in rehabilitating employees. If the employer is to be told, the Enabler is the one who must tell him; for the counselor to divulge such information to a third party would be an illegal breach of confidentiality.

9. Ready at last, they set the time for the actual confrontation. One effective time is Monday morning, when the Dependent is most likely to be sober, with his defenses at low ebb because he is suffering a heavy hangover. If possible, it is also a good idea to choose a time when his defenses are already under strain from a drunk driving arrest, a threat-

ened divorce, or perhaps a serious warning from his doctor. Such circumstances will intensify the sense of crisis that the intervention team is trying to produce and increase the likelihood that the Dependent will feel he has "hit bottom." After all, it is not the actual severity of the crisis that counts but how severe he *perceives* it to be.

The confrontation will probably be conducted under the leadership of the intervener who made the first contact for help, and the counselor should be present. In fact, the best place for the event is the counselor's office, where the atmosphere is serious and professional and the Dependent can find little opportunity for diversionary tactics. Getting him to go there is, of course, not always easy. Surprisingly, however, I have found that the alcoholic is often quite curious about what is happening in those sessions that he knows his family has been attending without him under the guise of "getting some help with family problems." The effects have probably already impinged uncomfortably on his life. A straightforward statement that the counselor "asked if you would come in with us next Monday to discuss some of our family problems" may be all the urging he will need.

It has been my experience that, if the planning is thorough and everyone is adequately prepared, the chances of intervening successfully are about 80 percent. The critical factor is the health of the family members. If they have all recovered to a position of personal strength, courage, and ability to love, they nearly always succeed.

The piling up of episode upon episode of his alcoholic behavior, described in all its sordid detail by those who have witnessed it, is usually defense shattering for the Dependent. The effect is heightened by having those he respects and loves confess the anguish his actions have caused them. Add to these the clear message, implicit in the whole atmosphere of the confrontation, that in spite of all their pain these people still care about him and are deeply concerned—the Dependent is usually shocked into facing the painful truth about his condition.

This is the point at which the chief intervener presents the Dependent with the program of treatment and after-care he is being asked to accept. (Where it is possible, all arrangements for treatment—hospital bed, insurance coverage, and any other practical matters—should have been made, with the counselor's help, prior to the intervention.) The family members will each make clear to him that they realize they need help, too, and that they have already agreed to a treatment program of their own. Their willingness to admit their need and accept help makes it easier for him to do likewise.

Sometimes a Dependent refuses to enter a formal treatment program but makes tearful promises to stop drinking. These promises are undoubtedly sincere at the time they are made and should be received in that light. If he joins AA and is faithful in working the program, he actually may find sobriety without professional treatment. Because of the nature of his disease, however, it will be almost impossible for him to stop without some kind of help. Before any promises are accepted, they should be accompanied by a firm agreement that he will enter a specified treatment program immediately the first time he takes a drink.

The most effective recovery program, in my opinion, combines professional treatment for the whole family with membership in AA, Al-anon, and Alateen. (In chapter 16 we will see how one family used these combined resources to effect a successful intervention.) A follow-up survey of former patients at St. Mary's Hospital in Minneapolis, where this combination is used, found that 79 percent of them had not taken a drink for a year after being discharged, and 51 percent had not drunk for four years. Of those who "slipped," 81 percent returned to total abstinence without returning to treatment. Perhaps most important of all, 91 percent of the patients said that as a result of treatment they had enjoyed "significant improvement" in their family lives, work lives, and personal happiness.[3]

Sometimes, of course, an attempted intervention fails. What then? Certainly matters are no worse than before, and probably better. Much has been learned by everyone, and there is no reason the learning should stop. The family can remain in treatment whether or not the Dependent agrees to join them. Before the intervention meeting ends, they should make clear to him the steps they plan to take to continue their own recoveries; those steps may mean some changes in attitudes, behavior, and relationships that will affect him, too. They can choose to stand by him and try another intervention later when new circumstances suggest they may be more successful. Or at some time they may choose to act on the other option that always remains open—to leave their relationship with the Dependent.

Whatever the outcome of the intervention attempt, the family's continued pursuit of their own individual recoveries is vital to their personal well-being and to the Dependent's chances for eventually achieving sobriety. Without it the debilitating effects of the family disease will once more set in.

---

[3]Unpublished survey by St. Mary's Hospital (Minneapolis), 1975.

FAMILY INTERVENTION

The process that we have just been observing might be termed *direct intervention,* since it confronts the family problem at its source, the Dependent. This approach was developed in response to our new understanding of alcoholism as a disease, which made it clear that someone should take direct action to persuade the alcoholic to seek help while there was still time.

In the last decade we have gone a step further. As we have discovered that alcoholism is not merely an individual problem but a family disease affecting every member and every facet of family life, we have also realized that change at any point in the system can affect the shared disease. This offers many new possibilities. A crisis in the life of any member of the family can become the "bottom" that brings everyone, including the Dependent, to treatment. Reaching the Dependent in this indirect way I have called *family intervention.* It is a chain process, often initiated by the person to whom a family member has turned for help.

A high proportion of helping professionals have already learned to recognize the symptoms of chemical dependency and to urge its victim to get the help he needs. Now we are training them to recognize the symptoms that characterize other members of an alcoholic family as well. Where many people in the community have this knowledge, families no longer have to be able to seek help of their own volition—it literally confronts them!

Employers, especially, have become involved in family intervention. Long alert for the symptoms of individual dependency, they are now becoming equally watchful for the signs of enabling. When a good employee begins to miss work, to be touchy and irritable, to complain of frequent headaches or backaches, to seem preoccupied and make mistakes, to turn out less work and have more accidents, to use excessive amounts of medical insurance benefits for stress-related illnesses, the supervisor can be pretty sure that employee is under some kind of severe personal stress. In companies that are knowledgeable about alcoholism, its presence somewhere in the family is immediately suspected.

Physicians, too, are learning that their adult patients, particularly those with stress symptoms (digestive problems, headaches, backache, high blood pressure, heart symptoms, unexplained weight gain or loss, nervousness, or depression), may well have an alcoholic spouse or parent. In children or adolescents, allergies and asthma, frequent stomach upsets, low resistance to colds and childhood diseases, bedwetting, over- or underweight, hyperactivity, complications of promiscuity or drug abuse, and unwanted pregnancy are all clues that a parent might be alcoholic.

Lawyers and pastors, for their part, are learning that marital discord, financial problems, juvenile delinquency, reckless or drunken driving charges, or unwanted pregnancy all occur more often in alcoholic families and are likely to be repeated unless the underlying problem is identified.

The juvenile courts are a particularly rewarding spot for intervention—not surprisingly, given what we now know about Scapegoat behavior. In Minnesota, intervention has been literally built into the system. When a youngster in trouble for any offense is deemed to be chemically dependent as well, the judge assigns an assessor to the family, and all members are screened for chemical dependency. If a parent turns out also to be dependent, then the child *and both parents* are sentenced to undergo treatment. If they do not appear, the parents are held in contempt of court. As a result of this program many alcoholic families who otherwise would have remained invisible are getting the help they need.

In the school systems, teachers, counselors, and administrators are learning that the children who require the greatest amount of their time and attention—the troublemakers, the underachievers, the absentees, the shy loners, the hyperactive youngsters with learning problems—are all exhibiting problems known to be characteristic of alcoholics' children. (As educators become more knowledgeable about family Heroes, they may also find their former admiration for the energetic class president, the hard-working straight-A student, or the star athlete now mixed with concern if the youngster seems driven to succeed.)

I remember one family where the school problems of a seven-year-old child provided the intervention point for three generations of alcohol-linked distress:

Joel had been misbehaving in school to such an extent that his teacher finally gave up trying to manage him. She referred him to the school psychologist to have him tested. The psychologist could find nothing abnormal in the boy, but he did notice that the parents seemed to be under a good deal of stress. Since I was working with families, he referred them once again, this time to me.

At the opening of our initial session, I asked for introductions. The mother spoke first, then the father; but Joel, their only child, said nothing. When I asked him his name, he crawled under a chair and hid, whereupon his parents immediately began to argue over his behavior.

Their interaction gave me some clues. I suggested that Joel join our children's therapy group and that the parents work with me.

In the weeks that followed, they talked about their relationship with each other and their family histories. The wife expressed a great deal of bitterness about her husband's attention to his mother, and he admitted that he did feel more obligation to her than to his wife and son. As we explored possible reasons for this attitude, he discovered that he was feeling guilty about his mother's unhappy situation—his father drank too much.

I suggested that they intervene to get help for his father. The very idea frightened my client, but realizing now the price his wife and child were paying, he agreed. We began to prepare for the intervention.

During the training period, both husband and wife came to recognize how many qualities in their own personalities and in their marriage had been brought with them from the families where they grew up. For the first time, they could understand what they had been doing to each other, and a new spirit of openness and concern began to develop between them. In time, their relationship was strong enough that they could afford to feel some concern for his father.

Through the entire process, Joel was seldom mentioned. In the children's group, however, he learned to talk about his feelings and to share his fears about what was going on in the family. His school behavior gradually improved.

This story had a happy ending. The intervention went very well, and Joel's grandfather consented to go for treatment. By the time he was discharged, all three generations were well on their way to happier lives.

A CHALLENGE TO PROFESSIONAL COURAGE

Suspecting alcoholism presents the professional person with a delicate situation. Though the symptoms he sees may be characteristic of one or more roles in an alcoholic family, alcoholism is not their only possible cause. He probably has no conclusive evidence to confirm his suspicion, nor can he count on an honest admission from the family. The rule of secrecy in alcoholic families is so tight that often no one dares admit the truth; in fact, they may still be denying it to themselves.

Yet, professional responsibility demands that he do something. This family, if indeed it proves to be alcoholic, needs help as soon as possible. They are in any event dysfunctional, whatever the cause, and his efforts will no doubt lead them to counseling that will improve their lives. His only choice is to confront them with the evidence and try to enlist their cooperation.

The first step is to call one's client (patient/parishioner/student/ employee) in to discuss the situation. Most often this person, if adult, will turn out to be playing the role of the Enabler. Where the immediate problem concerns a child, the parents should be called in with or without the child, depending upon his age. If one parent is alcoholic, as suspected, probably only the spouse will show up for the conference—again the Enabler.

The professional person's goal will, of course, be to check out his suspicions. Is the client himself involved with chemicals? Is the spouse? A child? A parent? In subtly probing for information, the professional will begin with some general inquiries about what may be happening in the person's life (or his child's) that might be creating stress. If the client senses an atmosphere of nonjudgmental acceptance, caring, and concern, he may find the opportunity to unburden himself irresistible and give a clear picture of what is happening at home.

Even in cases where the family is rigidly stuck in its characteristic denial, the professional has considerable leverage. The client is in crisis and has a strong need to trust the professional and to retain his sympathy and his services. With a physician, lawyer, or pastor, the family have probably themselves sought him out; with an employer or school counselor, they face the danger of losing their livelihood or having a child suspended—either of which is compelling motivation to cooperate. The professional should appreciate how much leverage he has and use it, first to determine all he can about the family situation, and then to get the family to see an alcoholism counselor unless the possibility of alcoholism is conclusively ruled out.

He must present whatever evidence he has as frankly, clearly, and compassionately as he can, emphasizing the seriousness of the situation. Next, he must explain why he feels the problem may be related to alcoholism—educating the family as he goes. Finally, he will make his recommendation: "I have reason to believe that there may be a problem of chemical dependency in your home, so I am referring you to such-and-such information center to find out."

In some cases the professional will then go ahead with trying to resolve the specific problem that was brought to him in the first place. In others, he may feel it is wiser to make his further services conditional upon the family's first following through with his referral, either because they need the additional motivation this contingency can provide or because he feels that it is useless or impossible to deal with the specific problem while the underlying one continues.

Once the family makes its first contact with the alcoholism information center, intervention can proceed in much the same way as if they had recognized their own problem and sought counseling voluntarily. They may, however, require more motivating and longer training in order to confront the Dependent successfully.

Throughout this process, the professional person who intervenes with a family faces many of the same challenges as family members who intervene with a Dependent. He must break through their well-practiced defenses and bring them inescapably face to face with the crisis—often multiple crises—they are in; he must cite each bit of data he has collected in full, unvarnished detail; he must offer a concrete recommendation for how and where they can find help; and finally he must make very clear their lack of alternatives and the probable consequences of failing to seek help, including any change that might mean in their relationship to him.

Like any other intervener, the professional may find intervention a rather unpleasant business, and he must care enough about the family to risk antagonizing them. But if he has enough concern and courage to confront them with the truth, he may be the pivot on which their troubled lives turn back toward hope and happiness.

CHAPTER 12

The Continuum
of Care

MANY TIMES in this book I have spoken of *treatment* as a door to hope and health for the alcoholic family. Now it is time to take a closer look at exactly what treatment is. Who gets treated and for how long? What are the goals? What are the counselor's tools and philosophy in pursuing them? And how does he know when the goals are reached?

First, let's consider what an effective treatment program does *not* try to do:

1. *It does not encourage the individual to adjust to the alcoholic family system.* As we have seen, the system is sick, and one can only adjust to it by becoming sick, too.
2. *It does not aim at restoring the family to where it was before alcoholism set in.* If the family system had been truly healthy then, the disease could not have developed as it did; the family members would have either changed the system or moved out of it.
3. *It does not attempt to "fix" the many problems facing the alcoholic family when it enters treatment.* The counselor limits his efforts to helping the family members, first, to realize that they are sick—as individuals and as a family unit—and then to get well. It has been my experience that if we concentrate on treating the immediate problems of chemical dependency, other problems such as those involving money, job, parenting, or sexuality seem to lessen. Once family members learn to communicate openly with one another

about their disease, they can often resolve their other problems in the same way without professional help.

4. *It does not encourage the individual to change or recover for the sake of someone else.* Though the Enabler's courage to intervene may be the Dependent's one chance for survival, and though his decision to stop drinking can transform life for her and the rest of the family, a successful treatment program will avoid using such appeals. The reason: they simply do not bring lasting results. In the long run each member of the family must be motivated to get well *for his own sake* if he is to get well at all.

What the effective treatment program does endeavor to do can be summed up in three broad goals:

1. *It exposes the alcoholic family system for what it is.* The counselor must approach this task from two directions. He must educate the whole family about the addiction process and about chemical dependency as a family disease. At the same time, he must begin to break through each member's individual wall of denial, delusion, and compulsive behavior so that the person can gradually see and admit the part he is playing in perpetuating the disease.

2. *It helps the family make its system more open and flexible,* a system where each person is free to be himself and to grow, and where these autonomous individuals communicate with honesty, clarity, and mutual caring.

3. *It nurtures each family member to wholeness.* The first priority of treatment is, of course, to heal the psychological wounds caused by the disease. Then, since everyone comes to treatment with very low self-worth, he will be encouraged to embark upon a program of personal growth that will continue for the rest of his life, increasingly enhancing his sense of worth and all aspects of his day-to-day living.

These may seem like ambitious goals, given the stubborn resistance to treatment for which alcoholism has long been notorious. They are indeed ambitious, but they can be—and are being—achieved by effective treatment programs.

Alcoholism is a holistic disease, affecting the whole person and the whole family; to treat it effectively, a program must treat the whole person and the whole family.

Until recent years alcoholism programs treated only the Dependent. They often succeeded in stopping his drinking, "drying him out," and starting him on the road toward physical health again. Some even tried to deal with the emotional and spiritual roots of his problem, especially those that included AA membership as part of the treatment. But no matter how sincerely the Dependent vowed to change, in a few short weeks he faced a bitter test: he had to go home again. Since the rest of the family members were still acting out the same old alcoholic denial, delusion, and compulsion that he had only recently put aside, his fragile new sobriety was in danger. The odds of relapse were high. And through it all, the damage to other family members remained, continuing to cause them all pain.

Today we have a much greater choice of programs available, varying widely in their formats (and consequently in their effectiveness). Some still treat only the Dependent, but an increasing number include family members as well. Some treat Dependent and family separately; others treat them together using the techniques of family therapy. Some accept family members even if the Dependent himself refuses to go into treatment.

What I will describe in this section is not some clinic's actual program (though a number have been patterned on it). Rather, it is a model of an ideal program that brings to the healing process all that we currently know about chemical dependency, family systems, and psychotherapy of both individuals and families, plus my own clinical findings about alcoholism as a family disease. It is designed as an outpatient program but can be adapted to inpatient facilities or coordinated with a separate inpatient program for the Dependent. One popular version of this model is a four-week residential program for the Dependent with the family coming for a week or ten days of that time.

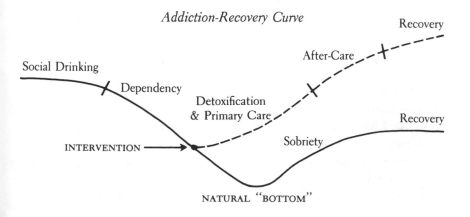

Addiction-Recovery Curve

Another is an outpatient program in which the entire family comes three or four nights a week for five weeks. Both of these programs are followed by a three-month structured program of after-care and a recommendation for ongoing active involvement in AA when after-care is over.

When we left our troubled alcoholic family in the last chapter, the Dependent had been confronted in a carefully planned intervention and had at last agreed to stop drinking and go into treatment. The addiction/recovery curve shown in the diagram on page 165 gives a clear picture of what has happened to him up to this point and what is yet to come. Let us look first at the left side of the curve, which shows his progressive disintegration as alcoholism advances. If left to its natural course, his disease will eventually reach "bottom"—a crisis so dire that he is finally moved to give up his use of the chemical. Intervention, however, raises that bottom by forcing a crisis earlier and thus bringing him to treatment sooner.

On the right side of the curve we see the gradual recovery of his damaged potentials in treatment, after reaching a natural bottom (solid line) or after intervention and a treatment program of the type described in this book (broken line). When pursued earnestly and with persever-ence, recovery can continue indefinitely, and the person can reach higher levels of functioning than before the onset of alcoholism.

This curve is virtually the same for family members as for the Dependent, with these small differences:

1. The critical stages of the disease for family members may begin later.
2. The point of "intervention" for the family member is the point at which he first comes into contact with the treatment facility or helping professional, which may be some time before the actual intervention with the Dependent.
3. The Dependent's recovery curve includes detoxification.

The right side of the curve, representing treatment and recovery, has been divided to indicate the three major phases of the treatment program. I like to refer to these as the "continuum of care," since they offer treatment experiences synchronized to the changing needs and capabilities of the recovering alcoholic or family member as he pro-gresses. These phases address, in sequence, the three major goals of treatment:

- *Primary care* treats each family member separately, in individual sessions with the counselor and in supervised groups of the person's peers.
- *After-care* treats the family members *within* the family system, for their own recovery and for a transformation of the system itself. The family will also attend group counseling with several other families. Sometimes individual counseling or couple counseling for

Goals of Treatment

	DEPENDENT	EACH FAMILY MEMBER
PRIMARY CARE (4-6 weeks)	(In individual sessions and peer groups)	
		Breaking through the wall of delusion
		Accepting the disease
		Recognition of feelings
INTERVENTION →		
	Abstinence & detoxification	
	Breaking through the wall of delusion	
	Accepting the disease	
	Recognition of feelings	
AFTER-CARE (10-12 weeks)	(In single-family sessions, multi-family groups, & peer groups)	
	Sharing feelings	
	Accepting and forgiving	
	Rebuilding the family system	
	Recovery of the whole person	Recovery of the whole person
RECOVERY (open-ended)		

the spouses continues into after-care. If the Dependent is not living with family members, a close friend may take their place in treatment. In a halfway house other residents can serve this same function. The important thing is to teach them to interact with the meaningful people in their lives in healthier ways.

- *Recovery* is a final, open-ended period of continuing growth, planned during after-care and pursued by each family member after leaving the counselor's supervision. The personal and family system changes that have been set in motion during primary care and after-care are deepened and extended; from this more and more nurturing base, the individual persons can regain and develop their personal potentials in a perpetual deepening of their self-worth.

Although some individual counseling is necessary for each family member, much of the work of alcoholism treatment can be done in a group. At first, usually during primary care, the person being treated meets with a small group of his peers, between five and twelve participants. He has an opportunity to hear the experiences of other families and other individuals of his age or family role. He can observe their actions and see in them the denial, delusion, and compulsive behavior that he is blind to in himself. They, in turn, will see his defenses and confront him with them.

Most people find the group an uncomfortable arena to be in, at least in the beginning. It forces one to trust. In the family, blood ties often carry an unwritten obligation to trust—or at least to appear to trust. In treatment groups, however, the other members are just there. Trusting is an explicit choice that must be made—a hard one for members of an alcoholic family, where trust has so often been betrayed.

Once a person learns to trust, to stop pretending and really let others in the group know him, he has crossed an invisible line. He suddenly has a sense of belonging. He feels safe at last to express his fear and anger and hurt; indeed, the group expects him to. This experience gives him the practice and confidence he will need to participate with openness and honesty in the more emotionally charged group of the family.

The next grouping we use is, of course, the immediate family. Here the group brings with it an established system to complicate the interaction. It offers a more advanced laboratory for feeling and communicating.

Groups of families are also brought together, to undertake as family units the same kind of experience that the members had as individuals in the peer groups. The number of families in a group will naturally vary somewhat, according to the number of members in each family. An ideal grouping might be four families of four or five members each, under the supervision of one counselor. It is important if at all possible to have all members of a family attend the group.

Finally, we group clients in larger groupings for educational workshops, lectures, and films. Since the purpose is the presentation of information, not direct interaction, the size of the workshops is limited only by the space available. Use of workshops can save time and allow the actual treatment sessions to focus on problems unique to the individual or family. Too, presentation in the large group lends authority to the information presented and counters any suspicion a resistant client might have that the counselor is "only telling me that to get me to do what he wants."

Workshops usually begin late in primary care or early in after-care and continue into the recovery phase, presenting subjects appropriate for each stage of treatment.

Size is not the only way workshops and smaller groups differ from each other. Workshops are, in effect, classrooms where information and insights are presented; they appeal to the client's mental potential, offering him tools for dealing with his problems and becoming a more whole person. Small groups, on the other hand, are laboratories, where he can begin to use his new tools in a controlled setting; they appeal to his emotional potential. Naturally, workshops sometimes offer experiences, too, and groups certainly result in learning. But their fundamental purposes are different. That of workshops is *clarity*, while that of groups is *therapy*.

Now let us look more closely at each of the phases of the continuum of care.

CHAPTER 13

Primary Care

CURIOUSLY, primary care, the very foundation on which the rest of this treatment program is built, has often in the past been completely omitted in dealing with an alcoholic family. The Dependent may have had some for himself if he had been in residential treatment, but the rest of the family was usually brought into the picture as a group—if at all—with no individual preparation. Thus they brought with them all the repressed feelings, delusion, and compulsive behavior that had infected the family for so long. Trying to change and heal the dynamics of the family as a whole under those circumstances was much slower, more difficult, and less likely to succeed than when we start with family members who have already begun to deal with their individual dysfunctions in primary care.

The treatment goals for each person in this first stage are the same:

1. *To let down the wall of defensiveness.* By the time the family enters primary care, the level of pain is so high that each person has sealed his feelings off from himself and others behind a stout wall of defenses. Nothing can be accomplished until the counselor can somehow penetrate this wall. The process begins as early as intervention training, for the counselor must break through the family's denial and delusion before they, in turn, can break through the Dependent's and thus intervene successfully.

Fortunately, the compassionate counselor has at his disposal the one tool against which his clients have no defense—the same one he teaches them to use in breaching the Dependent's defenses—*caring.* It has usually been a long time since anyone in this family has had a caring listener who was willing to hear their pain and able to understand it. Listening alone can often melt apparently rigid defenses in a single session. At least it can make a small opening through which to communicate. The pressure of pent-up feelings, waiting to pour out, will soon widen it.

The purpose here is not, of course, to totally demolish the client's psychological defenses. Rather, it is to open an avenue of communication through them. Gradually as treatment proceeds, he will be made aware of these hitherto unconscious defenses, then helped to relinquish the unhealthy ones and replace them with healthier ones that are under his conscious control.

The counselor needs to appreciate that these clients are not simply putting up resistance, refusing to express what they are feeling. They are *not able to feel* their true feelings. They will have to be brought very gently to see the truth of their condition and to have the courage to feel their pain. The presence of a caring person with whom to share it makes that courage possible.

2. *To let the pain emerge.* It is important to resist one's natural impulse to ease the client's pain; he should be allowed to feel it all, and fully. The counselor can usually expect to encounter a seething mixture of hurt, rage, hate, shame, grief, loneliness, fear, jealousy, guilt—the whole Pandora's box of human anguish. Which emotion is strongest in a particular family member will depend in large measure on his role— anger in the Enabler, for example, or inadequacy in the Hero.

As the client begins to feel his pain and let it emerge in words, tears, or other appropriate channels, he will need to recognize it for what it is. People from alcoholic families seem to have a very difficult time distinguishing one emotion from another. They are sensitive only to gross differences and tend to describe their feelings in vague terms of being sad, glad, upset, depressed.

Simplistic though it may sound, I have found it helpful to give these clients a list of some of the feelings possible in the rich spectrum of emotion accessible to a sensitive human being:

love	hurt	discomfort
concern	embarrassment	resentment
tension	courage	sadness
confidence	uneasiness	fear
discouragement	cockiness	need

relief	anger	shame
excitement	affection	fulfillment
irritation	happiness	humility
hate	guilt	comfort
curiosity	grief	hopelessness
anxiety	disgust	amusement

Even such an incomplete list serves as a starting point from which we can begin to discriminate between some of the often mistaken pairs—differentiating between, say, shame and either embarrassment or guilt; between hurt and either hate or anger; between excitement, tension, and anxiety. I find the list works equally well with individuals and with groups, either peer groups or families.

Once he begins to recognize his feelings, the client must learn to accept them. Our culture has tended to judge feelings as good or bad, that is, as worthy or unworthy to have. One can readily admit when he feels happy or loving or brave, but not when he feels sad or angry or scared.

Here again I find some elementary teaching is helpful. I explain that everyone has feelings; they are part of being human. Though sometimes unpleasant, they are neither good or bad; they just *are*. It is what we do in response to them that is good or bad. We need to know clearly what we are feeling so we can act in a way that is healthy for ourselves and others. We also need to be able to share our feelings freely because they are our common denominator, the one place where people can truly connect.

The counselor's nonjudgmental acceptance of whatever feelings are expressed makes it easier for the client to accept them himself. It also provides a model to be recalled later, during after-care, when the client must learn to hear the feelings of other family members with that same nonjudgmental acceptance.

3. *To begin to experience some positive feelings.* Allowing himself to feel his pain will make it possible for the person in primary care to begin feeling positive emotions as well. His capacity to feel, so long turned off in order to avoid the pain, will gradually come to life again. I use that metaphor knowingly, for feelings *are* life. The person who has turned off all his feelings is in many ways dead.

The counselor's role in this process will be simply to show continuing care and appreciation in order to nurture the tender new growth of trust, hope, and love.

Perhaps a special word might be said here, too, for forgiveness. I see alcoholism as a blameless disease, yet alcoholic families are full of blaming, self-blame (guilt), and feeling blamed. The counselor's compassionate, nonjudgmental attitude can do much to dissolve the blaming and set the tone for forgiveness. As the client releases his burden of blame thoughts—as he can forgive and feel forgiven—his pain will ease dramatically.

4. *To accept the family illness and one's own part in it.* The very fact of being in primary care indicates that there has been some minimal acceptance by the family of the fact that alcoholism is their chief problem, and preintervention counseling will probably have already provided them with the basic facts about chemical dependency as both an individual and a family disease. Further education can be done in primary care workshops featuring lectures, films, or visits from alcoholics who are successfully re-forming their lives in the recovery stage.

To accept the diagnosis of alcoholism is hard enough—the whole family has for so long denied it. But to accept one's own part in it is immeasurably harder. Until now they have all seen the Dependent as the problem (even though no one may have been willing to label him alcoholic). They do not understand that his illness could only grow as the family system allowed it to happen. As part of that system, *they* are part of the problem. Admitting this is a necessary pre-condition for the work the family must undertake together in after-care.

5. *To make a personal commitment to an ongoing recovery program for the family and for themselves.* It has taken years for the family's disease to develop to its present crisis, and it will take a long time and a lot of hard work to create a new, healthy family in its place. The work begun in primary care must go on, first in after-care and then, on the family's own initiative, long after supervised treatment is over. Quite obviously, it can be successful only if everyone involved feels a strong personal commitment to the enterprise.

WORKING WITH THE ROLES

By now it must be apparent that what happens in the individual treatment sessions depends a good deal on the particular role that a family member is playing. While the ultimate goals are the same for all, each role presents a special configuration of challenges to the counselor and calls for special approaches.

The Dependent

As a first step the Dependent will often need some kind of medical attention, especially detoxification—sobriety is absolutely essential before any meaningful treatment can start. This often means hospitalization and consequent separation from the family, but primary treatment can and should begin anyway. (It may well be already in progress for the family members who intervened.)

Because he has suffered the chemical as well as the emotional ravages of alcoholism, and because his disease has been progressing for so long, the Dependent is in a state of deep delusion. It is necessary to keep feeding back to him, over and over again, the counselor's objective observations about what he is doing and what is happening as a result.

The intervention and the beginning of treatment have shown the Dependent that the crazy world of suffering and desperation he has experienced for so long is not the only world there is. Something, someone outside himself is going to help him find health, hope, and sanity again. At first, that something may be only the treatment center as a whole, or the peer group in treatment, or AA. For the AA member, it is also some Higher Power.

Part of the Dependent's despair has lain in the heavy burden of guilt and shame he carries. Explaining the known pathology of his disease helps dispel these feelings by showing him the degree to which dependency robbed him of his freedom of choice. The support of other, concerned people will also help; if they can still find something in him worth caring for, perhaps he can begin to care for himself again. Meanwhile, the counselor must not be intimidated by the anger and rejection (or in some cases, charm) he encounters in the Dependent, but rather speak to the hurt and shame and guilt that lie beneath.

As the Dependent recovers, he gradually learns to trust, first within the family, then in a widening circle of relationships. Eventually he finds a deeper meaning and purpose in his life.

The Enabler

Though she is in a little closer touch with reality than the Dependent, the Enabler may actually be even more resistant to treatment. She too has suffered, and she too carries a burden of shame and guilt. Hers, however, are different. She feels shame for what she sees as *his* problem, guilt for her inability to change *him*. As a result, her most pronounced feelings are self-righteousness, self-pity, and anger, though she may not be aware of the full depth of her anger. From this posture it is very hard for her to see her own behavior objectively and admit that she is part of the problem.

The counselor must first listen to her story with understanding and compassion, giving her appreciation for what she has endured and support in her desire to improve the family's plight. She will soon sense that in him she has an ally. At the same time, he will have to constantly but gently redirect the focus of their work from specific problems and issues, on which an Enabler is inclined to digress, back to the more essential matter of her feelings. As these are aired to the counselor, particularly her massive block of rage, they will slowly soften, relieving the inner pressure enough for her to consider some other possible versions of reality.

An early task for the counselor will be to teach this person, whose controlling purpose in life has been to change the Dependent's behavior, that her dream is impossible. She can change only herself. By explaining the simplest principles of family interaction, however, he can show her that changing her own behavior will trigger changes in the whole family system.

From this point his teaching can go on to the characteristic roles people play in an alcoholic family. He will feed back to her, as he did to the Dependent, his empathetic but honest perception of her present role behavior and its consequences. In time she will come to acknowledge her contribution to the family illness.

Throughout this hard work the Enabler must be motivated to change *for her own well-being* and not for the sake of the rest of the family, which may have been her chief conscious purpose in the past. The counselor can tell her of other Enablers he has known who, even after they are divorced or widowed, go on playing their roles, contracting new marriages with dependency-prone partners and creating new crises to replace the old one, which they find they cannot live without. The stakes of treatment for her are nothing less than her very self—her health, wholeness, and chance for happiness.

It is, of course, of critical importance that the counselor sees alcoholism as a blameless disease and communicates that fact both in his own attitudes and explicitly in his educational work with the clients. Blaming would intensify the Dependent's sense of guilt and would make the Enabler's resistance to accepting the responsibility for her part in the disease even more rigid. She has been engaged internally in so much blaming of the Dependent for all these years that she is hyperconscious of blame. Even when she finally accepts the truth about her role in the illness, she may simply turn the blame back on herself rather than giving it up.

The Hero

When the Hero arrives for his first individual session, he may well seem to be the most "together" member of the family. His self-worth is higher than the others', and his pain may be less acute. But the counselor should be forewarned that, second only to the Enabler, this child will be the most resistant to treatment. For one thing, as we saw in earlier chapters, he may properly be called a "Little Enabler"; he will present the same attitudes and resistances as the Enabler. In addition, he has a special incentive to cling to a role that has brought him some positive payoffs along with his pain.

True, the Hero has, in the course of playing out his role, developed qualities that are potentially valuable to others and fulfilling to himself. It is certainly not the intent of treatment to change these. But as long as they are accompanied by the compulsiveness that now characterizes them, they will bring him not only joy but some measure of pain as well. If he chooses a career in some helping profession, as so many Heroes do, his compulsiveness will also make him highly vulnerable to burnout.

The counselor's goal is to help the Hero pursue his goals by free choice, not because he must but because they bring him satisfaction. Expressing appreciation for the Hero's good qualities—an easy enough step because it is so warranted—can establish the counselor as an ally in the pursuit of excellence and thus lay the basis for trust. Then the counselor can proceed with the rest of the agenda for primary care, explaining the alcoholic family system and giving the Hero feedback on his behavior. As he becomes aware of his role-playing, his compulsion to overwork and overachieve will fade.

The counselor can be effective in helping the Hero only if he does not feel intimidated by any competence or possible intellectual superiority this admittedly able person may seem to possess; as always the counselor must stay aware of the real feelings underneath—inadequacy, fear, and guilt.

Until now the Hero has occupied a special and honored place in the family. When he gives up his role, he must also give up being the most special. The counselor must be sure that the Hero's newfound freedom, added to his acknowledged virtues and achievements, leaves him with such a strong sense of worth that he no longer needs the chair of honor. Heroes who are not sufficiently prepared for this loss risk becoming depressed or angry and perhaps switching to the role of Scapegoat.

The Scapegoat

Like the Dependent, the Scapegoat comes to treatment with his self-worth almost totally shattered. The family, and often the community as well, have labeled him bad for so long that he has accepted the label as truth. His delinquent behavior may have actually precipitated the crisis that ended up in intervention.

When this sulky, uncooperative youngster walks into the office, the counselor may understandably jump to the conclusion that he will be the most resistant member of the family. His oppressive burden of hurt, shame, and guilt is hidden behind such a solid wall of either silence or bravado that initial attempts to communicate with him are likely to be discouraging.

How can the counselor break through to win this youngster's trust? His one hope lies in being *totally honest and caring,* attitudes for which the Scapegoat has never developed a defense because he has so seldom encountered them. The counselor's honesty must be caring, giving the Scapegoat necessary feedback on his behavior but with no hint of blame. Conversely, the caring must be impeccably honest. This child has been hurt so often that he is wary—how could anyone really care about a no-good kid like me? He will detect the slightest shadow of insincerity or manipulation.

Beneath all his suspicions, though, the Scapegoat wants desperately to trust the counselor. His need for help is so great! Some of the other family members have had positive as well as negative payoffs from their roles, but not he. He has nothing to lose in treatment but his pain. In my experience, as Scapegoats realize that the counselor does truly care, they are relieved and grateful to be able to pour out their hurt and anger and self-hate to what may be the first understanding listener they have ever known. Sometimes a Scapegoat, using the courage and communication skills that he has learned in dealing with his peers, has proved to be a strong ally for change during my after-care work with the family.

Learning about the characteristic problems of alcoholism in a family can do a lot to relieve the Scapegoat's guilt—the disease is the culprit, not me! And the unfailing respect and concern with which the counselor treats him can evoke the first faint glimmers of returning self-respect.

However effective primary care may be for the Scapegoat, though, the truth is that he probably has a pile of real-life troubles much higher than anyone else in the family, unless perhaps the Dependent himself. School failure, drug abuse, delinquency, bad companions, a reputation as a troublemaker—some or all of these problems still hang over his head and must be dealt with. He will need strong, continuing emotional support and quite possibly some practical guidance while he resolves them. The counselor in an alcoholism treatment center may not have the time or specific training to follow through with these problems. If not, the youngster should be referred to an appropriate professional person for additional help.

The Lost Child

Though he does not display the hostility of the Scapegoat when he comes to treatment, the Lost Child may be just as hard to reach. Where the Scapegoat has dammed the flow of communication behind a wall of distrust, the Lost Child seems to *have* no flow; it is frozen by a lifetime of solitude. The counselor's warmth—again his openness and caring—must thaw it, make the child comfortable, and draw him out gently and patiently.

The relationship with the counselor in primary care can show the Lost Child the rewards of relating that he has been missing and help him begin to develop the skills he lacks. In after-care he can practice them with family members under the counselor's guidance. Peer group therapy, Alateen, and later social activities that are included in his program for the recovery stage will offer an ever-expanding stage on which the Lost Child can exercise his newly discovered social potential.

This does not mean he must give up the "alone time" he has come to value. He can continue the reading, meditation, or quiet hobbies with which he has learned to fill his solitude creatively, but now he has a wider choice. He can also build close relationships and at last find some relief from the intense loneliness he has always known.

The Mascot

Some Mascots can be a delightful addition to the treatment process, adding a needed light touch with their sense of humor. Others are maddening, either refusing to take anything seriously or being so fidgety and disruptive that little constructive work can be done. Some Mascots I've known have been alternately delightful *and* maddening.

Whatever form his symptoms take, this youngster is consumed with anxiety. The counselor's first task is to relieve it, letting him see that the treatment setting is a safe place and the counselor a person he can trust. As the anxiety dissolves and the youngster relaxes, his symptoms will be less marked and more responsive to his conscious control. Now he can begin to concentrate on learning the many things about the family and himself that he needs to know. But treatment is already well underway by this time, for relieving his anxieties and quieting the behavior they arouse is what treatment for the Mascot is all about.

Symptoms that have been developing since infancy will not usually disappear in a few weeks of treatment, but I find they do ease considerably. This is an important preliminary to after-care. While some characteristic behavior by the Mascot can provide grist for the family sessions, too much acting-out can be so disruptive that little progress is made in the work with other family members.

Like the Scapegoat, the Mascot may have real-life difficulties, such as learning disabilities or serious emotional problems. Again, these should be referred for special help unless they fall in the area of professional expertise of the counselor or therapist doing the treatment.

THE WHOLE PERSON INVENTORY

Although much has been said in this book about the family—family dynamics, the family disease, family treatment—ultimately the family is not important for its own sake but only for the way it promotes or interferes with the personal wholeness and happiness of the individual members who comprise it. And so in treatment, even when the unit we are treating is the whole family, our true objective is developing the damaged or stunted potentials of each person.

For this reason I have found the whole person model (presented in chapter 2) very useful in working with family members. I usually introduce it early in primary care. It serves as an inventory of the individual potentials, a map of where we hope treatment will lead, and a theoretical framework to help the client understand what we will do to get there. It lends itself equally well to use in private sessions or in groups—the peer group in primary care, the family in after-care, or special groupings of husband and wife, parent and child, employer and employee, according to the counselor's judgment.

The inherent structure of the whole person wheel points up the truth that we are all more alike than different: we all have the same kind of potentials. But it can also be used to identify individual differences —the diverse ways each of us has developed his potentials. Strong and unique development is a sign not only of differentness but of health.

When I use the wheel as an inventory, I give the client a pencil and ask him to shade the sections, showing how much he feels each potential is currently developed. Where he feels that one has never been developed or is weaker now than at some time in the past, he is asked to write a few sentences (or sometimes simply to tell me) about how that weakness feels to him, why he thinks it happened, and how he would like to be able to change it.

Because the inventory gives a profile of an individual at a given point in time, it can also be valuable as a way of measuring growth. Sometimes I have a client fill out one inventory when he enters treatment and another when he is ready to leave. Comparing them gives him an encouraging measure of his growth and also points out those areas on which he needs to continue working.

Sometimes the power of this exercise to prompt fresh insights still surprises me. I remember one young man who took a giant step in the one week between our appointments, thanks to the whole person inventory:

Chuck was seventeen when I first met him. His father had already completed treatment for alcoholism and was recovering. The treatment program was somewhat different from the model described in this book, however, and Chuck had not participated. He continued to act out his Scapegoat role and create problems for his parents, his school, and sometimes the police. That is why the family came to see me.

When they showed up for their first appointment, Chuck was dressed in greasy blue jeans, a baggy sweater that had obviously been expensive before it was abused, bloodshot eyes, and a scraggly beard. It was soon obvious that he did not want to be there.

"This kid's been giving us all a hard time," the father began. "I don't know how he turned out the way he has. We've tried hard to bring him up right, but he's just impossible to live with! He's sure nothing like me when I was a boy."

I asked to talk with Chuck alone for a few minutes, and he began to open up. "I'm a free person," he said, "and I worked hard to get free. I don't respect my dad's values. I do things my own way."

He seemed to want very much for me to agree how different he was and how clever to have "freed" himself from his father's values (after all, hadn't his father been an alcoholic and caused the family all sorts of trouble?). But it was a time for honesty.

"Free?" I asked him. "You're no freer than your father. You're as much like him as I've ever seen a son like his father."

"How can you say that?" He sounded outraged. "*I* wouldn't work fifty hours a week like Dad. *I* wouldn't dress up in a monkey suit and tie every day. I make my *own* decisions!"

"I realize that your father is still recovering," I told him, "and that one of the things he still has to work on is his rigidity. He is reacting rigidly to the pressures of the world he lives in—he wears the right clothes, has his hair cut the right length, does everything just the way he thinks he is supposed to. *But you are reacting, too.* The only difference is that you're reacting to him. You feel you have to wear your hair long because he wears his short. You have to be sloppy because he is neat. You have to break the rules because he conforms to them. *You're just as rigid as he is.*

"If you were really free, you could wear your hair long or medium or even crewcut if you chose. You could be sloppy some days and neat others. You could wear blue jeans today and dress slacks tomorrow.

"Different? You both even turned to chemicals to make you feel good. The only difference is that your dad used alcohol and you smoke dope.

"If you could learn to listen to your own feelings and make your own decisions without worrying about what anyone else was doing, I might say you were free. But right now I see you as being hooked on being the exact opposite of your father.

"You can start getting unhooked by being honest with yourself— and with me."

All the while I talked, he had been slumped silently in the chair, looking at his boots. Now he slowly looked up, and in his expression I saw, not a belligerent teenager, but a confused and miserable child.

"Help me," he said. "My life's really messed up!"

We were ready to go to work. I began by explaining to him about the various dimensions of human potential that I had found in working with people. At the end of the session I gave him a copy of the whole person wheel and asked him to think about how it applied to him.

A week later Chuck came in again. This time his hair was brushed, he was wearing clean brown cords, and he told me he had found a part-time job.

Working with the inventory, he said, had opened up things he'd never thought about before. One night he decided to sit down and talk with his father. They used the inventory to find out just where they really were different. It showed them that they had exactly the same human nature, but that within it they had differences. They also found, however, that they had a number of similarities, as I had pointed out.

Chuck tried to reconstruct the conversation for me. His dad had said, "Physically—the way you look—you're certainly different from me. But if that's your honest choice, if I know that what you're doing really feels right for you, I guess I can handle it."

When they came to the social potential, Chuck told his father, "I don't like your friends much, and I sure wouldn't want to spend my evenings at a council meeting or playing bridge with the Harrises. But we're different, and I can understand that you enjoy doing those things."

As they talked, they found a bond of mutual respect growing between them—respect for each other and for themselves as well. They felt closer than they had in years. Soon neither the differences nor the similarities seemed very important. What mattered more was that they could talk about them. Chuck said that it was the first time he had ever really listened to what his dad said. And he felt it was the first time his dad had listened to him.

When the five basic goals of treatment have been met for all members of the family—when they have got in touch with their feelings, let their pain emerge, and found some positive feelings beneath it; when they have accepted their part in the family illness and made a personal commitment to a recovery program for themselves and the family—they are ready to move on to after-care.

At this stage the whole person inventory is useful in giving them a gauge of how far they have come and how much remains to be done, and in motivating them to persevere in treatment in order to realize the rich satisfactions all those as yet undeveloped potentials on their whole person wheels now promise.

CHAPTER **14**

After-Care

AFTER SO MANY years of pain, a family feels great relief when the Dependent agrees to go into treatment. Agonizing though the decision is for him, once it is made, he too feels relief; his long ordeal is over. As he begins to get a tenuous hold on sobriety and everyone in the family experiences some faint glimmerings of returning health, there is a great surge of hope and joy. By the time the Dependent leaves the treatment center, they feel that at last their problems are over and life is going to be wonderful from now on.

In this flush of optimism, some families are inclined to believe that there is no need to continue treatment. The sweetness of the moment has fooled them into thinking they have the whole pie. Actually, however, only about 10 percent of the necessary work has been done by the end of primary care.

The honeymoon the family experiences during this time may last anywhere from a few weeks to a year or more. When frictions arise, everyone simply dams up his feelings to avoid rocking the boat. Sooner or later, though, those dams are going to collapse under the pressure of the many problems they came to treatment with and have not yet resolved. The family may, in fact, seem to have even more problems than before the intervention.

For one thing, old problems look bigger now, since the overriding problem of alcohol use is no longer present to take everyone's mind off the others. And they may feel even less able to deal with their difficulties because primary care, if it has been effective, has begun to dissolve their

183

old, compulsive ways of coping and there has not yet been time to learn new, healthier ways.

Besides the left-over problems, making room in the family for a suddenly sober Dependent as well as other members who are beginning to become autonomous will for a time precipitate a lot of new problems.

All these accumulated challenges form the context for after-care, as well as the immediate motivation. At the root of most of them lies the question of change—giving up the old and accepting the new. At first it may seem surprising that this family should want to cling to any shred of a past that was so painful. Unhealthy and unsatisfying though it was, however, there were some payoffs in the alcoholic roles, and family members will be reluctant to give them up when there are not yet new satisfactions to replace them. Let's look at some of the specific problems that arise in parting with the old ways:

Fear. The first problem for everyone in the family is usually fear— fear of ghosts of the past and fear of prospects for the future. The Dependent wonders, "Can I stay sober? Do they all hate me? Can I hold a job after all these years? Can I earn back my family's respect? Will my wife ever respond to me sexually again? Can I deal with all the family problems we face?" Other family members are asking their own questions. The Enabler wonders, "Will he really stay sober? Has he forgiven me for intervening? Can I trust him to handle family affairs now? Will he be able to hold a job? Can I give up mine? *Must* I give up mine? How will he treat the children, and how will they respond? Can I ever again find him sexually attractive?" Meanwhile, the children are worrying how it is going to be for them. Probably all they can remember is an angry, unreasonable, perhaps violent father, whose moods and actions were erratic.

Hurt and anger. Under the fear, thinly veiled, lies a sublayer of hurt, resentment, and anger. Primary care has helped family members to get in touch with this, but it remains for after-care to help them deal with it. Meanwhile it rankles as they tell themselves they *ought* to be feeling love and appreciation toward the others for all they have each done to turn their lives around.

Loss of denial. After primary care gets the individual back in touch with his feelings, he finds it very hard to go back to denying them. But it takes courage for him to feel them. He has to give up the safety from challenge and conflict that he had formerly bought—dearly!—with silence and denial.

Loss of a focus. They have all literally had the props of their dysfunctional lives knocked out from under them with the loss of their chief focus, the Dependent's drinking. Like one who has carried a heavy burden for a long time, they miss it when it is lifted.

Loss of a scapegoat. When problems arose in the past, everyone could find some relief in blaming, either the Scapegoat or the Dependent. But primary care has spoiled this game by making them aware of what they were doing.

Loss of roles. They have also had to give up whatever positive satisfactions their compulsive roles offered. This is especially hard for the Enabler and the Hero, who have been admired and praised for their patience, fortitude, loyalty, nurturing, responsibility, hard work, and often achievement outside the family as well. Even the less rewarding roles offered a sort of familiar security. Now they are not sure how to behave—or what to expect from the other family members, who in giving up their roles have become less predictable.

Loss of the old family system. They are confused about what a family "should" be and how it "should" act. Primary care has helped them to realize how narrow, rigid, unhealthy, and downright unworkable their old definition of a family was, but replacing it with a better one has yet to be done.

Loss of a dependent Dependent. They all have to give up taking care of the Dependent and babying him, managing his life and making his decisions. For the Enabler this is hardest, especially since there is no way for her to be sure that he can be trusted to handle matters himself.

For each familiar condition or behavior that must be sacrificed, there is a replacement that must be accepted. These two faces of change are closely related and equally stressful. Here are some of the new things family members must adapt themselves to:

1. They must make space for a newly sober and presumably responsible Dependent—in a family that had closed ranks and carried on without him. The Enabler must move over now and let him share the responsibilities and the authority. The children must learn to respect him again and accept his authority, seeing him as he is now and not as they so recently remember him.

2. They must all apply what they have learned in primary care about staying in touch with their feelings and owning those feelings whatever they may be.

3. They must extend this same right to everyone else in the family

—not easy in a family where for so long no one dared to feel anything but a few approved emotions, such as loyalty, compassion, love, trust— none of which was a very natural response to the reality of the family situation.

4. They must each find a place in their hearts for forgiveness, the only salve that will heal the old wounds and allow continuing contact without irritating friction.

5. The family must provide growing room, not only for a recovering Dependent, but also for role-free, growing family members, too.

6. Parents and children alike will have to learn to be—and to let others be—free, autonomous persons (within, of course, the limits of their maturity).

7. They must learn to trust themselves and one another with this newfound autonomy.

8. They must work out new family rules and new ways of relating in order to cope with the many problems facing them; then each individual must learn to live comfortably within this new system.

9. They must accept the fact that all these changes are only a beginning, that change is a continuing fact of life in a healthy family with ever-growing members.

These, then, are some of the core problems that underlie the more specific ones of which they complain—silence, withdrawal, money, sex, in-laws, kids in trouble, school failure—all of which they will want the counselor to solve for them in after-care. It is important that he resist this demand and remain very clear about his true agenda. *His goal is not to solve the family's many practical problems.* The focus of after-care must be process, not issues. It is the process of what people do and say to each other that raises or lowers self-worth. Issues are important, but only as a context in which process can be observed and modified.

The counselor will keep in mind the deeper, system-related problems listed above, but even those he will not presume to solve. Rather, he will provide a safe and supervised setting where the family can begin to practice with one another the more open, honest, feeling communication they have each been learning in primary care, and thus begin finding some solutions themselves. They will learn not only to cope with change but to initiate it and thus gain control of their lives.

As the shared "high" of finding sobriety for the Dependent wears off, the family often experiences a period of deep discouragement. They had thought that all their troubles were over, only to find that they have merely begun what will be a long process involving change for all of them. Through the intervention period they have been highly motivated to bring about change, but the change they envisioned was only in the Dependent. During his detoxification and primary treatment he came to share that vision. Unless there has been an effective program of primary care for the family as well, we have the paradoxical situation that when the Dependent finishes his residential treatment, he is the healthiest member of the family—healthiest because he is the only one motivated to change *himself*.

Primary care, however, sets in motion the slow process of change for all of them. It loosens the fixed structure of what has been and prepares the way for what can be. Through all the phases of treatment, change is the name of the game. The family, individually and collectively, will resist it all the way, much of the time not even aware of their own resistance. But gradually they *can* change and they will. They *must* if they are to remain out of the alcoholic trap and realize the happier, healthier life they now dare to hope for.

As the family wrestles with its multiple problems, with its desperate need to change and its frustrating resistance to doing so, the mobile that we saw in chapter 3 is going to do some violent rocking. Its individual components will be tossed about and perhaps collide with one another; the framework that connects them will have to shift and flex to avoid breaking up. During this time it is important for the family to have the steadying hand of a trained counselor to help them find a new and comfortable balance with as little damage as possible to people and relationships.

This is what after-care provides.

THE GOALS OF AFTER-CARE

Primary care has been a time of focusing on the components of the family system—the individuals and their personal dysfunction. Each family member, as a result of his work, is more open and in touch with his feelings. He has begun to reclaim a little of his self-worth and become strong enough to take some new risks. It is important not to begin after-care until each person is thoroughly in touch with his own delusion, defenses, and compulsive behavior, and motivated to change them. While he is in their grip, he is powerless to function in the honest and flexible way a healthy family system demands.

As the family members come to accept alcoholism as a family

illness during primary care, they find new hope that they can recover. The cold isolation, resistance, and despair have begun to melt, and the family are ready to come together to continue their healing. After-care, then, becomes a time to work with the system itself, reassembling the components and helping them to function better in relation to one another.

The major goal of after-care is to open up the family system. That means, primarily, opening the channels of communication that have so long been blocked by fear, denial, and the unwritten rule of silence. The members of an alcoholic family come to after-care with many years' backlog of painful feelings, which they have started to feel again in primary care but which have most likely never been shared with the rest of the family. Now they must learn to express these feelings and to accept similar expressions from the others.

This is a risk none of them has taken for a while, or maybe ever, and it is bound to be scary at first. But feelings are the ground where deep, human contact can be made. The members of a family are all different in many ways—age, sex, abilities, interests, temperament. The only thing that they truly share is their feeling nature. It is here they can find their similarity—the similarity that makes it possible for them to tolerate, and even to enjoy, their differences.

While they are learning to communicate—indeed all during after-care—the counselor will function as both coach and referee. He will work constantly to keep communication straight and flowing freely. He will point out when family members block their own or each other's honest expression, where they slip back into their old roles, and how they are responding to feedback once it is given. As they begin to communicate more openly, they will gradually be able to referee their own interaction.

As the private pain is shared, it slowly becomes obvious to everyone that they have all been suffering, all carrying parts of the same oppressive load—the disease of alcoholism. Discovering that they are all victims, they stop victimizing and scapegoating one another; only the disease is to blame. Draining off the negative feelings clears the air for some new, more joyful feelings to arise. When these are communicated, the family can begin to share joy as well as pain.

So the process of sharing unfolds. Information, like feelings, is communicated more openly and with less distortion. Delusion gives way to reality. Disagreements can be negotiated. Family rules, now challenged in open discussion of ideas and feelings, can be rewritten by consensus, ensuring that they accommodate everyone's needs. Rights and responsibilities are gradually shared, rather than being the sole privilege or burden of one or two individuals.

Naturally, this work cannot be fully completed during the limited span of after-care. What is important is that it be begun and that family members learn the skills to carry it on, on their own.

Toward the end of after-care, the counselor will encourage the family to take a serious look at their values and their hopes for the future, again both as individuals and as a family group. In dysfunctional families, I have found, the values of the most controlling member—in alcoholic families, the Dependent—are imposed on everyone else. Now, however, the family's newly learned communication skills will allow them to explore honestly both their shared dreams and their differing ones, adapting current rules and plans for the future to make room for all.

Through all this period of focusing on the family system, it is important to remember that the real target of treatment is the members. A family is nothing but a collection of unique individuals who happen to be related to one another in a special way. Everything that happens in after-care is, in the end, designed to make each member healthier, happier, whole. It is a time when they can begin to *experience* the selves they rediscovered in primary care, to *feel* their own interactions with the rest of the family and to watch those of the others. They can become more aware of their defense patterns, the roles they play, and the things they do to keep them separate from the rest of the family. This awareness is a necessary first step to the larger goal of treatment: putting an end to role-playing.

It is not enough to eliminate the roles of Dependent and Scapegoat. The Heroes and Enablers and Lost Children and Mascots must be quietly ushered offstage, too. When a Dependent gives up his dependency, he is likely to shift to playing a Hero to keep the spotlight on himself. The relieved family members often act as Enablers for this ploy. It is up to the counselor to expose the new twist in the old game and show the family that true recovery means giving up *all* roles. (As I mentioned in an earlier chapter, this shift from Dependent to Hero is even more common when the Dependent is a youngster who has been abusing drugs.)

Through the long years of pain, there was no way for anyone in the family to pursue his own values in his own way without paying a high price for his differentness. Whatever the coin in which it was exacted,

it left his self-worth near bankruptcy. As the system slowly becomes more open, however, the individual will find more space to be different, more freedom to be himself. His honest sharing of his feelings will hasten the process; so will his willingness to allow other family members space for being unique. This space is absolutely essential for a person to be able to grow. And he must know that he is growing, creating, and producing in ways that are fitting for him, if he is to be whole and symptom free.

By the time after-care is completed, the individual should be enjoying a considerably expanded—and still expanding—range of choice in his life. And his nearly smothered self-worth, which was given first aid in primary care, is now recuperating and beginning to regenerate its lost potentials.

SOME TOOLS FOR THE COUNSELOR

Recalling the miserable, dysfunctional state of the family when primary care started, we may be tempted to view successful treatment as some blend of magic and miracle. Admittedly, as in any helping profession, the counselor's personal capacity for intuition and empathy is a critical ingredient. So are a sound treatment rationale, thorough training, and practical experience. But given these things, the counselor will also want to find some more concrete tools for success. Here are some that I find useful:

The intake form. Most agencies, and many private counselors as well, use some kind of intake form to provide data for planning, treatment evaluation, and research. An alert counselor will find the answers on this questionnaire to be a plentiful source of advance information on the family. For example, was any family member left out? Surprisingly often the person who fills out the form will neglect to give information on himself,[1] possibly because he has dissociated himself from the problem. Young children may be left off because they are considered "too little to be involved in this." Adolescents or adult children may be left off because they are no longer living at home. If anyone has left the home, the counselor will want to explore the reasons and circumstances of the departure.

The ages of the family members can also hold clues. Two children close in age? This may have affected either the marriage or the sibling relationship. Spouses of widely divergent ages? This may suggest special personality needs of the spouses as individuals or special adaptations they have had to make in the marriage. Birth order of the children can explain a lot about rivalries, alliances, and probable family roles. In filling out the form, most parents list the children chronologically. When they do not, it may be a tip-off that someone is seen as "special."

The treatment setting. A well-planned consulting room can facilitate work with a family. It should be pleasant and comfortable, the light cheerfully bright but not harsh. There should be plenty of space for people to move around and plenty of seating, also movable.

The seating game. When a family arrives for their first session together, I like to have the chairs or pillows either stacked neatly at one

---

[1] In actuality, more of these intake forms are completed by women (the classic Enablers) than by men.

side or arranged chaotically (the presumption being that they were left this way at the end of my previous appointment). In either case, they must be rearranged before our session can start. I ask the family to sit down anywhere they wish, thus leaving the responsibility for the room's arrangement to them. Then I simply watch: Who sits where? Who directs others to their seats? Is there conflict? Between whom? Who settles it, and how? The way the family goes about bringing order to the room can be a preview of how they will go about bringing order to their lives.

At this first session there is bound to be a fairly high level of anxiety, which exaggerates natural defenses. The demands of the seating decisions add to the stress. By simply watching and listening to the actions that follow, I can get more insight into how a family works than by several hours of hearing about their problems. I can see which members feel close to each other, which are estranged, and which individuals are alienated from the whole family. I can see where the power lies and how it is used. If no one seems to be directing the action or disciplining the children, that tells me something, too.

The seating game often reveals immediately who is playing which role. The spouse of an adult Dependent is, of course, the probable Enabler. The child who sits nearest her is likely to be either the Mascot or the Hero, depending on age and other behavior. The child sitting distant from everyone else is probably either the Scapegoat or the Lost Child. The little one squirming on someone's lap or toppling off a pile of pillows in the corner is sure to be the Mascot. Role behavior in alcoholic families is so stereotypical that the actors can be relied upon to play out this seating game in highly predictable ways.

Hearing the family story. Once the family have settled into their chosen places, it is time to hear their story. They want to tell it, to pour their pain and frustration out to the counselor, but the telling is difficult. They are not only asking for help: they are admitting failure. That takes self-worth, something they sorely lack. So the family comes well rehearsed, with the intervener usually speaking first. The others listen nervously.

Her story is both a description of their problem and a justification for their coming. She seems to be saying, "Our family is so bad! Please agree with me that we need help. Don't tell me that I'm exaggerating, that our problem is small and insignificant. That would embarrass me. I'm very worried, and I need to know that you can and will help us."

As she shares the family's most intimate secrets and deepest fears, the rest of the members will naturally be reacting to what they hear. Some interrupt, argue, contradict, lose their tempers. Some confirm her story, blame the Scapegoat, squirm, joke, move their chairs back from the speaker or maybe from the whole group. Sometimes the storytelling is temporarily disrupted by tears, angry outbursts, digressions, irrelevant debate, or attention-getting behavior by the Mascot. At times like these the counselor feels like the conductor of a chaotic orchestra. He must maintain enough order to hear the instruments. He must notice which players are yearning to play, so he can call them to attention and give them permission to be heard. Through it all he must try to be sensitive to the larger patterns of the symphony: the family's story itself is not as important as the *process*—the way they hear and tell it.

Team counseling. When working with large families or those in which there is a good deal of acting out, I find it helpful to have a co-counselor. Where so much is going on, four eyes and four ears can catch more of the action. Team counseling also offers a second set of perceptions of what is happening, an informed person to discuss the case with, an alternate personality for the family to relate to, and a stronger therapeutic presence than a single counselor. Unfortunately, this is something many treatment agencies feel they cannot afford.

People who attend my workshops for professionals often ask me what techniques I use in this difficult work with families. It is not an easy question to answer. Some of my strategies can be traced back to my training as an alcoholism counselor. Some I have learned from Virginia Satir and other gifted therapists. Some I simply improvise to meet the treatment challenge of the moment. Often an impromptu exercise proves so effective that I make it a regular part of my repertoire. (Several of these exercises are presented in the Appendix.)

Whatever specific intervention tactics I may use at a particular juncture, with a particular family, there are some general guidelines that I have found valuable:

1. *Do the unexpected.* This keeps the family off guard, with their defenses down. For example, in the first session I often ask people to "teach me what your family is like." They are usually quite willing but then look shocked when I choose the Mascot rather than the Enabler to be "teacher."

2. *Stimulate action, not words.* Exercises like making a family portrait (see page 245) are far more effective if done without talking. By involving the body, we can bypass the mind's defenses and get directly at feelings. More action, less talk also keep treatment sessions livelier and more fun.

3. *Involve the outsider.* By asking the person who seems most isolated in the family—because of age, shyness, scapegoating, or whatever —to take the lead in an exercise or discussion, I can bring him back into the action.

4. *Check out how people are feeling.* Whenever one member says or does something challenging or risky or inappropriate, ask what he is feeling at that moment. Then check out how the other person or persons involved are feeling—perhaps the whole family. I ask this question time and time again—often many times in a single hour.

5. *Have family members role-play one another.* This is a powerful tool to help one person understand what another is feeling and what it would be like to have to stand in his shoes. I find it an especially helpful way to build bridges between the Scapegoat and the other family members.

6. *Watch behavior in treatment for clues to behavior at home.* For example, if one member refuses to talk, I ask the others, "Does this happen at home?" Their answers and the discussion that follows help us turn a possible obstacle into a useful focus for work.

All these precepts are equally helpful to me whether the families I am working with are alone or in groups.

Counselors and therapists among my readers have no doubt already identified what I do as a process approach. The process of thinking/ feeling/responding in the individual and the process of interaction between individuals are the real objects of treatment. Teaching families about their unique process—helping them to recognize it, to watch for it in their daily lives, and to alter it when it begins to cause someone pain —is the chief business of after-care. When family members have learned these things, they are nearly ready to come out from under the counselor's wing. Here are some clues that after-care is drawing to a close:

Each individual

- has his own unique identity.
- is aware of who he is at that particular moment and accepts it, with his inadequacies and faults as well as his talents and virtues.

- is congruent, his words, facial expression, and body language matching what he feels inside.
- is in touch with the reality around him, which he no longer feels a need to falsify or deny.
- relates to the positive in social institutions, seeking to transform them rather than rebelling.
- has a fresh interest in exploring the meaning of life (spirituality).

The family as a whole
- are a group of people who choose to belong to one another and who know, as individuals, that they do belong.
- are aware of the level of their relationship to each of the others, with all relationships being built on love and understanding, respecting that who a person is, is more important than what he does.
- can give and follow flexible rules, allow open communication from others, and tolerate mistakes.
- have created an open system where all topics can be discussed, all feelings can be expressed, and all members are allowed to be themselves, even though this means that they are different.
- accept change as a part of life and even a *sign* of life.
- display joy, fun, and a celebration of life.

This is not to say that the family or its members have all these qualities in full measure; they have much growing yet to do. But in each area a beginning has been made, and they are now equipped to carry on recovery under their own power.

In the later stages of after-care the counselor will help them plan their strategy for the recovery phase, both as individuals pursuing their own wholeness and as a family helping those individuals and fostering the potential for joy-giving relationships among them. These plans will be as specific as possible, made by the individuals involved with encouragement and guidance from the counselor. They will provide the necessary momentum for family members to continue the active pursuit of recovery—on their own.

CHAPTER **15**

Recovery Unlimited

IN THE EARLIER years of this century, when a person went into treatment for alcoholism, he was said to be "taking the cure." This quaint phrase may have been useful as a euphemism, but it bore little relationship to the usual outcome. More often than not, drinking resumed and, with such optimistic expectations, everyone was understandably dismayed. Treatment appeared to be only a brief recess in the degenerative progress of the disease.

The alternative view—that alcoholism is incurable—is more realistic but seemingly pessimistic as well. If it's incurable, what use is treatment? Yet without treatment, clearly all is lost. Into this dilemma the fellowship of Alcoholics Anonymous was born and offered a resolution: the disease is indeed incurable, they said, but its progress can be arrested and its ravages healed.

In AA, then and now, the alcoholic considers himself still an alcoholic no matter how many years he may have been "dry." The danger of relapse is ever present. As a result, those who have recovered their sobriety speak of themselves as "recovering alcoholics." The terms *recovering* and *recovery* are used freely, but never *recovered*. Recovery is seen as a journey without an end; a process, not an accomplished fact.

In my more than ten years of working with alcoholics, I have found nothing to invalidate this view. Occasionally one hears a claim from some isolated piece of research that suggests sober alcoholics may be able to drink again without losing control. Perhaps, but frankly I doubt it. Among the many alcoholics I have worked with, I have yet to know one who has succeeded in returning to controlled drinking. Those who have tried have paid an exorbitant price. Other counselors who attend my workshops report similar experiences. So in this book I never use the words *former, cured,* or *recovered* but always *recovering* when referring to the Dependent.

Now I would like to introduce an extension of that idea: the *recovering family.* If family members manifest all the symptoms of the Dependent's disease except chemical intake, and if they therefore need treatment similar to his, then does it not follow that they too remain ever at risk of relapsing into their old role patterns? I am convinced it does, so in my work I speak also of the *recovering Enabler,* the *recovering Hero,* and so on.

This idea has some practical value for my clients as well as for me. It carries the positive suggestion that for each person the process of growth is unending, that he can and must go on recovering to higher and higher levels of health and personal development. At the same time it warns him that the danger of slipping back into his old defenses is ever present. He advances or he retreats; there is no standing still.

RECOVERING THE POTENTIALS

With the completion of after-care, the formal, supervised period of treatment comes to a close. It may seem strange that I include recovery as a part of treatment at all, inasmuch as the counselor is not involved and the work is open-ended. I do so because I am convinced that this ongoing growth is a necessary final step. Without it, treatment is not complete and the results may not be lasting.

At this point we see a group of people each of whom is becoming truly himself—not perfect, of course, but growing. As a family they are beginning to function as an open, healthy system that will facilitate rather than block their growth as individuals. In earlier chapters we watched the slow disintegration of the personal potentials of each member of the family. Now let us return to see what has happened to these potentials during the course of treatment and what may remain to be done.

The Physical Potential

The improved functioning of the family moving into the recovery phase is clearly visible in their physical health. For the Dependent, after several weeks of detoxification, wholesome meals[1] and regular hours, the

---

[1] Much attention is currently being given to the connections between nutrition and chemical dependency. We may look forward to some new information on this question in the next few years.

physical transformation may be dramatic, but a new wellness is evident in everyone. As the catharsis of long suppressed and repressed emotions has reduced the level of tension, their chronic aches, digestive disturbances, and other symptoms have begun to clear up spontaneously.

During after-care the benefits seem to snowball. As physical complaints ease and treatment restores hope for the future, appetites improve and, with them, nutrition. As nutrition improves, energy level rises. As energy level rises and available time increases (because family responsibilities are again being shared), exercise and enjoyable activities such as sports and dancing increase. These in turn further increase energy level.

Improved nutrition has also shown up in clearer eyes, more vibrant skin, and a reduction in compulsive eating. These qualities, reflected daily in the mirror, reinforce a self-esteem that has been rekindled in treatment and often provide the incentive to take off extra pounds and give more care to grooming. These steps further increase self-esteem.

As both spouses begin to feel better physically, have more energy, and again take some wholesome pride in their own bodies, their long-lost sexuality can be rediscovered. This step, however, is not likely to be an easy one. Both parties have probably lost their sense of a sexual identity —a problem that may need to be explored in private after-care sessions with a trained counselor. If sexual difficulties persist, they should seek specialized professional help early in the recovery period.

The Emotional Potential

The emotions, more than any other aspect of the person, are the objects of alcoholism treatment. In primary care a client begins to get in touch with what he is really feeling, to distinguish between shades of feeling, and to give them names. Most of all, he learns to own them and to express them to the counselor as they arise. As he pours out the burden of negative feelings that have so long been held in, he can begin to feel a few positive emotions, like relief, hope, appreciation, compassion, and trust.

In after-care he can experience what it is to share his feelings freely with the rest of the family—perhaps for the first time. At the same time he learns to hear similar sharing from the others and to accept it, as a reflection of their reality and, where appropriate, as feedback on his own expressed feelings or his behavior. Now he discovers in more depth the joy of the positive feelings that can come from a free, open, loving relationship with others.

There are many emotions to recognize again and old patterns of

repression to break. The work will go on for a long time, out into the recovery phase. Like an unused muscle, one's capacity for feeling can atrophy. So little honest feeling has been expressed in this family that it will take time to learn how to do it.

The Social Potential

Another unrealized capacity that gets direct attention in treatment is the social potential. The trust and honest expression of feelings that the family member learns in his relationship to the counselor in primary care are necessary first steps to honest, intimate relationships in the larger world. At this stage he also has an opportunity to try these new ways of relating in a treatment group of his peers.

When the family comes together in after-care, he has an even better place to try his social wings, this time in a context that matters a great deal to him. He learns to give and to receive, to assert and to allow, to appreciate and to be appreciated. As his emotional potential develops, so will his social potential. The feelings that he has come to own in himself and accept in others will form a bridge between him and them.

A continuation of therapy groups and support groups, like AA, Al-anon, and Alateen, into the recovery period will offer continuing interchange with others who can be patient yet honest in their feedback because they know personally what it is to have to relearn these skills. Each family member's personal plan for recovery should also include some club memberships, discussion groups, volunteer work, or other activities that involve working and playing with others. The family's growing capacity to have fun will enhance these new relationships.

The Mental Potential

In one sense the mind has been active—indeed, far too active—all during the course of the family disease. It has been a harsh dictator, controlling or inhibiting every word, every action. The problem was that it was the *unconscious* mind that did most of the controlling. It was a *mad* dictator, acting on too little information and too much fear and compulsion. Facts, logic, honest feeling, and straight feedback played little part in its functioning.

In treatment the long-ignored reason was reactivated. First among the counselor's priorities was to free family members from the denial and delusion that had so long kept them from using their mental potentials to improve their lives. From the first pre-intervention sessions, he began educating them—about the disease, family dynamics, the nature of emotions, the family roles, all the factual material that underlay the work he was doing with them simultaneously at a feeling level. Sometimes the teaching was didactic; more often it was experiential.

As after-care work began to be reflected in the family's everyday life, opening up the system and clearing the long obstructed channels of communication, the individual minds gradually had more, and more reliable, data to work with. Some of these data concerned the objective reality of their lives, but more important were those that concerned the other members' subjective realities—their feelings—which collectively formed the real context of family living. Firmly grounded in this, the mental potential could at last function effectively.

Workshops can be an excellent way of helping the mental potential continue to develop. Treatment centers often offer programs on goal-setting and decision-making, family communication, dealing with depression, developing self-worth, learning to be assertive, handling anger, having fun without chemicals, and other issues common to alcoholic families. In these, all the potentials are developed *through* the mental potential. The workshops usually begin late in primary care or early in after-care and continue into the recovery phase, presenting subjects appropriate for each stage of treatment. Similar workshops are often available through other sources in the community, and these too can be useful.

After the family is on its own, such workshops can be especially helpful. As recovery unfolds, the choice of subjects can gradually shift from solving their problems to enriching their lives. Once the mental potential has been freed from denial, delusion, and compulsion, the possibilities for learning are unlimited.

The Spiritual Potential

That unquenchable spark in each of us that we call spirit is often flickering so weakly that it is barely visible by the time an alcoholic family comes into treatment. In a few cases the Enabler may have gathered her exhausted resources around it and fanned it to sustain her. More commonly, however, I find that this potential source of comfort and hope has been abandoned.

When I mention the word *spiritual,* many families confuse it with *religious.* Their immediate image is of church-going as they have experienced it (or perhaps I should say, perceived it, for their perception may not have been an accurate picture of the real experience at all). They think of phoney holiness, reluctant charity, self-righteousness, people with plastic smiles and a sort of neuter niceness. Most of all they remember the strict moral rules rigidly applied under penalty of eternal damnation, a fate often described in colorful and terrifying detail.

It is hardly surprising that people whose daily existence has been so filled with guilt, shame, anger, delusion, and compulsiveness would fix upon the negative aspects of religious participation. Their feelings, and sometimes their behavior as well, seem to fly in the face of the religious code as they know it, and they expect to be judged as harshly by God, the pastor, and their fellow parishioners as they are currently judging themselves. In self-defense they reject the whole thing.

In an organized religious group the individual member may at least choose how much of his personal time, energy, and commitment he wishes to invest, but pursuing personal spirituality outside an institutional structure is even more demanding. It asks more than most harried, emotionally impoverished members of an alcoholic family can give, so few attempt it.

Recovery of the spiritual potential begins with the first rays of hope that life can be different—at the point of intervention for the Dependent, at the very prospect of intervening for the family. Hope is an emotion deeply rooted in the spirit. As hope returns, life can begin to take on meaning again, and the battered psyche can find the strength it needs to start rebuilding all its potentials. The wise counselor nurtures hope tenderly and helps the client use it to fuel their work together.

In AA, of course, the spiritual potential is used as a base for recovery from the very beginning. The second of the Twelve Steps calls for alcoholics to "believe that a Power greater than ourselves can restore us to sanity." Wisely, AA allows the individual to define this Power in his own way.

As the recovering person gets into clearer touch with both his inner feelings and the outer reality of his world, he becomes ready to pursue his spirituality more actively. If he was formerly religious, he may return to the church he left. Or, like those who have had no earlier affiliation, he may choose to explore new territories of the spirit through reading and attending gatherings of various sorts for a first-hand experience of other traditions. (This may well be a place where the various members of a family display their differentness.)

These explorations will continue into the recovery period. I have known many recovering alcoholics, and family members, too, for whom a joyful new relationship to the larger universe was the dominant reality of their lives.

During after-care the counselor raises the question of personal values with the family. I like to use the simple form shown here, on which I have each member mark the extent to which he feels he is living up to each of the values he holds. If anyone has a value that is important to him and not shown on the form, we add it. Then I ask him to shade the area between the level he has marked and the 100 percent performance line. This is the gap between reality and hopes. The wider it is, the greater his anxiety will be, and the lower his self-worth. Though the chart

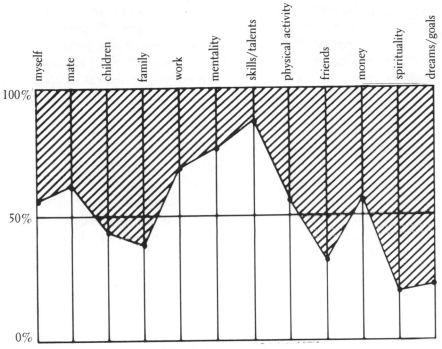

Life Satisfaction Chart

is an obvious way to check on whether he is trying hard enough, I find it even more useful as a vehicle to encourage people to take a second look at their values. Often alcoholic families are quite unrealistic about what they expect of themselves and others. I also have family members compare their charts, because family group values must somehow be adjusted to accommodate the individual values of every member.

This kind of clear definition gives each person some solid ground on which to go on constructing his future in the recovery period. Though his values may change over time, he is now equipped to understand *how* he is changing and to adapt his value system without throwing away positive values with those he has outgrown.

The Volitional Potential

Frozen stiffly into roles that dictated their responses to the people and events of their lives, the members of the alcoholic family long perceived themselves as having few choices. While they remained in their sick system, they were right. Their only alternative to the status quo was to stop the merry-go-round and get off. That is exactly what happened when someone in the family decided to initiate intervention.

Intervening is a clear and positive choice for all who participate in it. And on the day of intervention the Dependent faces an equally clear demand that *he* make a choice. These two choices, when made in favor of recovering health, can be the wedge that will open all their lives to a wider and wider range of choices.

During primary care the focus is mostly on freeing each person from the compulsion that keeps his will enslaved. As he begins to see that he does have alternatives, that he simply has not been free to look at them, he can begin to rebuild his volitional potential. In after-care he learns to use experience, information, and imagery of possible outcomes to help him make wise decisions. The counselor will encourage all family members to expand their horizons and thus their possible choices. As a natural next step to defining their values, he will help them explore their options and weigh their choices in order to actualize their values in their personal worlds. Begun in after-care, this process will continue to develop and gradually become a routine part of their post-treatment lives.

The problems they face, individually and as a family, offer plenty of opportunities for decision-making—getting or changing jobs, rebuilding family relationships, finding new kinds of recreation without drinking, and many more.

Ending formal treatment with after-care does not mean that the alcoholic family does not continue to need support far into the recovery period. But the time has come for them to reach out farther for that support. Today there are many kinds of therapy and growth groups where people can find understanding, support, and honest feedback from others who are also pursuing a greater wholeness. Such groups may be sponsored by the treatment center itself, but they can also be found through local colleges, holistic health clinics, growth centers, and other community organizations.

Whatever other resources the family finds, there is one that I consider paramount—AA, with Al-anon and Alateen for family members. We will take a closer look at these fellowships in the next chapter.

CHAPTER 16

AA as a Treatment Ally

IN THE LAST half century two strong yet distinct traditions have grown up, each offering an effective method for dealing with the tragedy of alcoholism. One is Alcoholics Anonymous (AA); the other, the alcoholism treatment profession. They have developed parallel to one another and actually share many of the same beliefs about the nature of the disease and what must be done to arrest it, yet they have markedly different styles and far less interaction than one might expect. Why? Does the separation serve any useful purposes? If so, what are they? If not, why does it persist, and should something be done about it?

Because of my deep personal dedication to both traditions, I would like to explore these questions here. But first, a little history.

The oldest currently accepted method of helping alcoholics, and probably the one with the most successes to its credit, is AA. Founded in 1935 by two alcoholics in search of recovery for themselves, it today embraces thousands of local groups in thousands of communities. Its members come from all social, economic, and cultural backgrounds, and from ninety countries of the world.

It is an informal fellowship of men and women who have discovered that they cannot control their use of alcohol, have admitted it, and have joined together to share their experience, strength, and hope in order to help one another and anyone else who may turn to AA to achieve sobriety. Some join at an advanced stage of alcoholism, after their lives have already been shattered; others join much earlier, when they realize that alcohol is interfering with normal, healthy living.

THE TWELVE STEPS OF AA

1. We admitted we were powerless over alcohol—that our lives had become unmanageable.
2. We came to believe that a Power greater than ourselves could restore us to sanity.
3. We made a decision to turn our will and our lives over to the care of God as we understood Him.
4. We made a searching and fearless moral inventory of ourselves.
5. We admitted to God, to ourselves, and to another human being, the exact nature of our wrongs.
6. We were entirely ready to have God remove all these defects of character.
7. We humbly asked Him to remove our shortcomings.
8. We made a list of all persons we had harmed, and became willing to make amends to them all.
9. We made direct amends to such people wherever possible, except when to do so would injure others.
10. We continued to take personal inventory and, when we were wrong, promptly admitted it.
11. We sought through prayer and meditation to improve our conscious contact with God as we understood Him, praying only for knowledge of His will for us and the power to carry that out.
12. Having had a spiritual awakening as the result of these steps, we tried to carry this message to alcoholics, and to practice these principles in all our affairs.

AA is not connected with any religious denomination or any other group or cause. It has no hard and fast rules, no fees, and only a minimum of organization. Its goal is personal sobriety, not the reform of others, and members are never recruited. Newcomers are warmly welcomed, however, and the only requirement for membership is a sincere desire to stop drinking.

Weekly meetings consist mostly of talks by recovering members, who share their experiences in achieving sobriety, and reports by newer members on the latest steps they have taken in that direction. All sharing is informal and voluntary. Underlying everything that is said is the AA prescription for recovery—the Twelve Steps. Through listening and learning, trusting, sharing, and fellowship, AA members together undertake to rebuild their lives.

Wherever a meeting may be held, and whoever the participants may be, the format is the same, so much so that even in a strange city members can go to an AA meeting and feel at home. In large metropolitan areas one can find a meeting nearly any hour of the day, any day of the week. Many members attend two or three meetings a week, to keep themselves focused on the solution instead of the problem—on recovery instead of their need for a drink.

For relatives and friends of alcoholics, there are two related yet independent fellowships—Al-anon for adults and Alateen for teenagers. Their purpose is to offer those whose lives are intimately entwined with the alcoholic's—and therefore with his disease—a source of support, information, and learning through others who have successfully handled the same problems. Admitting that they are part of the family disease, members follow AA's Twelve Steps. They also use the sharing format for meetings. People are welcome in these groups whether or not the alcoholic in their lives is participating in AA. In fact, family membership in Al-anon and Alateen can be a prelude to his taking the important first step toward sobriety.

The other approach to helping alcoholics is a much more recent development than AA. Professional treatment for chemical dependency (on either alcohol or other drugs) has emerged as a distinct specialty only in the last ten or fifteen years.

This field embraces two broad groups of workers. The first consists of those who have been trained specifically as counselors or specialists in any of a variety of available programs (one-year internships at treatment centers, two- and four-year college courses, and certification programs that are conducted in a number of states). The second group includes physicians, psychologists, nurses, teachers, and other helping professionals who by attending training workshops have qualified themselves to add this specialty to their existing professional work.

SIMILARITIES BETWEEN AA AND TREATMENT

The differences between AA and professional alcoholism treatment are immediately evident. Less apparent, but to me much more significant, are their similarities. There is a wider base of shared principles than most people in either tradition recognize. Both AA and the alcoholism treatment profession hold that:

1. Alcoholism is a disease.
2. Since it is a disease, no one is to blame.
3. The disease involves the whole person—body, mind, and spirit.
4. The disease involves the whole family, with those close to the alcoholic deeply affected by, and affecting, its course.
5. It cannot be cured, but it can be arrested and its damage healed.
6. To arrest it, the alcoholic must stop drinking immediately, completely, and permanently.
7. He also must change both his attitudes and his behavior, literally transforming his life.
8. The responsibility for these changes rests on the alcoholic himself because only he can make them.
9. He cannot make them, however, without help.
10. One powerful source of help is the caring concern of another person, one who cares enough to risk being honest.
11. Another source of help is the group, where the alcoholic can hear the experiences of other alcoholics, share his own, and get frank feedback.
12. The alcoholic must learn to be honest with himself, feeling his true feelings and seeing his actions as they really are.
13. He must learn to be honest with others as well, saying what he really feels and letting them say what they feel.
14. An important part of recovery is rebuilding the alcoholic's shattered self-worth.
15. Lasting recovery requires continuing effort by the individual with support from friends and family.
16. Literature, films, and lectures are valuable aids in teaching the alcoholic about his disease, motivating him to change, and facilitating his attempts to do so.
17. All the above principles, except number 6, apply equally to other members of the alcoholic family.

DIFFERENCES BETWEEN AA AND TREATMENT

At a practical level there are, of course, many obvious differences between these two approaches (as the long list on page 210 will attest). One is informal and social, the other structured and scientific, bred from a union of medical and social sciences. One is nonprofessional, offering the wisdom of those who have suffered the disease and found sobriety; the other is professional, offering the wisdom of those trained in a scientific paradigm. Even the environments in which they operate speak clearly of these differences: AA's casual gathering of peers over coffee cups offers the new member friendly acceptance and understanding; the consulting room or hospital setting of treatment, on the other hand, reflects the disease nature of alcoholism, offering both a reminder that the victim is not to be blamed and a source of hope that, like other diseases, this one can be treated with some success.

These differences are not so much a matter of principle as of form. Nevertheless, they have contributed to the distance that exists between the two traditions—distance, and often mutual suspicion.

AA members tend to feel a layman's distrust of any so-called expert, especially when his expertise concerns the mind, and most especially when he is purporting to treat a condition that he has not personally experienced and they have. They sometimes see the very objectivity of science as cold, its workings inscrutable, its motives suspect, its results doubtful. Treatment professionals, for their part, are equally dubious of what they often see as a motley bunch of true believers, amateurs with no tools but folk wisdom, religion, and tales of their own mistakes. Admittedly, I am exaggerating both views here to clarify the point, but the general attitudes of orthodoxy in one's own position and suspicion of the other's are real and widely held.

The matter of religion seems to be a particularly difficult hurdle for some professionals, largely due to a misunderstanding of the AA position. (This misunderstanding is also an obstacle to membership for many alcoholics who are otherwise attracted to AA.)

The key to understanding just what kind of spiritual commitment AA does imply seems to lie in the wording of the Second Step (in spite of the fact that the word *God* is used in some of the later steps). There the founding brothers wisely used very broad language: "Came to believe that *a Power greater than ourselves* could restore us to sanity" (italics mine). Other nonspecific terms are also used freely: a *Higher Power, God as we understood him,* and the *group conscience,* an idea that I have found only in the meetings and literature of AA. Granted, individual AA members do frequently talk about God, but in a society where the Judeo-Christian tradition is so dominant, this is hardly surprising.

In practice, the loosest kind of personal interpretation is enough to

SOME PRACTICAL DIFFERENCES
BETWEEN ALCOHOLICS ANONYMOUS
AND PROFESSIONAL ALCOHOLISM TREATMENT

Alcoholics Anonymous	*Professional Alcoholism Treatment*
Basis: Personal experience of other alcoholics.	Basis: Scientific research and theory; accepted psychotherapeutic practice.
Program: The Twelve Steps.	Program: Planned course of medical and psychological treatment.
Trust placed in "Higher Power."	Trust placed in counselor.
Individual totally responsible for recovery.	Individual totally responsible but initially motivated by intervention and later assisted by professional counseling.
Milieu: Nonprofessional and social.	Milieu: Professional and clinical.
Caring offered in a personal relationship.	Caring offered in a professional relationship.
Individual help given in informal private conversations.	Individual help given in structured private counseling.
Sharing in leaderless group.	Sharing in group led by trained counselor.
Individual participation in meetings optional.	Individual participation in treatment program expected.
Dependent and family attend separate groups.	Dependent and family treated together in some stages of treatment.
Help available any time.	Help available by appointment.
Individual takes Twelve Steps at his own pace.	Individual progresses according to treatment program timetable.
Individual assesses own progress and readiness to take next step.	Counselor assesses individual's readiness to take next step.
Period of participation open-ended.	Period of participation limited.

"work the program," as members put it. The "Higher Self," the "Life Force," "Nature"—anything that the individual believes is above and beyond, stronger and wiser than, himself will do. Even most atheists can comfortably find something to meet that criterion. One member puts it this way:

> The house that AA helps a man build for himself is different for each occupant, because each occupant is his own architect. For many, AA is a kind of going home—a return, like the Prodigal Son's, to the house and the faith of his fathers. To others, it is a never-ending journey into lands they did not dream existed. It does not matter into which group one falls.[1]

As AA spreads around the world and embraces cultures in which *God* is not the accepted name for the Ultimate, this definition is necessarily getting looser all the time.

Another important cause of alienation between AA and the treatment profession has little to do with alcoholism per se or the views peculiar to either group. It is simply the natural competitiveness and jockeying for position that seem to be so common in human affairs whenever two persons or systems must share the same ground. Unfortunately, the price for this kind of "turf protection" is often paid by innocent third parties—in this case, alcoholics and their families.

After long association with both Al-anon and the treatment profession, I am convinced that these two approaches are not incompatible. On the contrary, their very differences are a compelling argument that *we need both, working in harmony to achieve more than either could alone.* At some stages in the recovery process AA can be more helpful; at other stages, treatment. Some individual and family needs are filled better by AA, others by treatment.

Although all the personal potentials are addressed to some degree by both, the spiritual and the social are nurtured more by AA, the physical and the mental by treatment. The emotional and the volitional, on the other hand, receive much attention from both, each in its own way. At such times the efforts of each are reinforced by those of the other.

In my own work with chemical dependency problems, I have made membership in AA an important piece of the treatment package. In fact, I use the Twelve Steps as a framework for progress in treatment as well

[1] *A Member's Eye View of Alcoholics Anonymous.* New York, NY: Alcoholics Anonymous World Services, Inc., 1970. (Available from the General Service Office of Alcoholics Anonymous, Box 459, Grand Central Station, New York, NY 10017.)

as in the AA program, giving the client a unified goal and thus strongly reinforcing it.

We who work in the treatment profession should also remember that there are thousands of victims of alcoholism who will not find our help readily accessible, whether geographically or emotionally. For alcoholics who are young, single, or homeless, AA often seems to be an easier first step. And in smaller communities, the local AA group is usually the only help available.

Let's take a closer look at what treatment might be like for a family that was able to make use of both sources of help.

THE STORY OF GEORGE

George W., after drinking heavily for more than twelve years, had become totally dependent on alcohol. Last year he lost his job and soon after received a stern warning from Dr. Brown, the family physician, that his liver was in bad shape. His wife, Anne, felt desperate, but she did not know where to turn for help. At a friend's suggestion she called AA. A kindly sounding voice on the other end of the line invited her to an Al-anon meeting the next evening. That was the first step in a new direction for the whole family. (Another family might have begun their recovery from the other side of the fence—at a treatment center.)

Anne felt nervous as she drove to the meeting, but her fears were soon put to rest. At the door she was greeted by two smiling women and a man. "I'm Marie." "I'm Evelyn, and this is Jim. We use only first names." No questions, just a warm hello. Anne knew at once that she had been right to come.

During the meeting several members talked about their family problems and the pain they were feeling—the same problems and pain she had been trying to handle all alone for so many years. Others told how they had managed similar situations, sharing ideas that they had found successful—and unsuccessful, for there was no pretense, no covering up. Through the whole interchange was a gentle sense of caring, understanding, and appreciation for one another's hurting. Anne did not join in the discussion, but when the meeting was over, she felt as if a little of the load she'd been carrying for so long had been lifted. She walked out of the meeting room with a handful of reading material about alcoholism, AA, and Al-anon, plus several phone numbers of members she could call at any hour, day or night, if she needed help.

A couple of weeks later, Anne did tell her story, ending with her talk with Dr. Brown. He had recommended that, since George refused to get help for himself, *she* see a counselor at the Elmridge Hospital treatment center. She confided she had been agonizing over that advice for a month now. To go seemed like such a disloyal thing for a wife to do; George would blow his top! When she finished talking, one of the Al-anon members gently disagreed. So did another, then another. They pointed out that it would, on the contrary, take a great deal of love to risk George's anger in order to help him. "Tough love" they called it. By the end of the evening they had convinced her that the real disloyalty would be to let George go on drinking himself to death. The next day, knowing that she was backed by the moral and—if she needed it— practical support of her new Al-anon friends, she made the appointment at Elmridge.

(If Anne had lived so far from the nearest treatment facility that she could not go there for weekly visits, she might have found a physician, family counselor, or other professional in her community with special training to help victims of chemical dependency. Here again she could have turned to the other Al-anon members for advice.)

It took only a few minutes with the counselor for Anne to know that she had made another right decision. He seemed to know what had been happening in their family even before she told him, and he said he thought he could help. First, he explained all about the disease of alcoholism. Anne noticed that his ideas were quite similar to those she had found in the AA pamphlets. When she told him that she was going to Al-anon, he seemed pleased, saying that the center would be using the principles of the Twelve Steps in treatment, too.

Near the end of their hour together, he told her about a process called intervention, explained how it worked, and asked if she was willing to take the risk. She said she was, and they made another appointment. The counselor asked her to bring her son Robbie, 15, along the next time.

For five weeks Anne and Robbie met with the counselor. He helped them in dealing with some of their own feelings as well as preparing to confront George. Anne also went on attending Al-anon, where the concern and experience of the other members gave her some good ideas for managing problems at home. They also bolstered her resolve to intervene with George when she became frightened and tempted to give up. Meanwhile, Robbie started attending Alateen meetings and discovered, to his surprise, that he wasn't the only kid in the high school who had an alcoholic parent. The others had just never talked about their home problems, but then neither had he. It felt good to be able to tell someone how he felt—how confused and angry and scared he was—and to know he wasn't alone.

By the day they had set for the intervention, both Anne and Robbie were feeling stronger and more hopeful than they had in several years. The counselor had worked with each of them, helping them let out some of the feelings they had buried so long and so deeply that they didn't even know they had them. The whole picture of what had been happening at home was beginning to get clearer. They could now see that although George was the alcoholic, they too had been helping to make the situation sick and keep it that way.

The intervention had been carefully planned. Anne was nervous but determined. Dr. Brown came over to join them and added his medical prognosis to the avalanche of evidence they had prepared to convince George he needed help. At first George shouted and blustered and threatened to walk out, but he didn't. After a little while he just sat looking blankly at the floor, pale and shaking. In the end he collapsed in tears and agreed to stop drinking and accept help. Anne had packed George's suitcase so he could enter Elmridge as an inpatient that afternoon. The counselor and Anne had made sure a room would be waiting for him.

Only people who have lived for years with an alcoholic could understand fully the relief and joy and hope Anne and Robbie felt that day. They could hardly wait until Wednesday to share the good news with their Al-anon and Alateen friends.

George was hospitalized at Elmridge for a month. He had both private and group counseling and began attending an AA group for patients. The counselor worked closely with the AA principles, using the Twelve Steps as a framework for George's program of recovery. By the time he was ready to leave the hospital, George had put on a few pounds, his color had improved, and he felt as though life might yet be worth living.

Meanwhile, Anne and Robbie had a few more individual appointments with the counselor. They also started going to peer group meetings at the center, Anne with other wives of alcoholics, Robbie with other teenagers. In some ways these were like Al-anon and Alateen meetings, but not exactly; for one thing they were always led by a trained counselor. They offered still another way for Anne and Robbie to learn more about themselves and the things they were doing to make their lives unmanageable.

The day George went home—a sober man—was a landmark day

for the whole family. They were all in this together and had all been working hard on their own parts of the problem. But George's leaving the hospital didn't mean they would sever their ties with Elmridge. They still had a lot of work to do as outpatients. George continued to attend meetings of the AA group, where he had made his first close friends in fifteen years—closer perhaps than ever before; because of the honesty required in AA, they *knew* him as no one ever had before. And Anne and Robbie continued to attend Al-anon and Alateen, where they too had found satisfying friendships.

(If there had been no local inpatient facility, the counselor would have recommended one in another community, or possibly a local hospital if its staff were sensitive to the special problems of chemical dependency. Unlike George, the alcoholic who is hospitalized out of town must, on release, make a transition from the familiar support group at the treatment center to an AA group back home, which he has never attended. Now the family's already warm ties to the companion Al-anon group can serve as a needed bridge.)

The first week George was home, the whole family went to see the counselor together, for the first time since the fateful day of the intervention. He told them that they had all done a lot of growing as individuals in the last few weeks and that now he would like to help them grow together as a family. They had a lot yet to learn—and unlearn, because they had developed such unhealthy ways of dealing with one another during the course of the illness.

From that time on, they all met with the counselor once a week. They were free to talk about problems that had arisen during the week or whatever else was on their minds. The counselor seemed to pay less attention to *what* they said than to *how* they said it. He would often interrupt the discussion to ask how they were feeling about what they had heard or to point out how they were reacting. They found that gradually they began to notice their feelings and reactions themselves, even when they were talking at home without the counselor. What they were learning also made them more sensitive to other people's feelings in their various group meetings.

During this period they shifted from three separate peer groups to a single group of four families who met with the counselor one evening a week. They had learned of other alcoholic families' problems in AA, Al-anon, and Alateen, and also in their peer groups, but this was the first time they had had a chance to observe a whole family together in the same meeting. They could see a lot of reasons these families were having frictions—and realized that they were creating some of the same problems for themselves. At the same time the other families could observe them and give them feedback on how their family looked from the outside.

After a couple of months of after-care, they found that their family discussions were no longer ending in angry words or tears or someone's having to give in to keep peace. They could talk about their problems and find answers that satisfied everyone. Best of all, they discovered they could actually enjoy being together. They spent a lot more time now talking about happy things—family outings, news of AA friends, plans for the future.

The counselor began to talk to them about the future, too. What did they want for themselves as individuals in the months and years ahead? As a family? Those were questions that they hadn't dared face for so long that at first they had trouble answering. He helped them look at their present growth, their possibilities, their values, and their dreams. Gradually they started to lay some plans for how they could make their hopes become realities. The success and happiness of recovering families they had met in AA and Al-anon gave them confidence that it could be done.

After three months of family care, the counselor announced that he felt they were ready to continue their recovery on their own. He reminded them that although the alcoholism had been arrested, it would never be totally cured. If any of them slipped back into his old ways, he might find himself back in trouble. To keep their gains and go on growing, they would need some source of support. The counselor recommended that they continue attending their AA, Al-anon, and Alateen meetings indefinitely, and they each knew in their hearts that they would. The warmth and understanding they had found there was one of the most valued parts of their new lives.

AN INTERPLAY OF TWO TRADITIONS

The story I have just told you is typical of the families I see in treatment. The interplay of AA and professional care, acting independently but in harmony, creates a more complete environment for recovery than either can alone. The focus may shift from one to the other as the work progresses, but always the second is there reinforcing and being reinforced. To illustrate, I have plotted George and Anne's experience on the following chart, using italics to indicate the dominant force at a particular time or in a particular area of help. (For the clearest understanding, read the italic entry first.)

AA/AL-ANON/ALATEEN	PROFESSIONAL TREATMENT

Pre-Intervention

Al-anon offers the Enabler a readily contacted, nonthreatening source of information, understanding, practical help, and friendship—a supportive base from which to take the next step of seeking professional help.	
Group provides continuing help, friendship, and support for intervention.	*Counselor furnishes scientific information on alcoholism and the family's role in it, psychological first aid for family members, and experienced guidance in planning intervention with Dependent.*

Primary Care

AA group meets at hospital so that inpatients can participate.	*Residential treatment provides detoxification care and individual counseling for Dependent.*
Twelve Steps set forth spiritual and behavioral framework for recovery.	Inpatient program incorporates Twelve Steps into treatment.
Al-anon and Alateen meetings encourage family members to be honest with themselves about their feelings and their behavior. *Individual members are available for crisis peer counseling at any hour, any day.*	*Family members receive individual counseling as outpatients to break through their denial and delusion, to free depressed feelings, and to end compulsive, role-prescribed behavior.*
AA's Twelve Steps provide guidelines for family members as well.	Counselor uses Twelve Steps as part of family treatment.
Family members continue to attend leaderless Al-anon and Alateen groups.	*Family members attend peer group sessions led by trained counselor.*

AA/AL-ANON/ALATEEN	PROFESSIONAL TREATMENT
All three fellowships provide continuing source of individual friendships and group social activities.	Counselor encourages family members to begin rebuilding their social potentials, recommending Al-anon and Alateen as ideal places to do so.
	Treatment sees Dependent through physical crisis of withdrawal and volitional crisis of seeking sobriety. Set on the road to health, he is released from the hospital.
Friends who have experienced it themselves share the family's joy when the Dependent comes home, standing ready with support and help for the transition to a new life.	

After-Care

Meetings continue to give opportunity for experience in honest communication.	*All family members receive after-care counseling together to learn principles of open, honest communication. All also participate in multifamily group.*
Joint AA/Al-anon social activities give families new alternatives for recreation together and with friends.	Counselor encourages family to find new ways to spend time together and new ways for the Dependent to enjoy himself without alcohol; he supports active involvement in AA/Al-anon events.

Recovery

Participation in fellowships continues to offer ongoing friendship, social network, support system, and opportunity to grow by helping others find health and happiness again (Twelfth Step).	Counselor strongly recommends at close of treatment that family continue AA/Al-anon participation indefinitely.

The mutual reinforcement of AA and professional treatment programs springs naturally from their shared philosophy of the disease nature of alcoholism and the extent to which the entire family is involved. No conscious or planned cooperation is required. In fact, any formal collaboration would be contrary to AA's long tradition of independence from all other organizations and causes. In my opinion, the parallel but separate influences of the two are probably more effective than any kind of single, joint program might be anyway.

What *is* essential, however, is mutual respect between the two groups, with mutual support at the levels of the individual member on the one hand and the counselor on the other. The counselor should be aware and appreciative of the ways AA membership can facilitate the work his client is doing; at the same time, other AA members, in dealing with the client and his family, need to understand the powerful help professional treatment can give an individual in his efforts to "work the AA program."

In Minneapolis, where I practice, and other communities that are sophisticated in their understanding of alcoholism, this kind of mutual admiration is already developing. The benefits are clear, and thousands of alcoholic families have been the beneficiaries.

The common situation of an AA group's meeting (autonomously) within an alcoholism treatment center is one evidence of professional regard for AA. Conversely, the member quoted earlier has written:

> The oft-heard cry "AA is all you need" has the hollow ring of fear —fear that if any member dissents from the belief that AA is the one and only, the total and complete answer to all the alcoholic's ills, then all the other members will perish with him. . . . True freedom lies in the realization and calm acceptance of the fact that there may very well be no *perfect* answer. It remains then for each man to discover and to share whatever works for him.[2]

It is my personal hope that this book will help to widen the narrow bridge of understanding and acceptance that has been built. AA and the therapeutic professions are powerful potential allies, and they need each other.

[2] Ibid.

CHAPTER **17**

The Whole Counselor

ALCOHOLISM is a disease that stunts, fragments, and erodes the human personality. To try to help one of its victims become a whole and healthy person is a large task; to help a whole family of victims with interlocking pathologies is immeasurably larger. In fact, I know of few challenges any counselor or therapist faces that are more difficult. Treating alcoholic families tests not only what we know but what we *are*.

Working with families, whatever the problem they bring to us, is always an intricate business. Obviously, as you add more personalities to the therapeutic scene, you add to the difficulty of the job. But the progression is not merely arithmetic, for each new person also complicates the actions and interactions of the previous ones in a sort of geometric compounding. Small wonder it is that so many therapists prefer to see only one client at a time!

But even this is not the heart of the challenge. The real hazard is the *trap*.

In every dysfunctional family there is one central person who at some point became painfully trapped in his own personal dysfunction and began to spiral downward. Imagining that the source of the danger somehow lay in a hostile world outside himself, he threw up a massive system of defensive behavior. Its walls interfered with the normal flow of family life, and as other members tried to reach beyond them, they found themselves caught in a sort of emotional whirlpool—the same spiraling trap. They in turn developed defensive maneuvers, which were designed to protect them but only sucked them deeper into the trap.

Alcoholism is such a trap—a particularly powerful one, for total and inevitable destruction awaits its primary victim if he does not somehow find help. By a bitter sort of irony, the drink first slowly swallows the drinker; then, as though still not quenched, it proceeds to swallow everyone close to him, too, often by transforming *them* into drinkers as an intermediate step.

In order to communicate with a family at all, a counselor must take the risk of stepping into its whirlpool in spite of the danger. *The challenge is to enter the family system and yet stay out of the family trap.* If he, too, should get caught in it, he would be as powerless to help them as they are to help themselves.

His safety lies in entering the system but not becoming part of it. He must enter by his own rules and on his own terms. He must step in with one foot while keeping the other firmly planted in reality. In so doing, of course, he becomes an intruder, whom the family will perceive (correctly) as a threat to the present unhealthy balance of their system. Since any system tends to preserve its status quo, even though it be precarious and uncomfortable, the family members will unconsciously try to pull the counselor into their game.

If they succeed, he becomes part of the family problem rather than part of the solution—he becomes a *Professional Enabler.*

THE PROFESSIONAL ENABLER

Any counselor or other helping professional who engages in the same kinds of dysfunctional behavior as the family Enabler—denial, avoidance, covering up, protecting, taking responsibility for someone else, either the Dependent or another family member—is acting as a Professional Enabler. In so doing, the professional stands between the client and crisis, the only thing that will motivate him to make the hard but necessary changes in his life.

Why on earth would a professional person be an Enabler? The answer, of course, is that like the spouse he does it unknowingly. Sometimes, if he does not work regularly with alcoholics and their families, he may simply be uninformed, either about alcoholism as a disease or about the family as a dynamic system. He may not realize that helping in the usual sense of the word—that is, trying to fix things—is *not* helpful in this situation. It will only prolong the problem.

One example of professional enabling is the common practice of seeing an alcoholic by himself. It would probably never occur to most physicians or lawyers to require that a client with a possible drinking problem bring his spouse to every appointment. Indeed, such a demand might even seem unreasonable. But a deeper understanding of the delusion so characteristic of alcoholics and an appreciation of the extent to which other family members are implicated in the disease would tell the professional that he cannot possibly make an accurate assessment of the client's situation by seeing him alone. The picture he presents will not make sense because it is both distorted and incomplete. If the professional accepts it as presented, any solutions he tries are doomed to fail because he is trying to solve the wrong problem or cure the wrong ailment.

There are other ways, too, in which ignorance about how alcoholism affects a family can make the best-intentioned efforts counterproductive. We will consider some of them later in this chapter. First, however, let's look at another source of enabling impulses—the one most common in counselors and therapists—namely, low self-worth.

A counselor may doubt his worth as a person and so be afraid that the client family will reject him. Or, he may doubt his professional skill and so be afraid that others will judge him incompetent. Many counselors suffer self-doubts at both levels.

The difficulty lies not in the fact that a counselor has these fears but rather that he has not faced them honestly and dealt with them, so he takes them with him into the treatment relationship. While he still thinks his goal is recovery for the family, unconsciously his first priority is to relieve his own deep fears. His concern with winning the clients' approval and with treating the case "successfully" get in the way of his work. He will be tempted to tell the clients what they want to hear, not what he honestly sees and feels. He will try to find ready-made answers rather than leading the family through their pain to find answers for themselves. In the all-important matter of self-worth, he will be unable to nurture the family members because he comes to them so needy himself.

As we have seen, working with an alcoholic family is demanding. Each person is putting out signals to elicit the stereotyped response that his role invites, while the other family members are responding predictably to the cues and putting out signals of their own. An unwary counselor can be trapped into playing their game with them. He may soon find himself taking responsibility for the Dependent, sympathizing with the Enabler, admiring the Hero, rejecting the Scapegoat, ignoring the Lost Child, and failing to take the Mascot seriously— "just like one of the family."

In earlier chapters we saw how each family member was in turn snagged in some area of personal weakness and swept into the family trap. The same fate awaits a counselor who has unrecognized weaknesses and vulnerabilities of his own. If he is preoccupied with defending his own fragile self-worth and giving out his own double-level messages, he cannot be fully present to catch all the subtle body language, double-level messages, and other clues to private feelings and group process in the family. By failing to be in touch with his own feelings, he has lost the sensitivity to be in touch with the clients' as well. And if he cannot sense their feelings, then he is left with nothing to relate to but their defenses. In the end he becomes part of the dysfunctional system, one more player in the old family game of denial, where everyone responds to the defenses of others with defenses of his own. (See diagram, page 224.)

Both alcoholism treatment and family therapy rely on the counselor's honest, feeling-based communication to elicit a reply in kind from the client. But when the counselor is himself issuing manipulative, defense-based communications, the whole process breaks down. His words and actions become visibly inconsistent, a tip-off that they are also incongruent with his feelings. Clients are quick to pick up on such signs of weakness and lose respect for him as a model of authenticity and congruence. Because the counselor has broken his own cardinal rule, he loses control of the treatment process.

It is quite probable, however, that in his eagerness to please he has already forfeited the initiative to his clients. He yields to their demands for easy answers. He makes himself available at their pleasure, tolerating phone calls at all hours of the night or weekend. He referees their disagreements, coaches their decisions, meets their requests for "advice" (only to find that his comments are sometimes used as a club by one member of the family to beat other members into submission).

All the while he is scurrying around to solve problems, he has the nagging feeling that he is not really being effective. He is putting out brush fires while the whole forest is going up in flame. He feels tired, used, lonely because he has not made satisfying human contact with any member of the family.

Weeks pass, but nothing constructive seems to happen. The truth is that nothing will, because the deep, personal level where recovery takes place has not been touched. Clients and counselor alike feel discouraged,

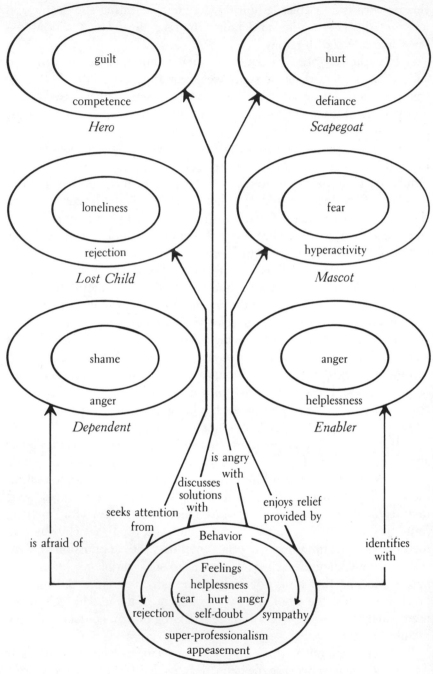

The Ineffective Counselor

and problems within the family worsen. Family members have lost faith in the counselor's ability to help them and, lacking any other source of hope, are reinforced in their old defenses. He, in turn, loses faith both in the family's natural impulse to health and self-worth, and in his own skills for helping them achieve those goals. His defenses, too, are reinforced. In his desperate need to see some progress, he may mistake the family's growing rigidity for strength.

Plagued by his fear of being seen as incompetent, the counselor may begin to hide behind a facade of false professionalism—jargon, intellectualizing, long impersonal discussions of test results—in an attempt to convince others and himself that he is truly well trained and effective. But inside he feels more and more angry because the clients do not change, guilty because he has not motivated them to, and frustrated by his own inadequacy.

The counselor's fragile self-worth grows even shakier as his original fears of rejection or incompetency are confirmed. Eventually, he may find relief by ending the treatment prematurely. Just as often, however, he needs the clients so much that he clings to the painful relationship, sometimes long after it would have been appropriate to terminate it.

Ironically, the counselor with low self-worth ends up converting his own worst fears into realities: his efforts at treatment do fail; his colleagues do see that he has failed; and the family, in their disappointment and despair, do reject him. Most of all, perhaps, *he* knows that he has been incompetent, and the old self-doubts are deepened.

Let me repeat that the counselor's problem is not that he has some doubts about himself, but rather that he has not brought those doubts out into the open, looked at them, felt them fully no matter how painful they might be, then stayed in touch with them vigilantly so they would not contaminate the work with his clients.

The same pitfalls that have undone our hapless counselor await any other helping professional who tries to work with an alcoholic or someone in his family. Let's see how people in other specialties can, in their own ways, become Professional Enablers.

Enabling by a Psychiatrist

Any psychotherapist who is treating a client for alcoholism is in exactly the same situation as the alcoholism counselor. A psychiatrist, however, faces another possible trap. If an alcoholic comes to him complaining of anxiety or tension and the physical manifestations of addiction have not yet become obvious, the chances are the psychiatrist will prescribe tranquilizers and/or sedatives. Indeed, a patient who already knows so well the pain-relieving properties of chemicals is likely to press him for them.

Prescribing drugs in such cases is common psychiatric practice and certainly does not indicate incompetence on the part of the doctor. It does, however, suggest that he has not seriously considered the possibility that the patient may already have a problem with chemicals. In view of the fact that one in every ten Americans abuses alcohol to the point that it is interfering with his life—and one in every four, as a member of an alcoholic family, is at high risk of becoming an abuser—*this possibility must always be taken into account before prescribing mood-altering drugs.*

The consequences of adding prescription drugs to the picture where alcohol is already a problem are grave. For one thing, the additive effect between the chemicals will hasten progression of the disease and can in some instances be fatal. In addition, the psychiatrist, by unwittingly lending his prestigious support to the Dependent's claim that alcohol is not his real problem, reinforces his denial and sabotages efforts by family and friends to get him to stop drinking.

Enabling by a Physician

Like the psychiatrist, physicians of other specialties are often asked to treat conditions that are, unknown to them, secondary symptoms of alcoholism. Frequently these will be stress symptoms in the Enabler or the children. Some, however, particularly ulcers, may also be presented by the Dependent himself. Here again mood-altering drugs may be prescribed, with the same potential dangers. Those risks are present even when the patient is not personally abusing chemicals. As we have seen, other members of the alcoholic family are highly vulnerable to drug dependency.

Even without prescribing drugs, the unaware physician can reinforce alcoholism by exonerating it, by assuming that some other condition, such as generalized family stress, is the root problem.

Once again I would caution every physician to keep the epidemic proportions of alcoholism in this country ever in mind. Just a few judicious questions at the outset, when he is taking the patient's history, may be enough to confirm the presence or absence of alcoholism in the family. Where it is seriously suspected, the physician can perform the critical function of intervening with the family. There are few professional services he could offer that would contribute so much to his patient's long-term health.

Enabling by a Lawyer

Alcoholics have far more than their share of tangles with the law, particularly on traffic and assault charges. Since legal difficulties often attract community attention that is embarrassing and sometimes costly to the family, a lawyer will find himself under great pressure to try to get any implication of the Dependent's being "under the influence" stricken from the charge. If the client is also a friend, the lawyer will no doubt feel a personal desire to get the charge reduced, too.

But any lawyer who gets the drinking component removed from an assault charge, who has a drunken driving charge reduced to reckless driving, or convinces the authorities that his alcoholic client should not be detained because "jail is no place for a lady"—that lawyer is doing his client no kindness. He is contributing to the Dependent's denial by whitewashing the offense; he is keeping the Dependent from experiencing the full consequences of his behavior; and he is softening the crisis that might have brought the Dependent to treatment. In a word, he is enabling.

Similarly, the lawyer who is called upon to defend a Scapegoat against drug, theft, traffic, or other charges may be tempted to get him off with a light or even a suspended sentence. After all, the kid is young, he hasn't had an easy time at home, and isn't it a lawyer's job to get the best treatment he can for his client? Perhaps. But the Scapegoat's legal difficulties may be the only point at which this family will come into contact with community helpers. The lawyer who is aware that kids in trouble have a better than fifty-fifty chance of having an alcoholic parent can, instead of aborting the crisis, use it to direct the family toward treatment.

These will not be easy decisions for a lawyer. The compassionate course will seldom be the most comfortable for anyone concerned, and the risk of the clients' dismissing him is real. But for the lawyer the stakes are relatively low—at worst a few lost fees. For the alcoholic family the price of his acquiescing to their wishes is immeasurably higher.

Enabling by a Minister

Most professional people groan a bit at the thought of having to deal with alcoholics and their problems. They have learned by experience that their best efforts have often ended in no-change and frustration. Some—particularly psychotherapists and physicians—accept an alcoholic patient or client only reluctantly, more often discouraging him by delaying the first appointment, referring him to someone else, or treating him only for the acute presenting symptom and washing their hands of the situation as soon as possible.

For the minister, however, such indifference is unthinkable; it would violate the very essence of his professional mission. He has committed himself to serve—to help the helpless, comfort the afflicted, heal the sick of heart if he can. At the very least, he is committed to try. Unfortunately, the chances are that his training in theological school or seminary has given him little understanding of the complex problem of alcoholism and few tools for working with it.

However unequipped he may be, the minister is nevertheless one of the most frequented sources of support for beleaguered alcoholic families, particularly Enablers. The problem that a family presents may be the heart of their troubles—the Dependent's drinking. More often, though, it will be simply a symptom of the deeper disorder: marital problems, money woes, teenagers in trouble, any of the catalog of trials that afflict the alcoholic family.

In his earnest desire to help, the minister is likely to accept the problem as stated, to sympathize, advise, perhaps take some action himself to ameliorate the situation. He may even seem to improve matters—for a while. But all too soon the family are back, with the same problem or another of the many to which they are prey.

Lacking understanding of the condition that underlies their problems, the minister most likely does all the wrong things. He works with only one part of the problem—with the symptom rather than the disease, and often with only part of the family. He "helps" rather than letting the family feel their pain, which is life's warning that all is not well. He steps in between the family and the full impact of their crisis.

The well-meaning minister is, of course, doing the best he knows how. When he sees that it is never good enough, never really effective for long, he feels discouraged and inadequate.

On the other hand, ministers with a sophisticated understanding of alcoholism and training in the skills of intervention can be extremely valuable links between people in pain and the sources of care in the community. Theological schools and seminaries have over the last few years enriched their curricula with courses in psychological principles and the skills of pastoral counseling. I hope that they will now extend that training to include what is probably the most ubiquitous problem of all, alcoholism.

Enabling by an Employer/Supervisor

An employer or job supervisor has much in common with the spouse Enabler. He spends many hours a day with the Dependent; his fortunes, status, and tranquility can all be sharply affected by the Dependent's advancing disease; and he makes many of the same enabling mistakes.

For a long time he denies the seriousness of the problem, covering up for the Dependent and, when necessary, assuming some of his responsibilities or redelegating them. He nags and threatens, perhaps, but puts off taking any decisive steps toward change, including recommending that the Dependent seek professional help.

The supervisor's inaction is rarely for lack of evidence. At first his employee showed only subtle signs that something was wrong. His output dropped; he performed erratically, sometimes still very well, sometimes poorly; he made mistakes and had accidents more frequently than before; he was often irritable; absenteeism increased; he seemed to be having money, marriage, and family troubles. In time more specific signs appeared: hangovers, long lunches, liquor on his breath (or telltale purifiers), "emergency" absences, and eventually drinking on the job. The signs are clear and well known to anyone familiar with alcoholic behavior.

Why does the supervisor put up with all this? His motives are much like the spouse Enabler's. First, he wants to avoid the personal embarrassment and possible criticism that will follow if outsiders discover he is tolerating an alcoholic in the department "family." Any attempt on his part to intervene may disturb the status quo, stir up unpleasantness, attract the attention of his superiors and other supervisors; and if it does not actually endanger his own position, it may at least cause him to lose the employee.

It is important to recognize that alcoholics often remain valuable employees long after dependency has a firm grip on their lives. Some manage to hold jobs for fifteen, even twenty-five years in spite of heavy drinking. The job is a matter of survival, for themselves, their families, *and their drinking.* For one thing, it offers a great basis for rationalizing: "How can you accuse me of drinking too much? Look how well I'm doing at work!" It also provides the income that is the lifeline to his supply.

The supervisor, like the spouse, is protecting a relationship that still offers enough positive values to be worth the hassle of preserving it. If he also happens to be a personal friend of the employee, he will share the motivation of affection as well.

So the alcoholic hangs on and the supervisor enables. He overlooks the Monday morning absences, lapses of memory, unpleasantness toward fellow workers, lagging productivity, and all the other problems of having an alcoholic on the work force. He fails for a long time to face the very real cost of these problems in lost time, mistakes, poor performance, accidents, reduced department morale, and administrative discontent.

When the advancing disease finally makes it impossible for the Supervisor-Enabler to go on playing his role, he usually "divorces" the alcoholic by discharging him, shunting him off to another department, or in some cases retiring him early. At last, the department's problem has been solved—but nothing has been done to help the employee.

Had the supervisor taken some action years earlier, as soon as he seriously suspected what the problem was, he might have saved the company a good worker, saved the family its livelihood, and saved the alcoholic his career and his self-respect—perhaps even his life. The loss is particularly regrettable when we consider the tremendous leverage that is available to the employer who is willing to use it.

Happily more and more employers *are* using it; many of the largest industries have now initiated their own programs of detection and intervention. So have the armed services. Personnel managers sit side by side with physicians and counselors in the workshops I give, for they know that salvaging a trained employee from impending addiction is not only humane—it's good business.

Enabling by a School Counselor

For many people the word *alcoholic* evokes an image of a grizzled skid row derelict, suffering the consequences of a lifetime of excess. In actuality, however, many of today's alcoholics are very young—some still in their teens. Alcohol, rejected by a large number of young people during the sixties in favor of other drugs, is once again the chemical-of-choice. As its use increases, in a society where mood-altering drugs have become a routine part of adolescent social life, I fear we can expect even greater numbers of juvenile alcoholics. In some communities nearly half the children now drink regularly before entering high school. Experience has shown that the younger abusive drinking begins, the faster it accelerates into dependency.

For the youthful Dependent, whatever his preferred drug, the school counselor is in a strategic position to intervene. Too often, however, counselors enable instead. They try to be helpful, hush up the problem, and get the young Dependent out of trouble. As long as his problems are in the spotlight, bringing him the attention he craves, he may seem to cooperate with the counselor. Then, just when it seems all is well, he will return to his old pattern, leaving the counselor feeling helpless and betrayed—classic Enabler feelings.

Granted, many school counselors' enabling is well intentioned, motivated by a compassionate concern for the student and a sincere desire to be helpful. The problem is that they do not understand the characteristics of chemical dependency or what actions on their own part will be *truly* helpful. Some counselors, however, allow their own professional insecurity to influence the way they deal with their students—the old problem of low self-worth. They choose the easier, safer, and more immediately gratifying course of buffering a crisis rather than letting the student face it and learn.

In order to take a firm position with alcohol- and drug-abusing students, or with Enablers whose youngsters are in trouble, the counselor needs to feel that his stand will be supported. Fortunately, both counselors and school administrators are becoming much more knowledgeable in handling chemical dependency. Tried in the fires of rampant juvenile drug abuse for the last fifteen years, they have had to be.

The informed school counselor can play another useful role. As we have seen in earlier chapters, a parent's hidden alcoholism often surfaces for the first time in an escapade by the Scapegoat, social withdrawal by the Lost Child, or learning difficulties, hyperactivity, or clowning in class by the Mascot. Any of these problems can bring a youngster into the counselor's orbit. If he recognizes them for what they are, he can use the child's welfare to motivate the enabling parent to get help for the family. Here again he will need the blessing and cooperation of the school district.

THE EFFECTIVE COUNSELOR

Effectiveness, like its opposite, enabling, seems to be primarily a product of who the counselor *is*. What he does is only a secondary consequence. Recalling the colleagues that I have known who were most successful in helping families to change, I might sketch the following composite portrait of the effective counselor:

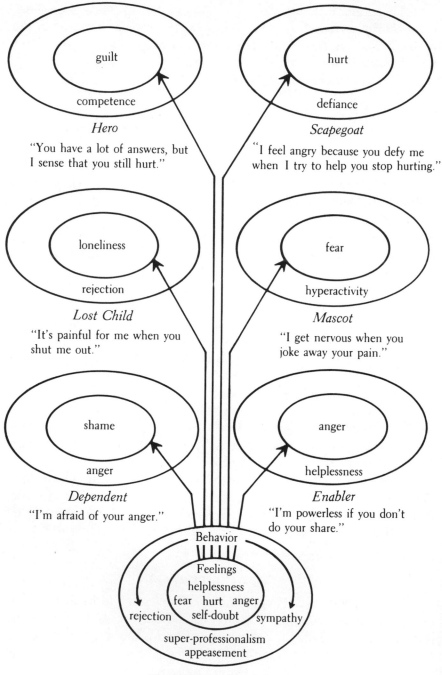

guilt

competence

Hero

"You have a lot of answers, but
I sense that you still hurt."

hurt

defiance

Scapegoat

"I feel angry because you defy me
when I try to help you stop hurting."

loneliness

rejection

Lost Child

"It's painful for me when you
shut me out."

fear

hyperactivity

Mascot

"I get nervous when you
joke away your pain."

shame

anger

Dependent

"I'm afraid of your anger."

anger

helplessness

Enabler

"I'm powerless if you don't
do your share."

Behavior

Feelings
helplessness
fear hurt anger
self-doubt
rejection   sympathy
super-professionalism
appeasement

The Effective Counselor

- *He knows himself.* He is in touch with his own feelings and willing to risk sharing them. Thus he becomes a model for his clients, establishing a climate of honesty and acceptance that makes it safe for them to feel and to share, too.
- *He is congruent.* What he says, what he does, and what he feels are all consistent.
- *He has a healthy self-worth,* appreciating his own potentials as tools to enhance his personal life and to help his clients.
- *He is aware of his weak spots,* flaws in his potentials where he might be vulnerable to being drawn into the family's unhealthy game or be an easy mark for the bully or the charmer.
- *He recognizes his own defensive behavior* as it arises and heeds it as a warning. By not having to give attention and energy to protecting his own sensitive spots, he can remain fully present with the family, picking up their double-level messages and tuning in to the feelings that lie beneath their words and actions.

In the diagram opposite, we see a model of how the effective counselor responds to the alcoholic family system. Inside, he is feeling all the human emotions, pleasant and unpleasant, that anyone else would in the same circumstances. Around this vulnerable feeling layer, to protect it, he has available a whole battery of defenses—again as everyone else does. But the counselor is *aware* of this defensive barrier in a way that many people are not: he can let it down when he chooses. (This is not to imply that counselors hold a monopoly on self-awareness, only that for them having it is imperative.)

Take, for example, the all-too-typical problem of confronting a resistant Dependent who is considerably larger and stronger than the counselor. The effective counselor faced with his client's barrage of anger and abuse, will not block it at his emotional boundaries with some defensive maneuver. Rather he will let it sink in to where it touches his feelings. Then he will respond by frankly sharing what he feels: "I really feel afraid when you are so angry." The very honesty of this interaction creates a probability that the client will in turn allow the message to touch *his* feelings. He may be surprised or sad to learn that he has caused the counselor to feel afraid. He may realize that he, too, is afraid and that his fear is somehow related to his anger. If he shares all this, a second honest exchange takes place. As counselor and client take turns responding to each other, first feeling and then sharing, they build a chain of trust. In family counseling, not only the person involved in the exchange but everyone present can develop congruence because the counselor was first congruent himself.

The qualities of awareness and honesty that the effective counselor displays when he is working with a family are reflected in his overall attitude toward his professional practice. His working principles would include:

1. *Being committed to his work,* with all the joy and pain that it entails. He gives it his time, energy, and concern in generous measure. He is willing to challenge what currently exists and to accept the struggle that goes with change—including change in himself.

2. *Knowing the limits of his commitment.* He knows not only what he can give but what he cannot—and what he is not willing to give. In the helping professions there is a constant temptation to believe we are indispensable to our clients. When this happens, our priorities get confused. The counselor must take care of himself if he is to be of value to his clients. He has other aspects of his life and other relationships that also need his attention. This will mean making some difficult decisions about the amount of time to be spent in work and the amount to be spent with his mate, children, friends, co-workers, and others. His time commitment should match the value he places on each relationship if he is to be truly congruent.

3. *Clarifying expectations of treatment.* At the outset it is important that the counselor find out what the family as individuals and as a group expect of treatment, and that he share with them his own expectations. He should tell them what he is able and willing to give, how much responsibility he will take and how much he expects them to take. Then he must make sure both he and they stick to that agreement. In my own practice I have found it useful to have an explicit contract with the client or family. The clearer the contract, the more satisfactory I have found the relationship. I tell clients:

As a counselor
- I will call to your attention whatever I see, hear, or feel that may be causing a breakdown in your personal or family well-being.
- I will be honest in my feedback to you, about what I perceive about you and also what I am feeling myself.
- I will support you in whatever way I believe is good for you.

- I will not make decisions for you.
- I am not a savior—I cannot work miracles.
- I am not Santa Claus—there are no free gifts. You will have to work.

As a client

- You will attend and actively participate in every session that you contract with me to have.
- You will give me at least 24 hours notice when you or someone else in the family cannot make a session; if you do not notify me, your next appointment will be no sooner than three months.
- You will do whatever work is required, both during and between sessions.
- You will make your own decisions and come up with your own proposals for change.
- You will be honest with me, as I will be with you, sharing information about what is going on in the family and what you are feeling, including what you are feeling about me.

I also review with the family exactly what we want to accomplish in treatment and the signs I will be looking for to tell us it is time to terminate it.

4. *Respecting the client as a person.* Each client is a unique and priceless individual; never in all of time or anywhere in the cosmos will he be duplicated. He deserves, simply because he exists, all the respect and concern we can give him. It is my personal belief that each client contains all truth within himself as his natural birthright. It is my job as a counselor to help him get in touch with that piece of it that he so desperately needs at this moment.

5. *Letting the clients take responsibility for their own changes.* As soon as a counselor takes on someone else's pain and feels responsible for fixing it, he is trapped in the same trap as the Enabler. He becomes a Professional Enabler. Then he is powerless to help the family. It is impossible for one person to change another, and even if it were possible, it would be counterproductive for the counselor. It is in the difficult but rewarding process of changing themselves that clients develop their potentials and their self-worth.

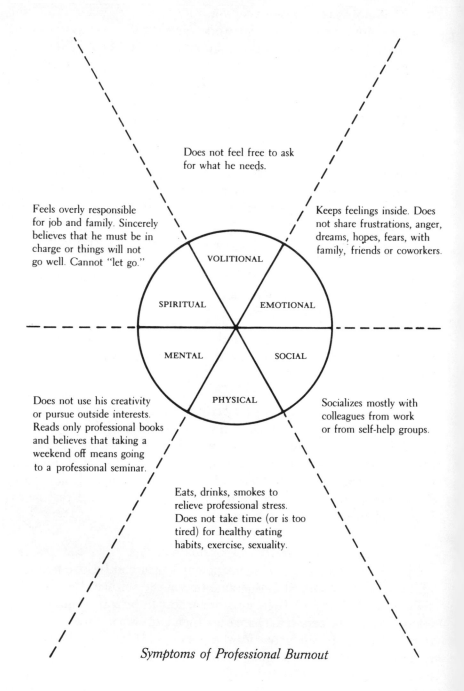

Does not feel free to ask for what he needs.

Feels overly responsible for job and family. Sincerely believes that he must be in charge or things will not go well. Cannot "let go."

Keeps feelings inside. Does not share frustrations, anger, dreams, hopes, fears, with family, friends or coworkers.

VOLITIONAL

SPIRITUAL

EMOTIONAL

MENTAL

SOCIAL

PHYSICAL

Does not use his creativity or pursue outside interests. Reads only professional books and believes that taking a weekend off means going to a professional seminar.

Socializes mostly with colleagues from work or from self-help groups.

Eats, drinks, smokes to relieve professional stress. Does not take time (or is too tired) for healthy eating habits, exercise, sexuality.

Symptoms of Professional Burnout

6. *Keeping his professional tools sharpened.* Psychology is a young and still growing science, and counseling a rapidly evolving art. In the field of chemical dependency new studies are constantly adding to what we know. Part of the counselor's sacred trust is to keep his knowledge and skills as current as possible through professional literature, seminars and workshops, membership in professional societies, and other avenues of continuing education.

7. *Feeding his own self-worth somewhere else.* Many people find their professional work an important source of their personal sense of worth, but for the counselor it can be a dangerous one. If he must assure a certain outcome of treatment in order to feel "successful," he is likely to censor what he says to the client rather than risk rejection by being honest; to try to fix problems rather than letting the clients learn slowly to handle them themselves; to hear any messages that treatment is "working" and be deaf to those that warn of trouble spots. Every helping professional has a responsibility to get his good feelings somewhere other than from his clients.

As we contemplate what it takes to be an effective counselor, we come back inescapably to the idea with which this book began—the pursuit of wholeness. This is not just something we recommend for our clients. We counselors, too, are embarked on a never-ending quest for greater wholeness, as persons and as helping professionals.

One price of ignoring our wholeness is professional "burnout," a syndrome that has been attracting a good deal of attention in the last few years. In the workshops I give on this problem, I use exactly the same whole person wheel that I use with alcoholic families, adding a few typical symptoms that indicate which personal potentials a counselor is neglecting (see diagram, opposite).

More recently, I have also developed a whole person inventory for professionals (see pages 248–253)—a practical checklist of feelings, attitudes, and behaviors for people engaged in counseling and related fields. Some such frequent self-checkup is an absolute must if we are to maintain either our personal well-being or our professional competence. The inventory is not intended to be an elegant statistical instrument—its purpose is not measurement. It simply seeks out those areas of the person that are currently being neglected and ties a warning flag to them.

Wholeness, after all, is not a trait or even a cluster of traits. Neither is it an accomplishment. It is simply a goal that, like the horizon, recedes as we move toward it. It will forever elude us and yet, the more diligently we pursue it, the more of life's landscape we will experience—and the more of our own expanding possibilities. It is this realization that allows us to trust in our client's equally limitless potential for change and growth, and here lies the hope for both of us.

THE COUNSELOR AS GUIDE

Wholeness in the helping professional is needed today as it has never been before. For thousands of years simply surviving on this planet presented such a full-time challenge that few human beings had the leisure to ask themselves, what is life for? Until recently, the chief task of counselors and therapists was to treat those who suffered from some mental disorder. As a result, we came to know a lot about illness, but our images of wellness were simplistic, matching neatly the types of personality that fit into the social system that subsidized us.

But the world is changing rapidly, and with it our professions. We are learning more about what it means to be human—and what perhaps it *can* mean in the future as our understanding grows. We are learning, too, the hidden problems and possibilities of relationships, including our own relationships with our clients.

Meanwhile, our clients have been changing, too. Many of them know more about our specialties than we ourselves did only a decade or two ago. Their expectations of life and of us are higher, their dreams grander, their possibilities more actively pursued than ever before. Our old selves and old professional styles are no longer good enough. The truth is, there *is* no more "them and us." Treatment has become an adventure that we are all in together, counselors and clients alike. We all share the responsibility for its outcome, and we can all benefit from undertaking it. Each time the counselor guides a family through its confusion and pain to congruence and health, he enhances his own congruence and health.

These new circumstances call for a new kind of specialist—a *guide*, who leads others to a fuller experience of life and fulfills himself in the process. Having already begun the journey toward wholeness, he can show others how to get onto the path.

There are already guides among us, and it has been my privilege to know a few. As a group, they are alert and responsive, living with the rhythms of their own bodies and helping their clients to do likewise. Most of them have entered and maintained close relationships with one or more persons; they love generously and are loved in return. They find life meaningful and satisfying, yet can accept suffering when it comes. They listen closely to their own boredom and anxiety, their dreams and fantasies, then search for the changes they can make to create greater harmony between inner and outer worlds. They would rather experience some knocks for being and revealing the persons they are than sell out their true selves for short-term approval.

Psychologically reborn, a guide willingly shares his enlightenment, freedom, and caring. Not so much an expert as a model, he serves as an example of the turned-on life. Simply knowing him will help a client find his own wholeness, health, and worth.

A PRAYER FOR GUIDES

Help me to create a setting for risk.
As each new person and family comes to visit me,
  help me to recognize and accept
  the fear and pain they bring with them.
Let me show them that I am not afraid.
Let me use my sensitivity and courage
  to mirror back to them all that I see and hear
  that keeps them in their bondage
  of pain and loneliness.
Give me the care and perception
  to show them their gifts and their power.
Let me reach out and touch—
  then let me leave them alone.
Let me trust in their strength and courage.
Let me let them make their own decisions and choices.
Help me to lead people to wholeness
  by being whole.

—Sharon Wegscheider

Exercises for
Healthier Families

THE FOLLOWING exercises are simple and fun, more like games than serious psychological "work." My clients find them a refreshing change from the usual talk-dominated family or group counseling session, and so do I. Those advantages, however, are only a fringe benefit. The real reason I use them as a regular part of treatment is that they are such powerful tools in helping family members gain the insight and skills they need to relate honestly and feelingly to one another.

Each exercise is based on a principle so elementary that if it were taught verbally most people would shrug and say, "Sure, we know that." But when it is presented in an exercise where it is actively *experienced*, the whole body seems to learn it. There is an entirely new, *felt* understanding, which can then be carried over into real-life situations.

The exercises can be used with members of a single family in after-care or with groups. When using them in a peer group, I simply ask the group to break up into "families" of five or six members each. For exercises 2 and 4, which require a realistic family structure, I ask each person to play one of the roles presented earlier in this book, including of course the Dependent. People can be allowed to choose the role they will play, or roles can be assigned. (Each approach has its advantages. I find that people tend to choose the role they know best—the one they are playing in their own family. Playing this role in the group can give them directly applicable experience to take home and use. On the other hand, playing the role of another family member will offer fresh insight into how it feels to be that person and why he may behave as he does.)

An example of the way I present each exercise is given in italic type.

I try to make the directions as simple and clear as I can (people from alcoholic families often have not developed good listening habits) and to keep the whole activity as light and playful as possible. When people are moving around and laughing, defenses drop and needed learning can slip in!

My purpose in presenting the exercises here is to share with other counselors a technique that I find valuable. But nonprofessional readers are invited to try the exercises on their own, either with other family members or with a "family" of unrelated individuals who are interested in improving their communication and relationship skills.

EXERCISE 1: A Tangle of Gifts

This simple little exercise leaves everyone feeling good. It draws on the ancient symbolism of gifts as a giving, in reality, of one's regard, love, even one's self. I find it particularly useful when I want to end a family session on a nurturing note or to create a spirit of involvement and mutual support in a group.

I ask everyone to join me in forming a circle in the middle of the room. To start the exercise, I offer my hand to someone in the group and say, *"I would like to offer you the gift of* _____ [joy, knowledge, humor, courage, etc.]."

He takes my hand and thanks me. Then I direct him to offer his other hand and a gift of his choice to someone else in the circle. We continue holding hands until everyone has received and given a gift. By the end of the game, there is a good-natured tangle of people, usually laughing and feeling a warm sense of closeness, emotional as well as physical.

EXERCISE 2: Let's Play Preacher

Because of the poor communication in alcoholic families, the members frequently have great difficulty in expressing themselves. The adults, after years of feeling they would not be heard anyway, have all but forgotten how; the children have never had a fair chance to learn. For such people, making any personal statement is uncomfortable. When it comes to the admittedly risky business of revealing their inner feelings, they will have a particularly hard time. This exercise is designed to give them some experience at a less sensitive level that lies somewhere between objective facts and subjective feelings—the level of personal opinion.

Today I'd like to play a little game with you that other families [or groups] have enjoyed. I call it, "Let's Play Preacher." We're going to pretend we're the congregation of a little church. It's Sunday morning, and we're all sitting here, nice and proper, waiting for the sermon to begin. Maybe you're wondering who will be the preacher. Well, that's the good part of this game. Everyone gets a chance. Each of you will have one minute to say whatever you really believe about the subject of our sermon, "One thing the world really needs is . . ." [or, "The most important quality in a friend is . . . ," or "The greatest evil threatening families today is . . ."]. Tell us your opinion with all the feeling and persuasiveness you can. Make us believe it, too!

After each sermon I encourage the "congregation" to show their appreciation by applause or *amens*.

EXERCISE 3: Talking in Stereo

Most of the conversation that goes on in families is either relaying information or asking for something. This exercise will help family members move from this shallow exchange to more intimate sharing. Since even troubled families customarily share information with one another about the events of the day, I start with that familiar situation. More than one family can do the exercise at one time. (When working with peers, I ask them to choose family roles for this exercise.)

Let's pretend you're all gathered around the family dinner table. It's a little after six, and everyone is full of news about what's happened today. You'll have 10 minutes to talk, exchanging information about the events of your day. Stick to the facts. We want everyone to learn as many facts as possible.
. . . All right. Ten minutes is up. Did you each get a chance to tell something about your day? Did you learn at least a few facts about everyone else's? [Discuss the experience for a few minutes.]
Exchanging facts is important for a family. We would have trouble carrying on our lives without them. But we need more than facts for healthy communication in our families. So, as they say in Hollywood, we're going to do a retake. Back to the dinner table, but this time we're going to change the rules. In addition to giving the facts, I want you to add the feelings that went with them. For instance, if Dad reports, "I

arrived late for the meeting today," he might add, "—and I felt really guilty!" Again, you'll have 10 minutes.

. . . Time's up. How did that feel? Different? [Discuss the two experiences, both from a speaker's standpoint and from a listener's.]

As this exercise helps us discover, conversation is a lot richer when it includes both dimensions—facts and feelings. In the first "take" we used only our mental potentials, to give and receive facts. In the retake, we added another dimension, the emotional potential. Using both is like talking in stereo!

EXERCISE 4: Asking for Help

Learning to recognize and express emotions is an important first step, but one must also learn to live with those emotions. Overpowering feelings often lead a person to say or do things that he regrets later. For example, when he is very angry, he may say harsh words that can never be erased. As family members become more open and honest with one another, they can learn to ask for help in times of strong emotion. This exercise offers practice.

On each of these cards I have written a word to describe some common feeling— happy, tired, depressed, frightened, and so on. I'd like each person to take a card. That will be your feeling to talk about as we go around the circle. Let's say that I draw a card that says "tired." When my turn comes, I will say, "When I feel tired, what I would like from you is understanding." Or I might ask for "quiet" or "help." You are free to ask for whatever would really help you handle the emotion on your card. Let's begin.

. . . And so you see, it isn't necessary to struggle with a strong feeling all alone. The truth is that other people are usually glad to do what they can to help you if you will only tell them how. This kind of honest sharing can prevent misunderstandings that are painful to both of you.

EXERCISE 5: A Room With a View

Since expressing an honest viewpoint on anything can seem risky in an alcoholic family, one member may be totally unaware of another's view of any given situation. He may not even realize that it is different from his own. When someone does occasionally dare to express a view, it promptly gets labeled "wrong" or "bad," simply because it is different.

This exercise helps make real for such people an obvious truth that they have accepted only in theory: no two people see, or even are able to see, anything in exactly the same way.

First, I'd like everyone to stand up and form a circle in the middle of the room. . . . Now stay where you are in the circle but turn around so that you are facing out, with your back to the center. Take one minute to look at the scene directly in front of you. Without turning your head, take in with your eyes as much of the room as you can. . . . Now close your eyes for a moment and remember what you saw, in as much detail as you can. Keep your eyes closed, and we'll go around the circle to give everyone a chance to tell us in a few words what he saw.

. . . Did it seem as though you were all describing the same room? . . . How did it feel when you heard someone describing things you hadn't seen at all? . . . You may have had brothers or sisters who were several years older or younger than you. Do you think they saw the family in a different way than you did?

The discussion can go on to explore how and why members of a family might see a particular situation differently.

EXERCISE 6: Posing the Family Portrait[1]

The obvious fact that each person has a different view of what happens within a family seems totally unrecognized in alcoholic families. The last exercise introduced this idea in a general way. This one applies it directly to the family, giving it practical, personal meaning.

Each of us has a mental picture of the family that we are living in. That picture will be somewhat different from the picture anyone else has of our family. When several artists paint the same scene at the same time, each picture is different, partly because they are all standing in different places and seeing it from different angles and eye-levels, partly because

[1] I have adapted this exercise from a technique called "family sculpturing," originated by Virginia Satir.

each human being has his own unique way of seeing. The same is true in a family.

Today we are going to make a family picture—the family as one person sees it. Who would like to volunteer to be the artist and make a picture of his family? . . . All right, come here and stand in the center of the room. You see, each of us is the center of his own world.

[At this point, unless the exercise is being done with all the members of an actual family present, I ask the "artist" to begin by choosing people from the group to role-play members of his family.]

Which one of these people do you feel the closest to? Which can you share your secrets and hopes and joys with? Have that person stand here, closest to you. How close will depend on just how close you feel you are. . . . Now, which person do you feel the most distant from? Where would you like him to stand? . . . Now place the other members of your family in your world, too, one at a time. Consider how close they are to you and also how close you think they feel to each other. You can rearrange them until all their places feel right to you.

So we see where everyone is located in our artist's world, at least as he sees it. Next we have to look more closely and see what they are doing —how as well as where they exist in his world.

Your mother and your dad are a long way apart here. Is that how you see them in reality? All right. Now pose your mother. Will she be facing Dad or turned away? Will she be pointing a finger at him, blaming him for the problems in the family? Or maybe be down on one knee begging him to do or be something different? Or maybe ignoring him as though he weren't there? Go over and pose her as though she were a department store mannequin, so that she looks true and right in this family portrait.

Now how about Dad? Here are his wife and children all on one side of the room, and there he is on the other. What does he do? Is he angry, also blaming? Or does he turn his back? Or something else? Go over and help him pose.

. . . Now pose the other people. If someone is on a pedestal [the family Hero] ask that person to stand on a chair. If two people are very close, they might hold hands or put their arms around each other. If one of your parents was very protective of one of their children, pose them to show that. Use your creativity to show us just what your family is [or was] like.

. . . [When the portrait is complete, I comment on any significant relationships that I see. My purpose is both to confirm that the relationship is correctly posed as the "artist" perceives it and to draw his attention to it.] *It looks as though you are closer to your father than your brother is. Do you feel that is true?*

[Now I address the other family members.] *Dad, how does it feel to be way over there by yourself with all those fingers pointing at you? Mom, how does it feel to you, with him so far away and all these children clinging to you? And how about the rest of you? How does the family feel to you from your position?*

Even when the "family" is only being role-played, the players often experience strong feelings of fear, loneliness, frustration, and other emotions from having to occupy the positions assigned to them. This is enlightening for them, and as they voice their reactions, the "artist" can begin to sense what life may be like for other members of his family.

When working with an actual family, I go one step further before ending the exercise. I ask each member in turn to change the positions and poses in whatever way is necessary to make them fit his own picture of the family. (Although each is really the center of his own picture, I ask them to continue working with the original picture so that we can see the similarities and differences more clearly.) *It is very important to allow time for this step.* Not only is it an important source of insight, but each member needs an opportunity to share his personal picture and have his right to it validated.

Throughout the exercise I continually reinforce the idea that *no picture is right or wrong, good or bad.* Differences are inevitable and okay.

Because the whole body is involved in this exercise, people usually get caught up in the action and reveal information or express feelings they would otherwise have kept carefully hidden. The result is fresh insight for everyone—and a fresh appreciation of the value of differing views as ways of gaining insight.

B

The Whole Person Inventory

FOR PROFESSIONALS

(This is not a standardized test but a checklist for self-evaluation. The answers are intended to yield, not a numerical score, but personal insight. There are no formal norms; the inventory reflects instead my observations of effectiveness, ineffectiveness, and burnout in a wide range of helping professionals throughout the country, who have attended my training workshops or work in the industrial or treatment programs for which I am a consultant.—S. W.)

PHYSICAL POTENTIAL

PERSONAL LIFE

____ Take good care of my general health, including exercise, diet, and rest.

____ Enjoy using my body in sports, exercise, or dancing.

____ Welcome sexuality as part of an intimate relationship.

____ Manage my time and energy to meet my own rather than someone else's priorities.

PROFESSIONAL LIFE

____ Provide a nurturing enviroment for treatment.

____ Maintain a balanced workload, within the limitations of my work setting.

____ Am alert for nonverbal communication in clients (facial expressions, posture, movements, tone of voice, etc.)

____ Take a straightforward attitude about providing a service for which people pay.

_____ Consider money primarily a resource for achieving my personal priorities.

_____ Consider my living and work environments as resources for enhancing my satisfaction in living.

SIGNS OF TROUBLE

_____ Am often tired and lacking energy.

_____ Am eating, drinking, or smoking more than I feel I should.

_____ Tend to put off visiting the dentist and having health check-ups.

_____ Am too busy or too tired to exercise regularly.

_____ Am often too busy to get away for a vacation.

_____ Use many of my vacations to attend professional workshops.

EMOTIONAL POTENTIAL

PERSONAL LIFE

_____ Am in touch with my feelings most of the time and respect them.

_____ Pay attention to my feelings as a necessary part of intuition.

_____ Give my feelings due weight in making decisions.

_____ Feel free and able to express my feelings in appropriate ways.

_____ Respect the feelings of others and their right to express them in appropriate ways.

PROFESSIONAL LIFE

_____ Respect my clients' feelings even though they differ from mine.

_____ Give clients permission to express their feelings in a safe atmosphere.

_____ Value my own feelings for what they can tell me about my client, our relationship, and the process.

_____ Respond to the client's deeper needs (as I see them) rather than reacting to his wishes or demands.

_____ Feel free to express my personal feelings to clients when doing so will not interfere with treatment goals.

SIGNS OF TROUBLE

_____ Find that most of my clients have to work through similar feelings—often the same ones that I have to work through myself.

_____ Believe that a client's avowed feelings, when they do not fit my professional picture of his situation, are probably defensive.
_____ Expect clients to be able to get in touch with feelings promptly as they arise.
_____ Believe that showing concern for the client openly undermines the professional relationship.

SOCIAL POTENTIAL

PERSONAL LIFE

_____ Am able to build and maintain satisfying relationships.
_____ Am open and honest with others without fearing the consequences.
_____ Reveal my opinions and feelings without seeking others' approval.
_____ Am willing to be vulnerable in sharing information about myself.
_____ Am direct and honest in expressing my needs and wants.
_____ Am in control of how much or how little of myself I reveal and do so prudently.

_____ Am willing to do my part in maintaining relationships.

PROFESSIONAL LIFE

_____ Have a clear understanding of my relationship to my clients.
_____ Am honest with clients and with myself about what I can and cannot do.
_____ Make no promises about the outcome of treatment.

_____ Give the client my total attention while we are together.
_____ Can confront the behavior of a client while still supporting him as a person.
_____ Have a clear perception of my own life and history, and of the part they play in the context of treatment.

SIGNS OF TROUBLE

_____ Find making and maintaining eye contact uncomfortable.
_____ Find the demands of my work leave little time for my family.
_____ Find the demands of my work leave little time for social activities.
_____ Spend most of my leisure time by myself.
_____ Spend most of my leisure time with others from my professional field or work setting.
_____ Tend to avoid discussing unpleasant topics with a client.
_____ Sometimes find myself making promises that I may not be able to keep.
_____ Discover sometimes that clients are embarrassed at the personal information about my life that I share with them.

_____ Sometimes find myself playing surrogate family member, friend, or lover to a client.

MENTAL POTENTIAL

PERSONAL LIFE

_____ Am knowledgeable about many subjects.

_____ Enjoy learning new things and developing new skills.

_____ Can remember and acknowledge most events of my childhood, including painful ones.

_____ Am open and receptive to new ideas.

_____ Am imaginative in envisioning new alternatives.

_____ Know my limitations and do not hesitate to ask for information, suggestions, and help.

PROFESSIONAL LIFE

_____ Plan my work in an organized way.

_____ Am able to communicate clearly.

_____ Can remember previous sessions and recognize patterns.

_____ Can accept supervision and criticism.

_____ Make an active effort to keep informed about new developments in my field.

_____ Know my limitations and do not hesitate to refer a client to another professional.

SIGNS OF TROUBLE

_____ Have little time to pursue hobbies or nonprofessional activities.

_____ Read mostly professional books and journals.

_____ Tend to use the same style of treatment with all clients.

_____ Try to fit clients into my theoretical model.

_____ Am coolly objective, feeling that it is more professional to see clients as cases rather than individual persons.

_____ Find I understand my clients so well that I often finish their sentences for them.

_____ Spend considerable time explaining my theoretical approach to my clients during treatment sessions.

SPIRITUAL POTENTIAL

PERSONAL LIFE

_____ Am convinced that life has meaning and direction.

PROFESSIONAL LIFE

_____ Feel a spirit of hope most of the time and communicate it to clients.

_____ Am aware of some Power greater than myself.

_____ Have a sense of my own relationship to the larger world, other people, and the Power greater than myself.
_____ Usually feel firmly balanced and grounded.

_____ Am aware that the roles I play in life are merely expressions of my true self.

_____ Feel accepting and accepted most of the time.

_____ Try to help each client see his present pain in a wider context that also allows realistic hope.
_____ Help the client learn that he can feel responsible for his actions and yet acknowledge a reality greater than himself.
_____ Guide the client in his search for the true self beneath his roles.
_____ Can accept a client's choices for himself even when they differ from what I would choose for him.

SIGNS OF TROUBLE

_____ Find the world a basically hostile place.
_____ Often feel that life is absurd and meaningless.
_____ Believe that I am totally responsible for whatever occurs in my life, and that my client is responsible for his.
_____ Believe that outside forces control whatever occurs in my life and my clients', so we are in no way responsible.
_____ Consider "counselor" ["physician," etc.] as my basic identity.
_____ Find I am often critical of my friends' and clients' values.
_____ Am convinced that my religion or spiritual path is the one true way and would convince my clients of this if I could.

VOLITIONAL POTENTIAL

PERSONAL LIFE

_____ Am usually decisive, even though I realize that I sometimes make mistakes.
_____ Am willing to take risks.

PROFESSIONAL LIFE

_____ Live up to the treatment contract I have made with the client.
_____ Expect the client to live up to the contract, too, doing his part according to his capabilities.

_____ Usually follow through on decisions with wholehearted action.

_____ Am disciplined and steady in whatever I undertake.

_____ Am persistent in the face of difficulty or discouragement.

_____ Can accept patiently such unavoidable frustrations as weather, physical limitations, and the idiosyncracies of people and institutions.

_____ Am willing to confront the client if he is not fulfilling the contract.

_____ Am willing to be directive when I feel the circumstances call for it.

_____ Am straightforward about my own needs and wants in the treatment relationship.

_____ Am responsible in routine matters, such as punctuality, note taking, and following institutional procedures.

SIGNS OF TROUBLE

_____ Feel constantly overwhelmed with things that I cannot find time to do.

_____ Am habitually late for personal and professional appointments.

_____ Conform to schedules and rules rather than making my own choices.

_____ Find it very hard to say no.

_____ Find it hard to change my position once I have taken a stand.

_____ Believe a responsible counselor should be available to his clients whenever they wish to see him, without concern for his personal convenience.

_____ Believe that a counselor should not be expected to see clients outside regular appointments, regardless of the circumstances.

_____ Rarely offer my own opinions and suggestions to friends or clients.

_____ Feel uncomfortable in setting and enforcing reasonable limits for my children, subordinates, or clients.

_____ Am strongly directive with clients and feel that failure to follow my directions should be seen as an unhealthy defense.

Index